Anni and Josef Albers

Acknowledgement of Country

The National Gallery of Australia respectfully acknowledges that we are on the Country of the Ngunnawal and Ngambri peoples of the Kamberri/Canberra region. We recognise their continuing connections to Country and culture, and we pay our respect to their Elders, past and present.

We respectfully acknowledge all Traditional Custodians throughout Australia whose art we care for and to whose lands National Gallery exhibitions and staff travel.

Warning

Aboriginal and Torres Strait Islander people are respectfully advised that this publication may contain images and words of, and references to, people who have passed away. Where possible, permission has been sought to include this material.

Aboriginal and Torres Strait Islander languages and placenames

The National Gallery of Australia recognises Aboriginal and Torres Strait Islander cultural heritage by including First Nations placenames in this publication. The placenames are current at the time of print although there may be minor changes to the spellings of these over time.

Anni and Josef Albers
National Gallery of Australia

Anni and Josef Albers is a Kenneth E Tyler Collection exhibition.
The National Gallery of Australia gratefully acknowledges the generous support of Exhibition Patron Penelope Seidler AM.

Contents

Below SI designer after Josef Albers, Teacup and saucer 1926, electroplated metal, wood handle, glass liner, 5.5 × 13.1 (diam) cm (each), manufactured by Berliner Electro Plated Waren Fabrik, Berlin

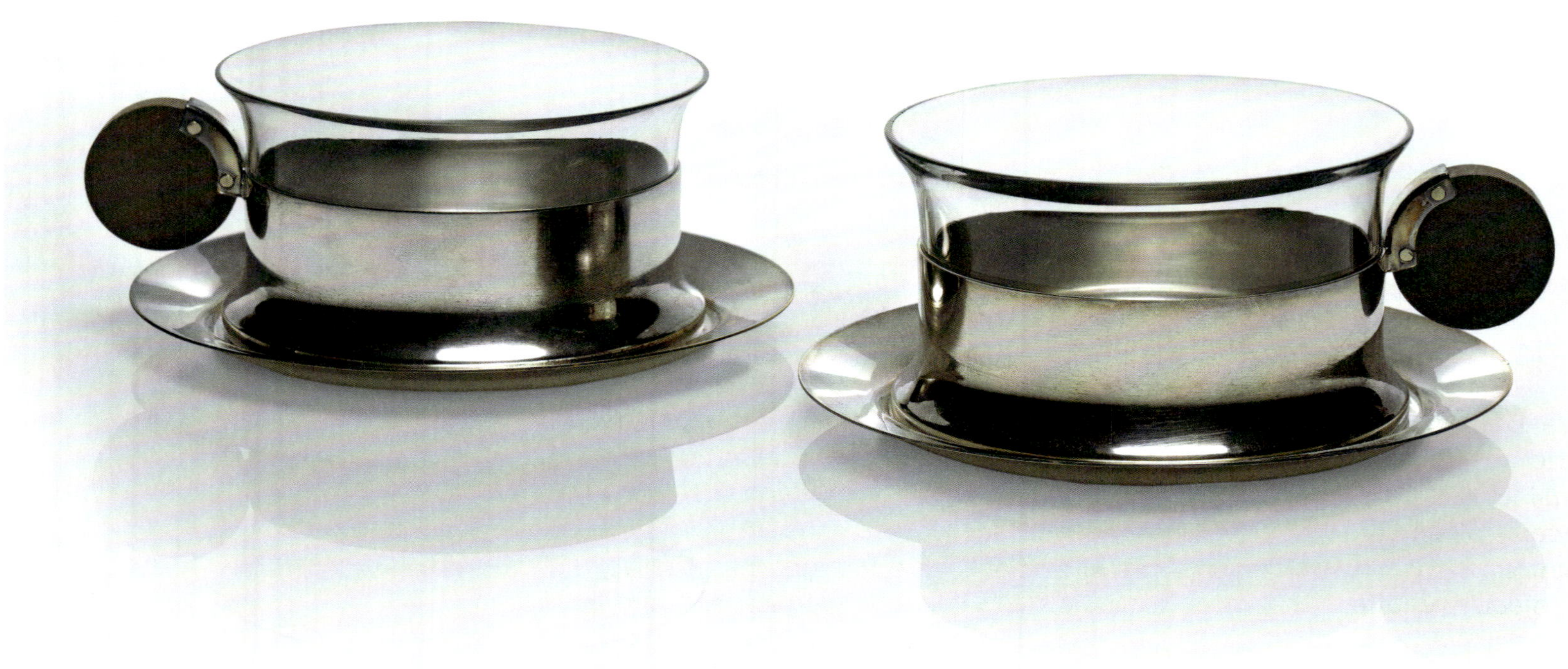

Foreword

Nick Mitzevich

Anni and Josef Albers brings together two exceptional artists of the twentieth century whose experimental works explore the languages of colour and geometry. The exhibition celebrates the contributions of Anni Albers and Josef Albers to minimalist abstraction and considers their far-reaching legacy within an Australian context.

Anni and Josef met in 1922 at the Bauhaus art school in Weimar, Germany, and their entwined biography forms a direct conduit between European and American modern art. Impelled by political turmoil in Europe to emigrate in 1933, the couple brought the interdisciplinary Bauhaus philosophy to the liberal Black Mountain College in North Carolina. Within this anti-ideological setting, they would teach innovative approaches to artistic production to a new generation of artists through practices that emphasised form, material and process. Many of the major works regularly on display from our American holdings are by artists who were directly influenced by these teachings, including Donald Judd, Robert Rauschenberg and Sol LeWitt.

Conceiving this project and publication to celebrate the riches of the Kenneth E Tyler print collection, curator Imogen Dixon-Smith also selected significant works from the National Gallery collection that relate to the revolutionary art of Anni and Josef Albers. The exhibition reveals their networks of influence with other Bauhäuslers and connections with fellow artists in Europe and America, as well as examining their sources of inspiration. It also brings Anni and Josef into an Australian context, through considering the links they had with Australian-based émigrés, including architect Harry Seidler and artist Ludwig Hirschfeld-Mack.

During the 1960s Anni and Josef formed a pivotal working relationship with visionary master printer Kenneth Tyler, whose legendary graphic workshops Gemini GEL and Tyler Graphics collaborated with artists on projects that combined art, science and technology. Tyler was quick to recognise a shared interest in pushing technical boundaries and worked with Anni and Josef Albers on producing several print series that charted new territory for both artists. *Anni and Josef Albers* includes screenprints and lithographs from this period, supported by documentation from the Tyler archive that shares insights into working methods.

The depth of the National Gallery's collection continues to support exhibitions that explore relationships between artistic periods and across cultures. It is now recognised that Western twentieth-century art movements and artists were influenced by the ideas and aesthetics of First Peoples. Indeed Anni and Josef openly drew inspiration from pre-Columbian art and architecture, for which they had a lifelong appreciation. The exhibition highlights the geometry and materiality of Peruvian cultural objects in the National Gallery's rich textile collection to enable contemporary audiences to reflect on these connections.

I offer my congratulations to Imogen Dixon-Smith for this thoughtful celebration of the work of Anni and Josef Albers and sincerely thank the Josef and Anni Albers Foundation for its support of this exhibition. Thank you also to the contributors to this publication for sharing their expertise: Nicholas Fox Weber, Executive Director of the Josef and Anni Albers Foundation; Philip Goad, Chair of Architecture, Redmond Barry Distinguished Professor and Co-Director of the Australian Centre for Architectural History, Urban and Cultural Heritage (ACAHUCH) at the University of Melbourne; Ann Stephen, Senior Curator Art, the University of Sydney, Chau Chak Wing Museum; and Jordan Troeller, Junior Professor of Contemporary Art History and Aesthetic Practices at the Institute for Fine Arts, Music and Education (IKMV) at Leuphana University Lüneburg.

We are thrilled to bring the Kenneth E Tyler Collection and archive into the public eye and owe a debt of gratitude to Kenneth Tyler for his continued support of the National Gallery. I would like to acknowledge James Mollison's vision in developing the Tyler Collection since 1973 and Jane Kinsman's expansion and stewardship of the international print collection over four decades. For her generous involvement with this project, we offer sincere appreciation to Penelope Seidler AM. Thank you also to the National Gallery of Australia Foundation for its enthusiastic support and the National Gallery team that has supported the exhibition project and publication.

Dr Nick Mitzevich
Director, National Gallery of Australia

Below Josef Albers, Collaged studies for *White Line Square II, V, VIII, IX, XIV* c1966, collage of coloured paper on board, sheet 48.4 × 52.6 cm

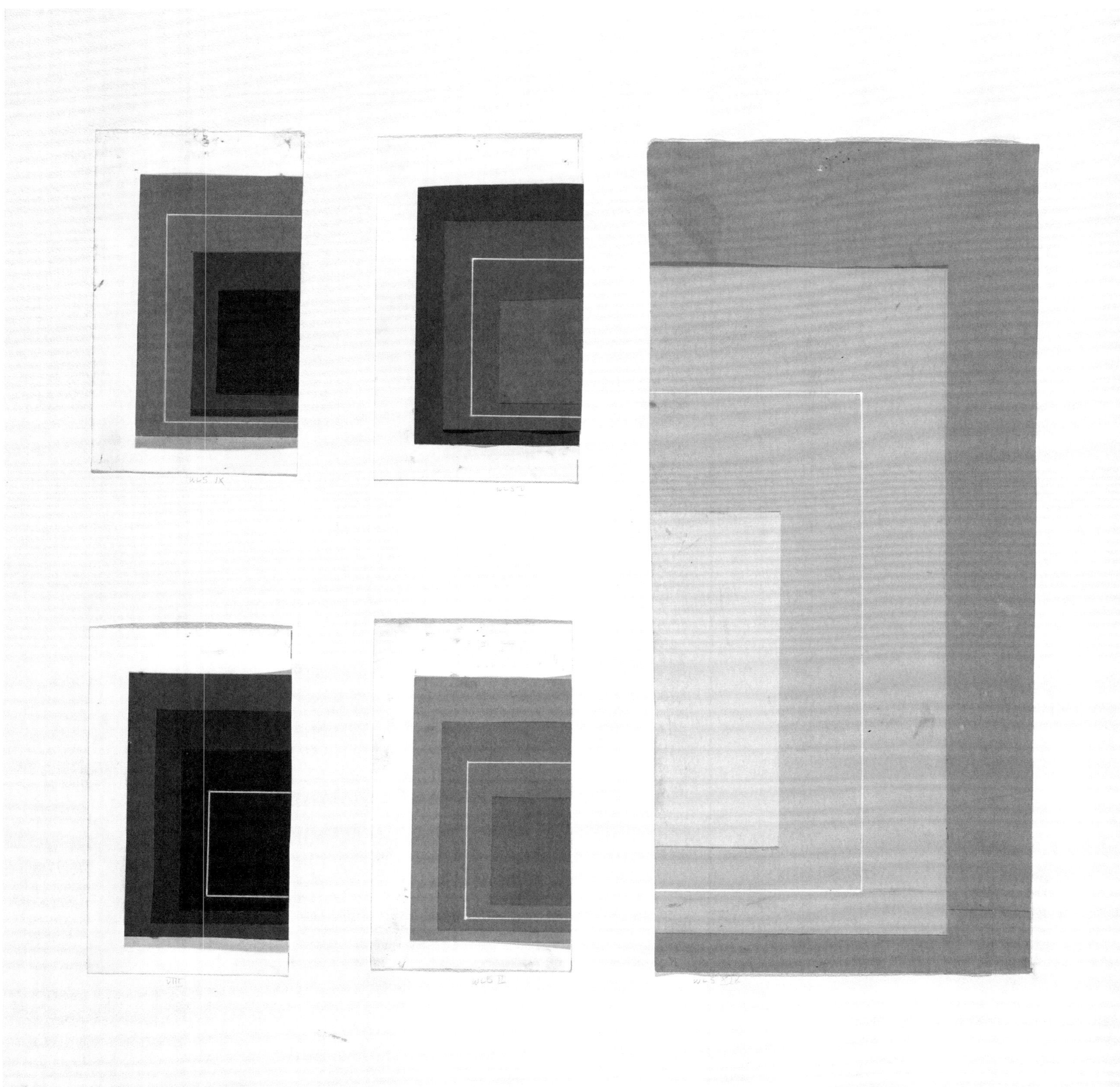

Introduction

Imogen Dixon-Smith

Anni and Josef Albers stood on the precipice of change at many points throughout their lives.

Born in Germany, in the years following the First World War, Anni moved from Berlin, and Josef from Bottrop, to live in Weimar and commence as students at the Bauhaus. Both were itching for an artistic training that looked beyond the strictures of the traditional art academies they had found little inspiration in. A decade later, they crossed the Atlantic Ocean as husband and wife. Propelled by the need to escape the frightening rise of fascism, they embarked on an accidental mission to 'open the eyes' of American students to the wonder of perceiving the world.

From their new home in North Carolina, the couple could cross the border into Mexico, and did so with a feverish appetite to immerse themselves in the ancient cultures of Central and South America that previously they could only observe in the colonial spoils of Germany's ethnographic museums—cultures that to the Alberses had achieved the unification of art and life. In a letter to Wassily and Nina Kandinsky, from 1936, Anni marvelled that Mexico was 'full of art, such as perhaps no other country. wonderful ancient art ... and folk art in addition, a still living tradition, and still good ... even today art is the most important thing in the country.'[1]

Anni and Josef were no strangers to the volatile energy of a new threshold. The formal reality of two entities meeting was a recurring investigation in their creative endeavours too. Anni forged her legacy as the twentieth century's greatest weaver on the loom. With a series of vertical threads set up in front of her, she launched into the composition of a design by passing a thread over and under the hurdle of each warp, drawing her graphic sensibility directly from this process. 'The horizontal–vertical intersecting of the two separate systems of thread,' she wrote, 'is of great consequence for the formative side of weaving'.[2] Josef was energised by meetings of a different sort. The magic that occurred when placing two colours side by side became a constant source of inspiration as he experimented with the interaction between colours so skilfully that endless variations elicited unique and affecting responses. Both artists were fascinated with the influence of two elements on one another at the point where they meet and how they could then exist as a whole.

Across two continents, Anni and Josef encountered countless colleagues who shared their reverence for an affecting art that is driven not by the psyche of the artist or the representation of our world, but by a pursuit to connect with the complexities of perception itself. Though the Alberses never set foot in Australia, their work was collected by the National Gallery as it developed a premier collection of European and American modernism. Josef and Anni also maintained strong artistic and personal relationships with fellow émigré artists and Bauhäuslers who had come to Australia. Events unfolding in Europe during the Second World War had led to the dispersal of many artists across the world. Australia was woven into the rich tapestry of the Bauhaus diaspora, as artists and designers internationally sought to maintain a connection with each other and bring the ideas of the school to their new homes. In this exhibition and publication, the National Gallery registers points of intersection in this dense, cosmopolitan weaving.

The first works by the Alberses to enter the national collection were a group of prints Anni and Josef made in collaboration with master printer Kenneth Tyler at Gemini Graphic Editions Ltd (Gemini GEL) in Los Angeles. These are part of the National Gallery's near-complete collection of Tyler's printer's proofs, purchased in 1973. This substantial acquisition sparked a significant and ongoing relationship between Tyler and the National Gallery. An entrepreneurial character who found a strong affinity with Anni and Josef's enduring commitment to push boundaries and chase perfection, Tyler became an important collaborator for the couple, working tirelessly to produce the most complex graphic manifestations of their revolutionary ideas. He signed his letters to Josef, 'As ever, your printer, Ken'.[3] The prints produced

1 Anni Albers, letter to Wassily and Nina Kandinsky, 22 August 1936, published in Nicholas Fox Weber and Jessica Boissel, *Josef Albers and Wassily Kandinsky: friends in exile; a decade of correspondence, 1929–1940*, trans Oliver Pretzel, Hudson Hills Press, Manchester & New York, 2010, p 87.

2 Anni Albers, *On weaving*, Studio Vista, London, 1966, p 38.

3 Kenneth Tyler, letter to Josef Albers, 31 October 1966, typescript, JA 42-7-1, Papers of Josef and Anni Albers, the Josef and Anni Albers Foundation, Bethany, Connecticut.

by the artists in collaboration with Tyler provide a grounding from which to push off in multiple directions to explore the ideas that influenced the Alberses, and the ideas that the Alberses imparted to the world. In this publication, Executive Director of the Josef and Anni Albers Foundation, Nicholas Fox Weber, charts the close working relationship between the artists and their printer. In an essay focusing on the links between the Bauhaus and Tyler, I explore how the principles absorbed by the Alberses at the school aligned perfectly with the printer's ambition and innovation. Art historian Jordan Troeller takes a closer look at Anni's textile *Camino Real* 1968, a work that marks the point of transition in the artist's thinking as she switched from weaving to printmaking.

One of the key relationships tying the Alberses to Australia was their ongoing friendship with German émigré artist Ludwig Hirschfeld-Mack, who found himself interned in regional Australia as an enemy alien during the Second World War. Josef and Hirschfeld-Mack were among the earliest students of the Bauhaus and shared a strong affinity from their time in such an experimental and evolving environment. In her essay about their friendship, curator Ann Stephen shows how the correspondence between the Alberses and Hirschfeld-Mack reveals—despite their very different fortunes and lives—a mutual commitment to experimental education and the creation of art for the benefit of society rather than one's own personal satisfaction, a sustained commitment that kept them connected across many years and great geographical distances.

In 2002 renowned Australian architect Harry Seidler presented a lecture at the National Gallery titled 'Josef Albers—teaching of visual perception'. In this talk, Seidler cited his time spent studying under Josef at Black Mountain College in the United States as the single biggest influence on his architectural practice. Seidler admired the uniqueness of Josef's practical and experimental exercises in the classroom. Instead of instructing his students in technique or style, Josef introduced them to the essence of his own practice: 'When the discrepancy between physical fact and psychological affect is at a maximum, therein lies the threshold of art.'[4] Seidler's designs brought art into the fabric of a building, a result of his multifaceted connections to the people and ideas of the Bauhaus, which also spurred him to bring the art of Josef Albers to Australian shores through a number of commissions. A conversation between architectural historian Philip Goad and Penelope Seidler AM brings to life this extraordinary relationship, which has remained largely untold, though it forms the most significant connection between the Alberses and Australia.

Both Anni's and Josef's work reveals how influence can move back and forth between two entities. Josef placed innumerable permutations of colours side by side to unlock novel interactions. A colour viewed on its own has its own identity. When placed next to a second, our perception of it changes in relation to this new visual combination, and this new identity becomes unique to that particular arrangement. Josef exclaimed to Tyler in 1966, 'It's so exciting ... colour fools you all the time. You never see neighbours in the same way, no, no, the same relationship.'[5] Similarly, Anni's intersecting threads are the basis of designs built up as the weft moves back and forth across the loom. As she described, 'A weft thread moves alternately over and under each warp thread it meets on its horizontal course from one side of the warp to the other; returning, it reverses the order and crosses over those threads under which it moved before and under those over which it crossed.'[6] She used this underlying logic, which she heralded as 'the quintessence of weaving', as the solid, impenetrable foundation and inspiration for her designs.

The weight of the name 'Albers' in art and design has been felt for decades and studied in great detail, but Josef's and Anni's work has never been approached in an exhibition from this distinct location. This exhibition and publication look back to the radical environment of the Bauhaus and illuminate those people and principles that set the Alberses on their path, while simultaneously following the forward momentum of their influence on creative practice.

4 Harry Seidler, 'Josef Albers—teaching of visual perception', lecture, National Gallery of Australia, Kamberri/Canberra, 2002, published online by Polly Seidler, 14 April 2018, reviewed 28 April 2023, https://www.youtube.com/watch?v=bs14c8DliZ0.

5 Josef Albers, phone conversation with Kenneth Tyler and Henry Hopkins, c 1966, transcript, box 3, folder 5, Kenneth E Tyler Collection archive, National Gallery of Australia.

6 Anni Albers, 1966, p 39.

Preface to transcripts

The process of printing Josef Albers's series *White Line Squares* 1966 to a level of precision not yet reached in his print oeuvre took great patience, perseverance and problem-solving skills on the part of Kenneth Tyler and his printers. Josef Albers lived in Connecticut on the East Coast of the United States, while the Gemini GEL workshop was in Los Angeles. The artist did not like to travel; instead, he directed the months-long production process via correspondence. Working with Albers initially proved difficult. Renowned for his exacting standards, Albers was a demanding perfectionist who insisted on meticulous craftsmanship. Tyler noticed that the challenges of the project were taking a toll on his printers, and in an effort to provide them with a sense of the artist as a person, he had transcripts made of his phone conversations with Albers. These gave voice to Albers's artistic vision as well as his technical requirements, and effectively managed the situation, as Tyler recalled:

> A lot of my nit-picking and struggle to have a very high standard in the printing was taken now with a better attitude because they heard the great joy from Albers when he saw a beautiful proof or a beautiful colour. I think that made a profound difference in the attitude of our little workshop. It certainly started us off with the right idea, that nothing was impossible and that the artist should really be in total control and that the demanding of better and better quality in the printing was absolutely essential and something that should be expected.[7]

Four of these transcripts have been reproduced in this publication. They reveal the close relationship Tyler developed with Anni and Josef Albers over a love of art that dared to challenge and excite.

Imogen Dixon-Smith
Kenneth E Tyler Curator, International Prints and Drawings
National Gallery of Australia

7 Kenneth Tyler, 1984, quoted in Pat Gilmour, *Ken Tyler, master printer, and the American print renaissance*, Hudson Hills Press, New York, & Australian National Gallery, Canberra, 1986, p 40.

Below Josef Albers, Study for Ken [*Gray Instrumentation II* series] 1974, collage of thin, cream hand-cut tissue paper adhered to thick buff cardboard, image 12.8 × 12.6 cm

13 Below Josef Albers, Study for Ken [*Gray Instrumentation II* series] 1974, collage of thin, cream hand-cut tissue paper adhered to thick buff cardboard, image 12.8 × 12.6 cm

Below Josef Albers, Study for Ken [*Gray Instrumentation II* series] 1974, collage of thin, cream hand-cut tissue paper adhered to thick buff cardboard, image 12.8 × 12.6 cm

Below Josef Albers, Study for Ken [*Gray Instrumentation II* series] 1974, collage of thin, cream hand-cut tissue paper adhered to thick buff cardboard, image 12.8 × 12.6 cm

Below Josef Albers, Study for Ken [*Gray Instrumentation II* series] 1974, collage of thin, cream hand-cut tissue paper adhered to thick buff cardboard, image 12.8 × 12.6 cm

Below Josef Albers, Study for Ken [*Gray Instrumentation II* series] 1974, collage of thin, cream hand-cut tissue paper adhered to thick buff cardboard, image 12.8 × 12.6 cm

Below Josef Albers, Study for Ken [*Gray Instrumentation II* series] 1974, collage of thin, cream hand-cut tissue paper adhered to thick buff cardboard, image 12.8 × 12.6 cm

Below Josef Albers, Study for Ken [*Gray Instrumentation II* series] 1974, collage of thin, cream hand-cut tissue paper adhered to thick buff cardboard, image 12.8 × 12.6 cm

Below Josef Albers, *Gray Instrumentation Ia* 1974, from the *Gray Instrumentation I* series 1974, screenprint, image 28 × 28 cm, sheet 48.2 × 48.2 cm

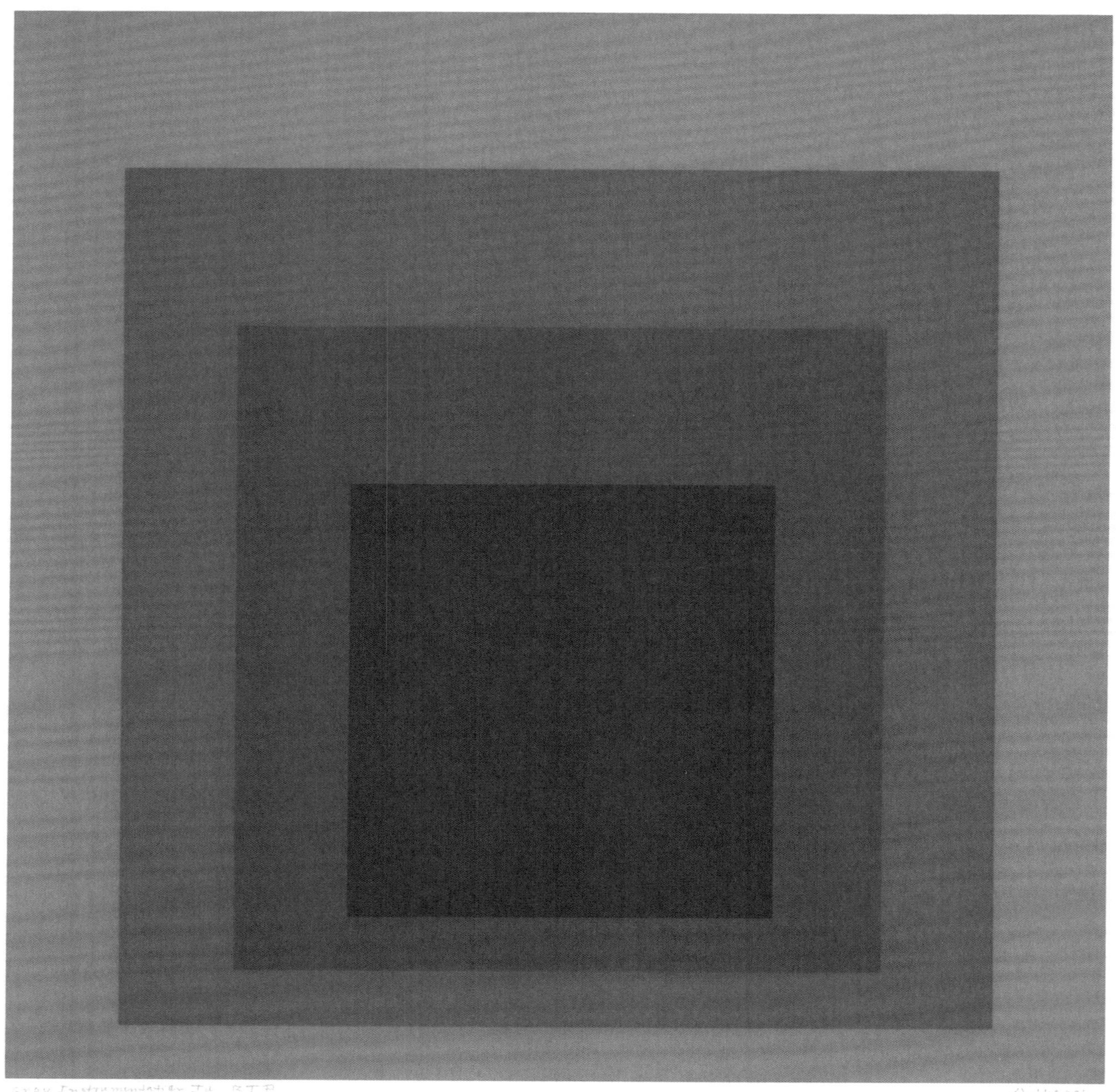

Below Josef Albers, *Gray Instrumentation Ib* 1974, from the *Gray Instrumentation I* series 1974, screenprint, image 28 × 28 cm, sheet 48.2 × 48.2 cm

Below Josef Albers, *Gray Instrumentation Ic* 1974, from the *Gray Instrumentation I* series 1974, screenprint, image 28 × 28 cm, sheet 48.2 × 48.2 cm

Below Josef Albers, *Gray Instrumentation Id* 1974, from the *Gray Instrumentation I* series 1974, screenprint, image 28 × 28 cm, sheet 48.2 × 48.2 cm

Below Josef Albers, *Gray Instrumentation Ie* 1974, from the *Gray Instrumentation I* series 1974, screenprint, image 28 × 28 cm, sheet 48.2 × 48.2 cm

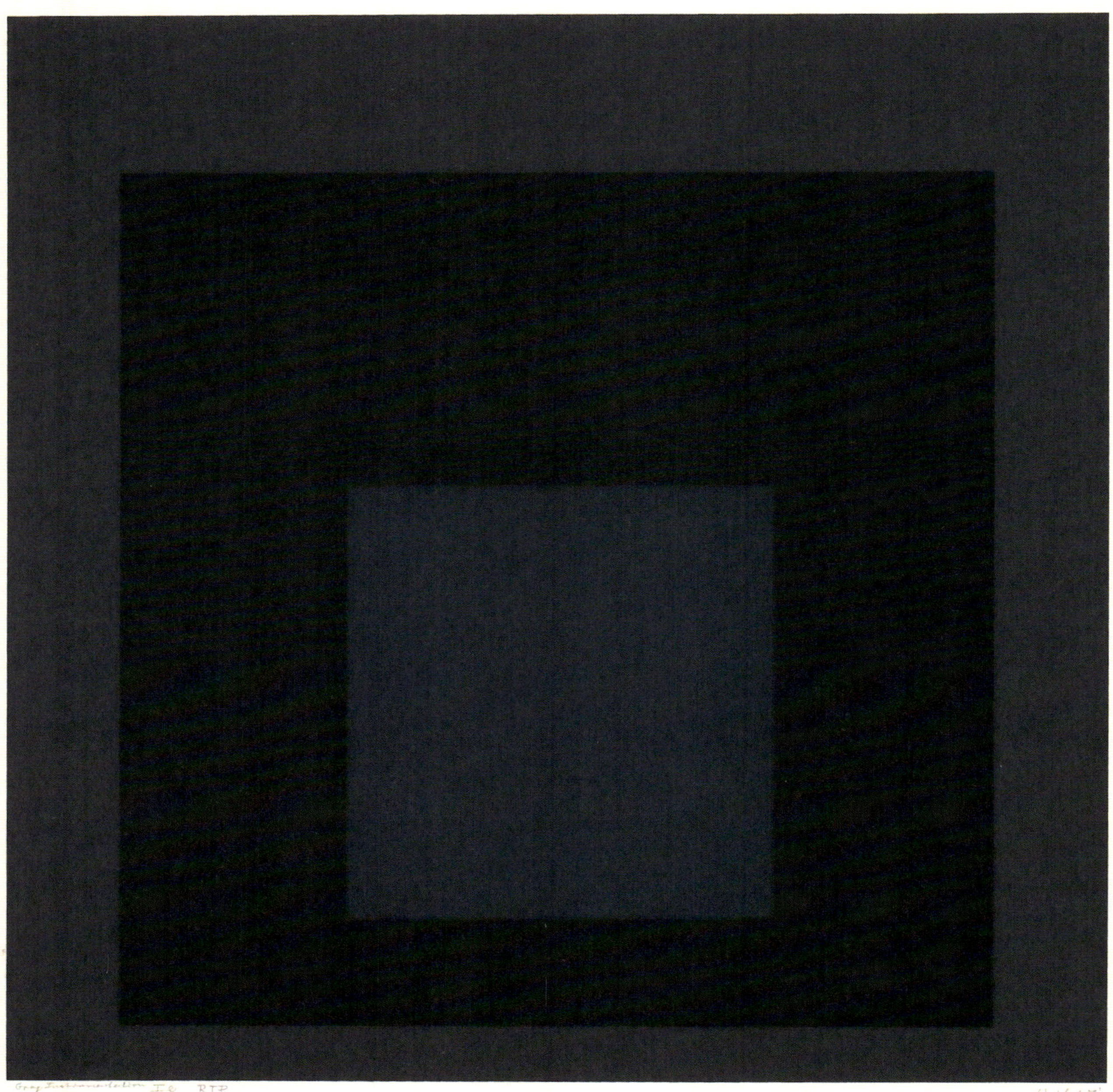

25 Below Josef Albers, *Gray Instrumentation If* 1974, from the *Gray Instrumentation I* series 1974, screenprint, image 28 × 28 cm, sheet 48.2 × 48.2 cm

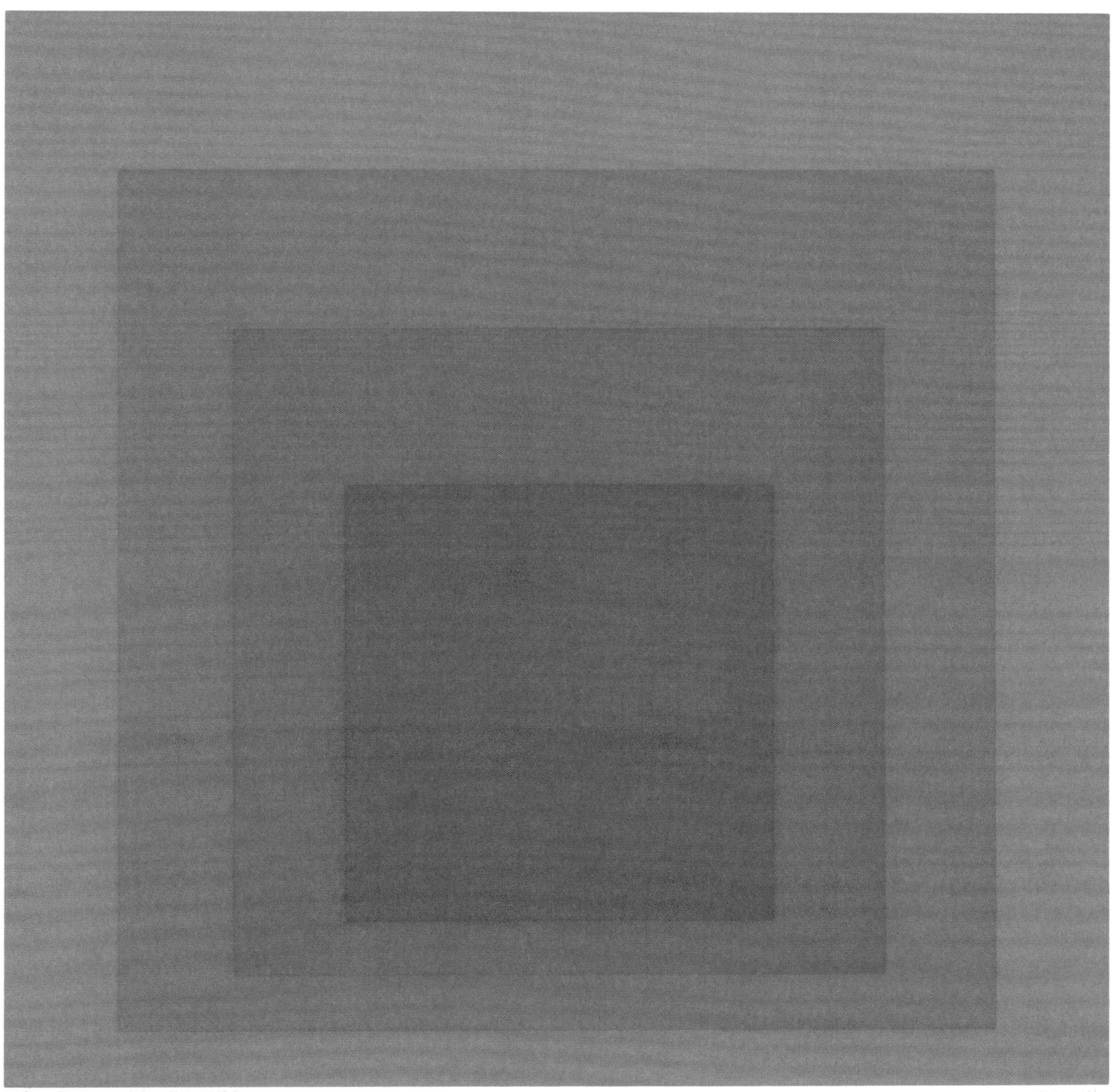

Below Josef Albers, *Gray Instrumentation Ig* 1974, from the *Gray Instrumentation I* series 1974, screenprint, image 28 × 28 cm, sheet 48.2 × 48.2 cm

Below Josef Albers, *Gray Instrumentation Ih* 1974, from the *Gray Instrumentation I* series 1974, screenprint, image 28 × 28 cm, sheet 48.2 × 48.2 cm

Below Josef Albers, *Gray Instrumentation Ii* 1974, from the *Gray Instrumentation I* series 1974, screenprint, image 28 × 28 cm, sheet 48.2 × 48.2 cm

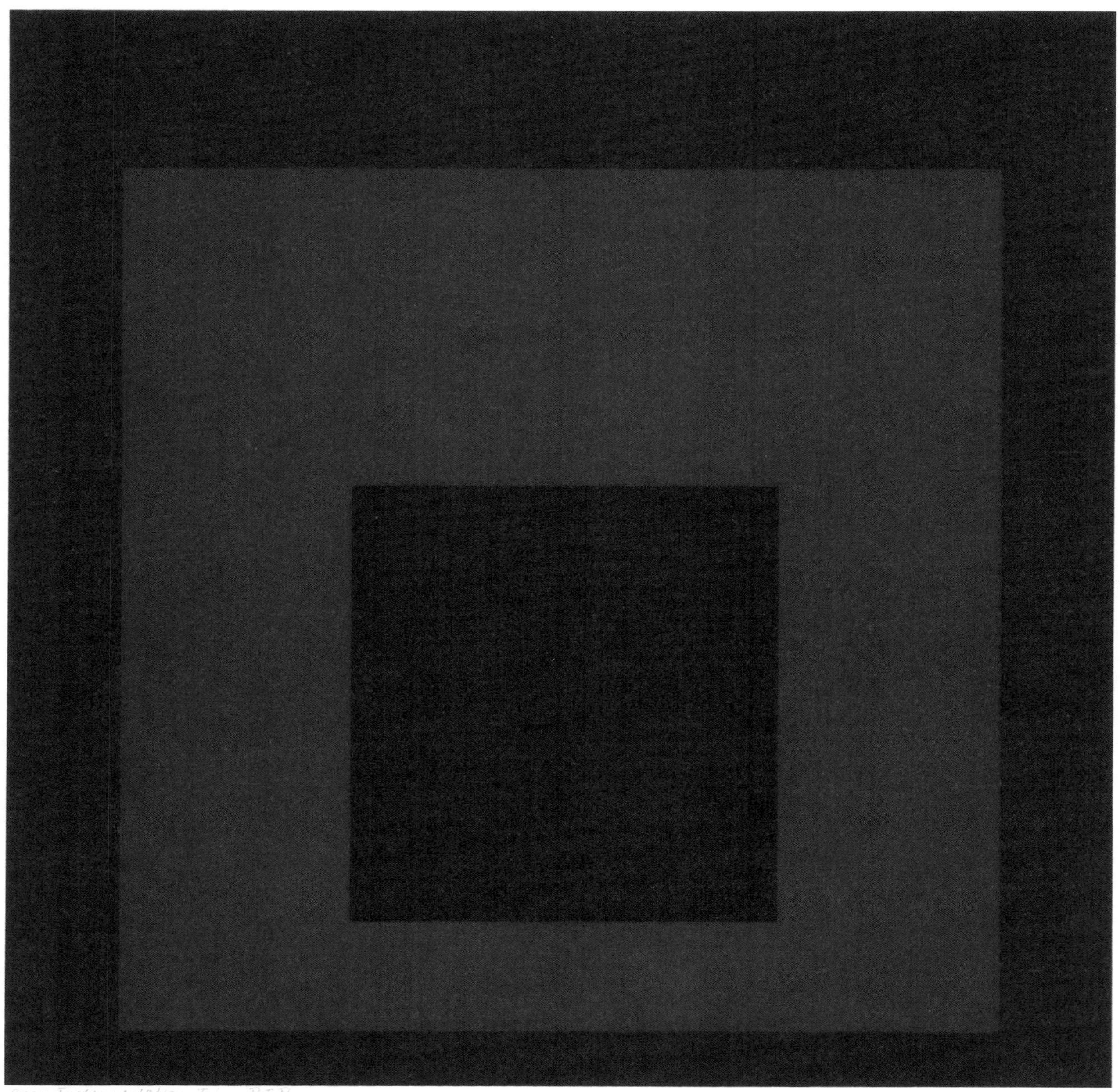

Below Josef Albers, *Gray Instrumentation Ij* 1974, from the *Gray Instrumentation I* series 1974, screenprint, image 28 × 28 cm, sheet 48.2 × 48.2 cm

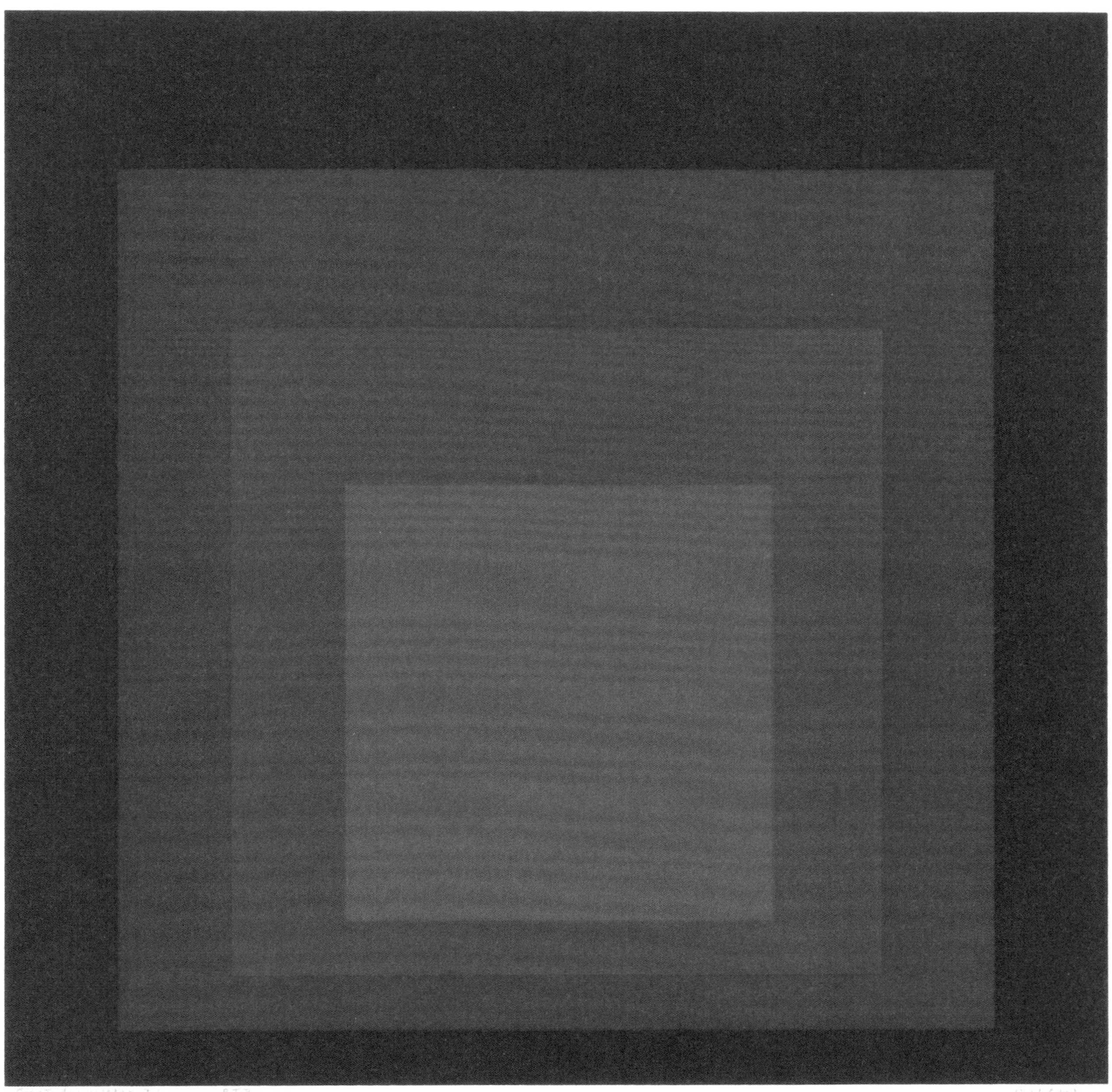

Below Josef Albers, *Gray Instrumentation Ik* 1974, from the *Gray Instrumentation I* series 1974, screenprint, image 28 × 28 cm, sheet 48.2 × 48.2 cm

Below Josef Albers, *Gray Instrumentation II* 1974, from the *Gray Instrumentation I* series 1974, screenprint, image 28 × 28 cm, sheet 48.2 × 48.2 cm

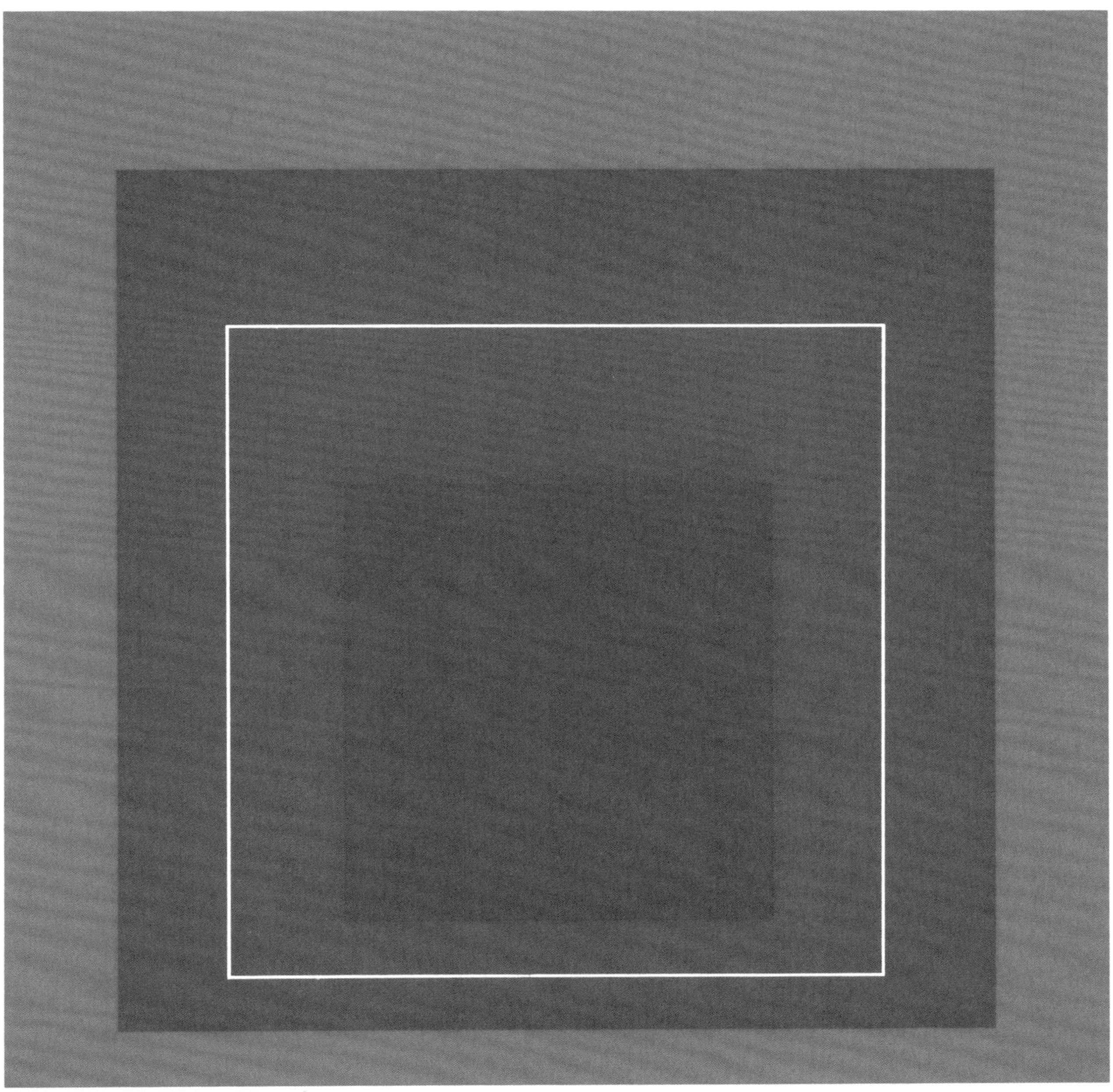

Below Josef Albers and Kenneth Tyler in the artist's New Haven, Connecticut studio, 1969, digital file from black-and-white photo print, photo by William Crutchfield, Kenneth E Tyler Collection archive, National Gallery of Australia

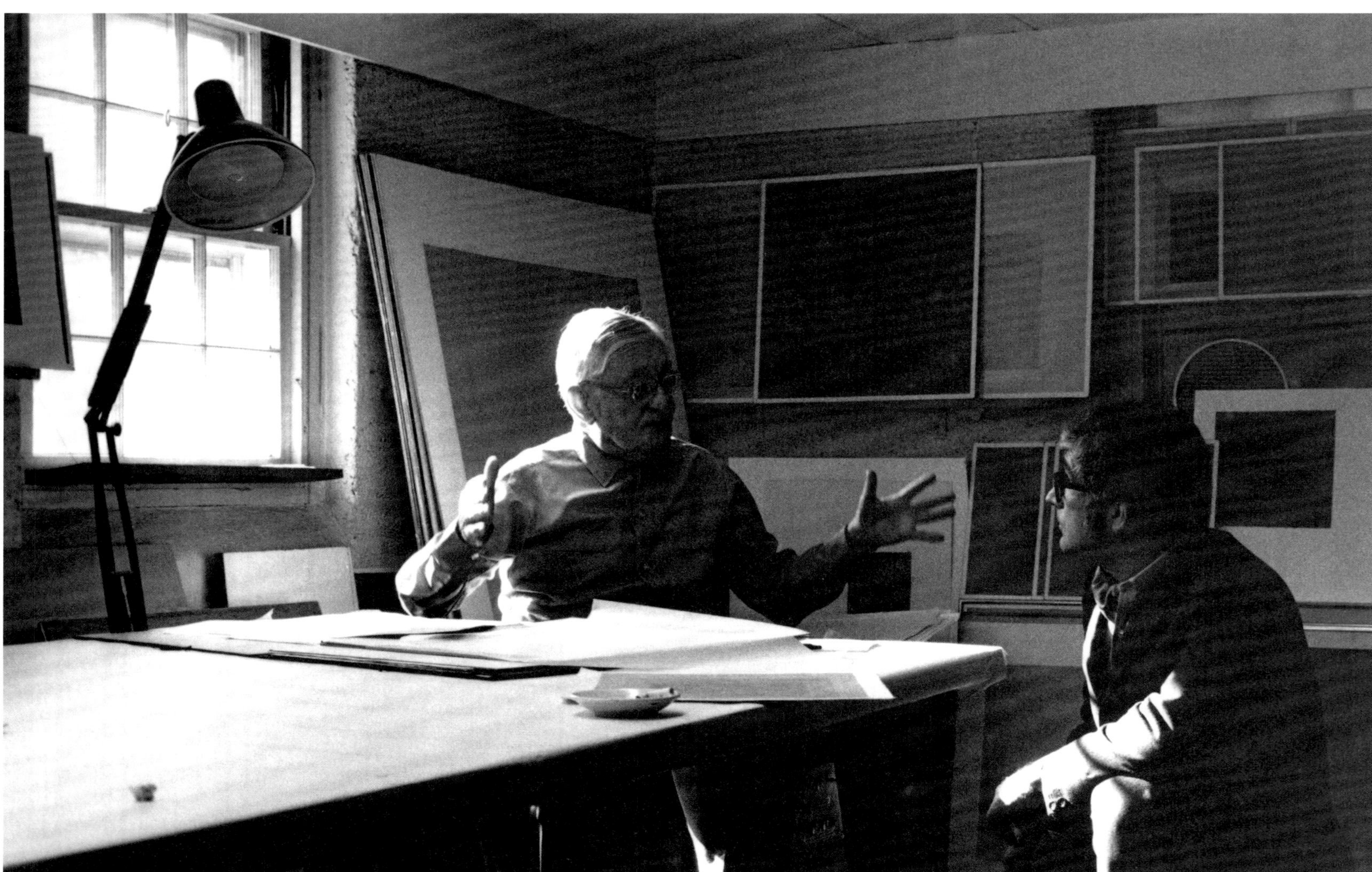

The Bauhaus: a lifelong preoccupation

Imogen Dixon-Smith

The Bauhaus was a brief but monumental modernist project. Across 15 heady years, students and masters came together in Weimar, Dessau and Berlin under the common goal of renewing artistic endeavour, rejecting the academies of the past to embrace a new spirit 'dependent upon the cooperation of many individuals, whose work reflects the attitude of the entire community'.[1] Two figures in particular stand steady in the unsettled life of the school. Enrolling as students at the Bauhaus in 1920 and 1922 respectively, Josef and Anni Albers became two of the most persistent forces dedicated to implementing the Bauhaus vision until the school was shuttered in 1933. During their tenure they were both students and teachers, and in both roles they grew with the school, straddling periods of change and borrowing what they needed to embody their own interpretation of the Bauhaus spirit.

For the Alberses, principles absorbed at the Bauhaus crackled like embers beneath their mature art practices in America. In 1963 the couple were introduced to up-and-coming printer Kenneth Tyler during a residency at Tamarind Lithography Workshop in Los Angeles. The intensity with which Anni, Josef and Tyler connected—over a shared commitment to innovation through practice, the marriage of craftmanship and industrial processes, collaborative thinking, and high-quality art accessible to the masses—generated an energy that reignited those Bauhaus cinders. Tyler embodied many of the principles that the Alberses cherished, albeit channelled through a very different personality, and it was these points of connection that allowed the two artists to produce their most technically ambitious prints with him. While Tyler did not profess to align himself with Bauhaus teachings, his background, intellect and ambition merged into the perfect prodigy of two Bauhäuslers ready to realise their ideas in print. This essay draws on the National Gallery's collection of Bauhaus material and its extensive collection of prints made by the Alberses in collaboration with Tyler to illustrate the extent of this intellectual and attitudinal connection.

The Alberses and the Bauhaus ethos

In 1920 Josef Albers, a teacher from north-west Germany with working-class roots, packed his bags for Weimar to start life anew at the Bauhaus: 'I was thirty-two ... threw all my old things out the window, started once more from the bottom. That was the best step I made in my life.'[2] Two years later, Annelise Fleischmann felt the same pull of the radical and progressive and left the comforts of her affluent life in Berlin to enrol at a school where the living conditions were meagre but the air electric. There was an instant bond between the two when they met and in 1925, once Josef had secured permanent employment at the Bauhaus, they married. Annelise assumed the name of Anni Albers. Although they learnt different mediums as students—Anni weaving on the loom and Josef assembling in the glass workshop—the Bauhaus marked the point at which their artistic practices were most strongly aligned. From these beginnings their work evolved to the point where both artists became leading contributors to the Bauhaus ethos.

Art itself cannot be taught, only the way to it.[3]

> What has made the Bauhaus famous is the teaching method of enveloping the youngsters to free them ... Not its lamps or its furniture. They are all out of fashion already. But the way of approaching formal problems or material as such, that has made it famous.[4]

1 Walter Gropius, 'The theory and organization of the Bauhaus', 1923, republished in Herbert Bayer, Walter Gropius and Ise Gropius (eds), *Bauhaus 1919–1928*, Museum of Modern Art, New York, 1938, pp 22–23. The Bauhaus was established in Weimar in 1919, before moving to Dessau (1925–32) and Berlin (1932–33).

2 Josef Albers, quoted in Nicholas Fox Weber, 'A new light: Josef Albers's work in glass', in *Josef Albers: glass, color, and light*, The Solomon R Guggenheim Foundation, New York, 1994, p 9.

3 László Moholy-Nagy, 'New Bauhaus catalogue', 1937, quoted in 'A visionary founder: László Moholy-Nagy', *Aperture*, no 87, 1982, p 6.

4 Josef Albers, 'At the Bauhaus', in Heinz Liesbrock (ed), *Josef Albers: interaction*, Yale University Press, New Haven, 2018, p 78.

Below Wilhelm Wagenfeld, *Kubus-Geschirr* (*Cube-tableware*) 1938, press-moulded glass, 16.5 × 18 × 18 cm

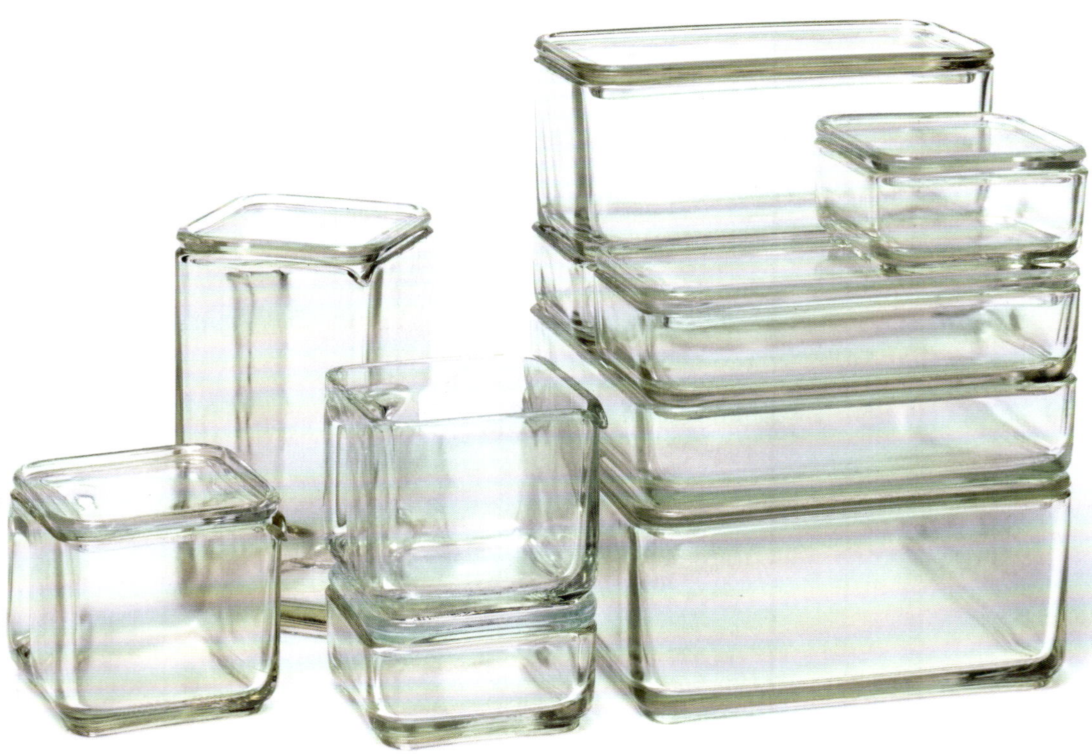

While a history of the Bauhaus is too extensive and complex to consider here, it is important to ground a discussion of the Alberses' creative spirit within the broader context of the school. Established in the turbulent landscape of postwar Germany by architect Walter Gropius, the school opened its doors in the city of Weimar in 1919 with an ambition to provide an artistic education distinct from that offered at traditional academies. As Gropius wrote in 1923:

> The tool of the spirit of yesterday was the 'academy'. It shut off the artist from the world of industry and handicraft, and thus brought about his complete isolation from the community. In vital epochs, on the other hand, the artist enriched all the arts and crafts of a community because he acquired through actual practice as much adeptness and understanding as any other worker who began at the bottom and worked his way up.[5]

Here Gropius expresses the idealism of a school grounded in the determination to bring art, craft and industry together into an interdisciplinary, practice-based curriculum, in which experimental artistic enquiry engaged with contemporary problems. This approach was intended to encourage students and masters to work in unity, like craftsmen working on a medieval cathedral—to realise what Gropius referred to as 'the new building of the future'.[6] The school was centred on a group of specialised workshops that, in theory, would work collaboratively on the delivery of artistic projects. In the early years, this included workshops in weaving, wall painting, glass, wood and metal, later expanding to photography, advertising and typography. While the utopian ideals of the Bauhaus were not always reached, its objectives still diffused into the psyches of the artists it housed.

A holistic approach to learning informed the structure of the curriculum. Upon admission to the school, all students undertook a preliminary course (*Vorkurs*) focused on material and formal studies, which introduced them to the foundational principles of art and design. The first iteration of the course was designed by Swiss artist Johannes Itten, who sought to establish the centrality of teamwork, experimentation and languages of design, while simultaneously assessing the most appropriate workshop for each student's apprenticeship.[7] It is worth noting that gender was often taken into consideration when assigning women to a workshop. This was true for Anni Albers, who was assigned to weaving despite her lack of interest in the medium. She recalled: 'My beginning was far from what I had hoped for: fate put into my hands limp threads! Threads to build a future?'[8] However, she quickly thrived in the experimental environment of the workshop, and 'distrust turned into belief and I was on my way'.[9]

The preliminary course also acted as a way of flattening out the varied levels of prior knowledge and training across the student body.[10] This diversity was a result of Gropius's radical approach to admissions. There were no prerequisite academic requirements and students from a range of backgrounds were encouraged to apply. This included women and international students and was also reflected in the cosmopolitan staff appointed by Gropius. Material support was provided to break down financial barriers for some students, and there was a wide range of ages represented in the student body—Josef Albers, for example, entered the school aged 32, while Anni Albers was 21.

The preliminary course was particularly influential in casting the typology of a Bauhaus student. Rather than being instructed in a particular style, the students were encouraged to build up an instinctive sense for visual possibilities through an intensive study of materials and their properties in relation to design and function. Itten taught students to study the 'essence' of natural materials such as feathers and thistles, to articulate their fundamental properties.[11] This approach became the basis of a Bauhaus student's training, and was embraced in various ways by many masters,

5 Gropius, 1923, p 23.
6 Walter Gropius, 'First proclamation of the Weimar Bauhaus', 1919, republished in Bayer et al, p 18; see Achim Borchardt-Hume, 'Two Bauhaus histories', in *Albers and Moholy-Nagy: from the Bauhaus to the New World*, Tate Publishing, London, 2006, p 68.
7 Michael Siebenbrodt, 'The Staatliches Bauhaus in Weimar—an avant-garde school of design 1919–1925', in Michael Siebenbrodt (ed), *Bauhaus Weimar: designs for the future*, Hatje Cantz, Ostfildern, 2000, p 12.
8 Anni Albers in *The woven and graphic art of Anni Albers*, Renwick Gallery of the National Museum of American Art, Washington, DC, 1986, p 13.
9 Anni Albers, 1986, p 13.
10 Siebenbrodt, p 12.
11 Siebenbrodt, p 12.

Below Josef Albers, *Gray Instrumentation II* series 1975, screenprints, image 28 × 28 cm (each), sheet 48.2 × 48.2 cm (each)

including Josef Albers, who made it the central tenet of the *Vorkurs* on his appointment to the position of master in 1923. He stated in 1928:

> Ours is an economically oriented age ... economic form arises out of function and material. Study of material naturally precedes understanding of function. Thus our attempt to come to terms with form begins with study of the material.[12]

Several works held in the National Gallery collection demonstrate the realisation of these fundamental ideas. Industrial designer and Bauhäusler Wilhelm Wagenfeld typified the successful resolution of form, material and function learnt at the Bauhaus in his *Kubus-Geschirr* (*Cube-tableware*) 1938. Manufactured by Vereinigte Lausitzer Glaswerke in 1938, the simple rectilinear forms of the containers shed any decorative associations and combine the sturdiness and clarity of glass with a modular design that allows containers in different sizes to be stacked in space-saving arrangements. The contents are easy to see and the containers easy to clean. Importantly, Wagenfeld took into consideration the needs of users and used the elegance of good design to address them.

Another exercise undertaken in the *Vorkurs* saw students test the limits of tonal gradation.[13] A study executed in Paul Klee's course in 1927 is an example performed by an unknown student at the Bauhaus in Dessau whereby a gradual alteration in the density of black was drawn across the page to test the extent to which a scale of gradation can be perceived by the human eye. This exercise shows the influence of Bauhaus masters such as Itten and Klee, particularly their interest in the use of contrast to arrive at a sense of harmony—thinking that was derived from colour theorists such as Adolf Hölzel and Johann Wolfgang von Goethe. Likewise, *Colour chart, blue, yellow, red on black* 1922 by Ludwig Hirschfeld-Mack, an early student of the Bauhaus, demonstrates the synthesis and application of new theories of colour at the Bauhaus, which took into account the psychic impact of colour. As Itten proclaimed, 'Each individual colour is a universe in itself.'[14] The colour chart refers to an exercise devised by Wassily Kandinsky which surveyed students' instinctual assignation of the three primary colours to the three most basic shapes—a square, a triangle and a circle. Interestingly, Hirschfeld-Mack's instruction board differs from the model proposed by Kandinsky, which assigned yellow to the 'sharp' triangle, blue to the 'restful' circle and red to the 'assertive' square.

Once students completed the preliminary course they were each assigned to a workshop where they commenced as an apprentice. Anni Albers wrote in 1938 that 'those starting to work in weaving or in any other craft were fortunate to have had no traditional training. It is no easy task to discard conventions, however useless.'[15] Training students to be proficient in their craft was a central component of the Bauhaus model and informed the workshop structure. Hirschfeld-Mack, for example, entered the print workshop as an apprentice in 1919 under Paul Klee, where he was trained in the operation of the presses and the preparation of printing blocks and plates for multiple processes including woodcut and lithography.[16] His hard work and dedication quickly made him essential to the running of the workshop, and his progression to the status of 'journeyman' (*Geselle*) was conferred on 23 April 1921.

While the structure of the workshops and curriculum implied a sense of hierarchy and upward progression, this was tempered by Gropius's focus on collectivism, which encouraged work done through 'the joint efforts of a group, each individual bringing to it his interpretation of a mutually accepted idea'.[17] Gropius later described the objective of the Bauhaus as 'unity in diversity and conquest of the cult of personality'—an ideal that was not always met.[18] Anni and Josef Albers both saw the early years as ones characterised by a plurality of ideas, structured by very little but an appetite for the new. Anni recalled that when she arrived, the Bauhaus 'was in a

12 Josef Albers, quoted in Oliver Barker, 'Albers's preliminary course: function and material', in *Bauhaus: a conceptual model*, Hatje Cantz, Ostfildern, 2009, p 244.
13 Siebenbrodt, p 12.
14 Johannes Itten, *The art of color*, Reinhold Publishing Corporation, New York, 1961, p 117.
15 Anni Albers, 'The weaving workshop', 1927–28, in Bayer et al, p 143.
16 Resi Schwarzbauer with Chris Bell, *Ludwig Hirschfeld-Mack: more than a Bauhaus artist*, HistorySmiths, Thornbury, Victoria, 2021, pp 38–39.
17 Anni Albers, 1927–28, in Bayer et al, p 144.
18 Walter Gropius, 'The idea of the Bauhaus—the battle for new educational foundations', trans Eva Richter and Alba Lorman, in Eckhard Neumann, *Bauhaus and Bauhaus people: personal opinions and recollections of former Bauhaus members and their contemporaries*, Van Nostrand Reinhold, New York, 1970, p 22.

great muddle and there was a great searching going on from all sides', and the masters 'were trying to find their way and were obviously not considered masters yet and didn't talk much to the students'.[19] However, a common purpose and appreciation for experimentation as a vehicle for change became the thread tying the school together: 'We knew that what the Academy was doing was wrong and it was exciting that you knew you had the freedom to try out something ... You were a contributor.'[20] In letters exchanged with Josef later in life, Hirschfeld-Mack shared similar sentiments, though also highlighting a cult of personality among staff members that went against the creed of collectivism:

> At the Bauhaus—even in the beginnings at Weimar, I felt sometimes, too much effort was made by some people to propagate their own name and importance. When masters and apprentices were gathered for this now famous Weimar photo—I deliberately did not appear, because I felt then, there was too much emphasis on [the] individual for show ... I still maintain that this special creative gift of the few, which lifts their work above average—belongs to humanity and is not for the benefit and fame for the individual.[21]

Written to Josef some 40 years after their time at the Bauhaus, this reflection suggests Hirschfeld-Mack's desire to connect with a Bauhäusler who maintained similar values. Josef carried a disdain for art that promoted the cult of the persona well into his career; movements such as Abstract Expressionism were anathema to him. To Josef, a plurality of views was significant to the success of the Bauhaus project: 'the best thing in the Bauhaus [was] that we were absolutely independent and we didn't agree on anything. So when Kandinsky said yes, I said no. We were the best of friends but we wanted to expose them to different viewpoints.'[22] As art historian Heinz Liesbrock writes, 'the arbitrary, the whim of the moment, and the exaggeration of the personal do not have any place in Albers' artistic ideas. He was averse to every emphasis on expression.'[23]

New priorities and new masters: moving towards industry

Of particular importance to the Alberses' experience of the Bauhaus are the significant changes that occurred in 1923, which marked a point of rupture in the school's trajectory. Rising economic pressures forced the school to turn its attention more acutely toward industry, while the appointment of a new generation of masters helped to rationalise and concentrate the school's radical spirit. Again, idea and execution did not always coalesce; however, the ambition was to align workshop activities with the mechanisms of industry to remain productive and relevant:

> A Call to All Members!
> The First Bauhaus Exhibition, planned for the summer of 1923, must, first of all, demonstrate the work and goals of the Bauhaus for the broader public, and at the same time serve as an appeal to these circles, as evidence that we do not wish to withdraw in a resigned or arbitrary manner, but instead are willing to take our place in the life of the community by means of creative work, and service.[24]

Labelled 'a question of do or die for the Bauhaus', the mission to grab the attention of industry had become a financial imperative.[25] With the school subsisting largely on ad hoc commissions from private citizens and the school itself—such as crockery for the dining hall and stained-glass windows for the director's office—senior staff were concerned that the work being produced in the workshops was moving away from the school's core values. In a talk to students in October 1922, Gropius

19 Anni Albers, 'Oral history interview with Anni Albers', 5 July 1968, Smithsonian Archives of American Art, Washington, DC, transcript, last updated 11 December 2002, p 4.
20 Anni Albers, 1968, p 4.
21 Ludwig Hirschfeld-Mack, letter to Josef Albers, 21 July 1961, JA 4-50_1958–1965_Lud, Papers of Josef and Anni Albers, the Josef and Anni Albers Foundation, Bethany, Connecticut.
22 Josef Albers, in interview, *Josef and Anni Albers: art is everywhere*, 2006, dir Sedat Pakay, film, 15 mins 30 secs, Hudson Film Works, New York.
23 Heinz Liesbrock, 'Honesty and modesty: Josef Albers', in Liesbrock, 2018, p 58.
24 Walter Gropius, proclamation issued at the Bauhaus, 13 October 1922, quoted in Éva Forgács, *The Bauhaus idea and Bauhaus politics*, trans John Bátki, Central European University Press, Budapest, 1995, p 100.
25 Lyonel Feininger, in 1922, quoted in Forgács, p 98.

Below Ludwig Hirschfeld-Mack's Journeyman's certificate, 1921, letterpress, gift of Chris Bell 2015, National Gallery of Australia Art Archive

Next left Paul Klee, *Die erhabene Seite. Postkarte zur Bauhaus-Ausstellung* (*The sublime side. Postcard for the Bauhaus-exhibition*) 1923, lithograph, sheet 15 x 10 cm

Next right László Moholy-Nagy, *Postkarte zur Bauhaus-Ausstellung* (*Postcard for the Bauhaus-exhibition*) 1923, lithograph, sheet 15 x 10 cm

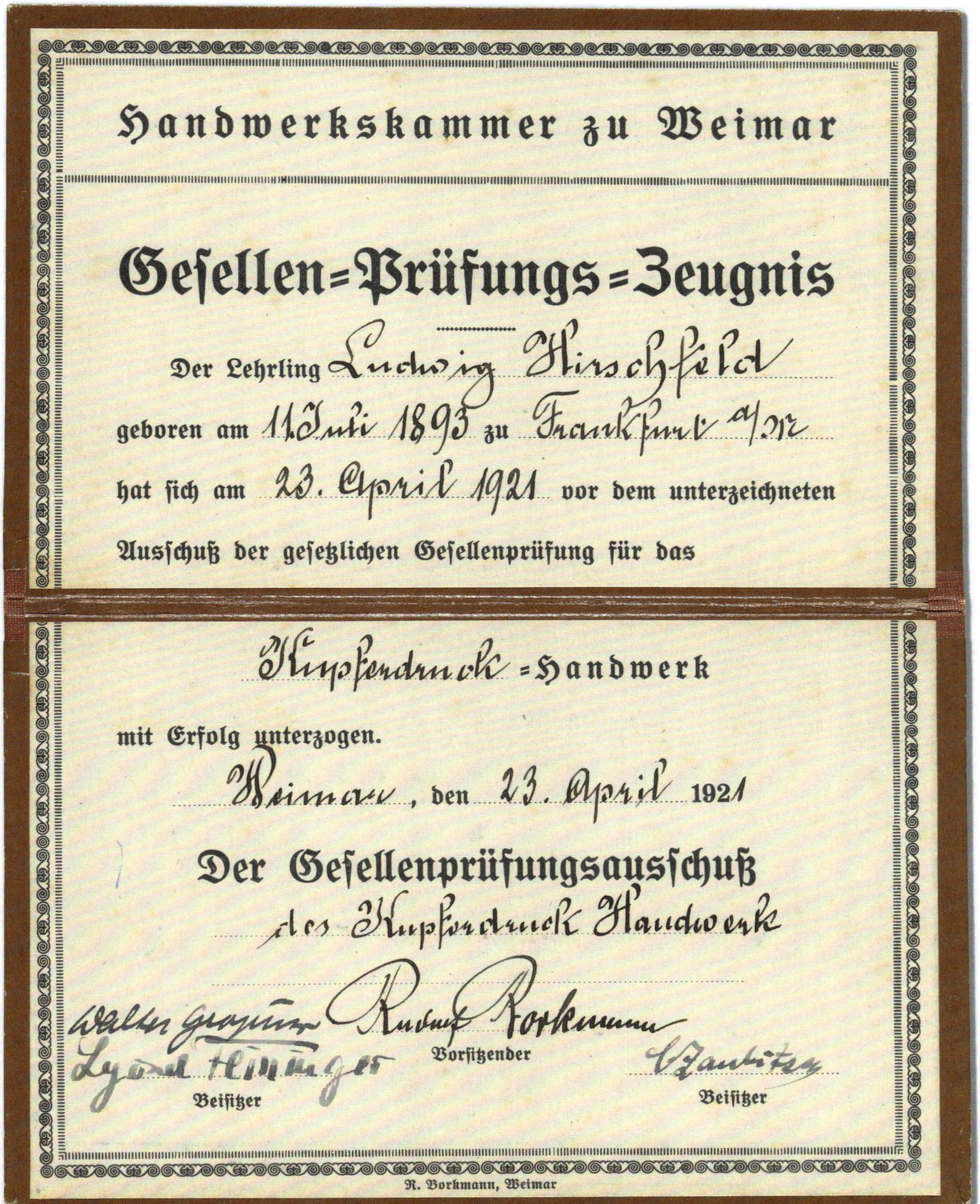

Handwerkskammer zu Weimar

Gesellen=Prüfungs=Zeugnis

Der Lehrling Ludwig Hirschfeld

geboren am 11. Juli 1893 zu Frankfurt a/M

hat sich am 23. April 1921 vor dem unterzeichneten

Ausschuß der gesetzlichen Gesellenprüfung für das

Kupferdruck=Handwerk

mit Erfolg unterzogen.

Weimar, den 23. April 1921

Der Gesellenprüfungsausschuß

des Kupferdruck Handwerk

Walter Gropius Rudolf Borkmann

Vorsitzender

Lyonel Feininger Zaubitzer

Beisitzer Beisitzer

R. Borkmann, Weimar

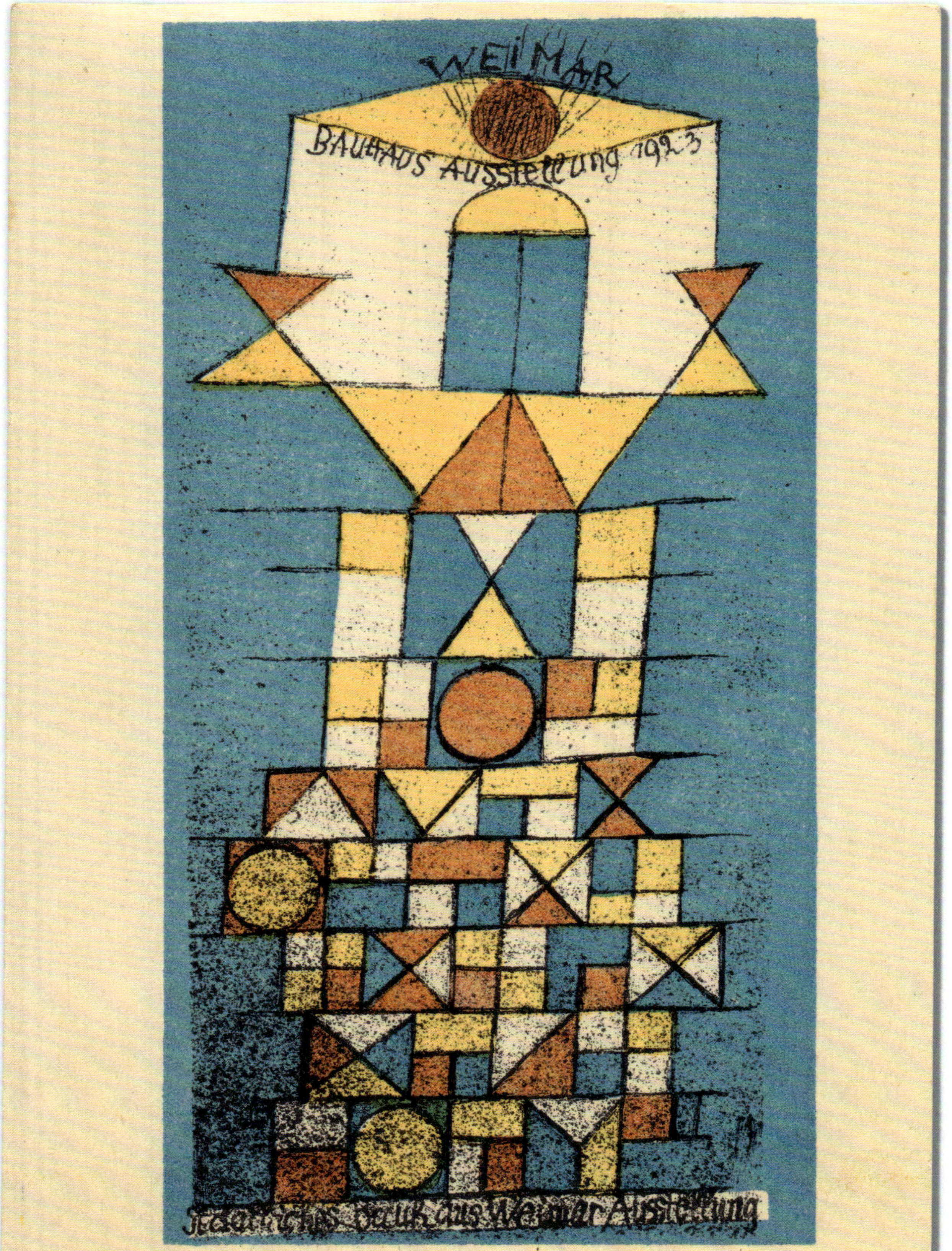
WEIMAR
BAUHAUS AUSSTELLUNG 1923

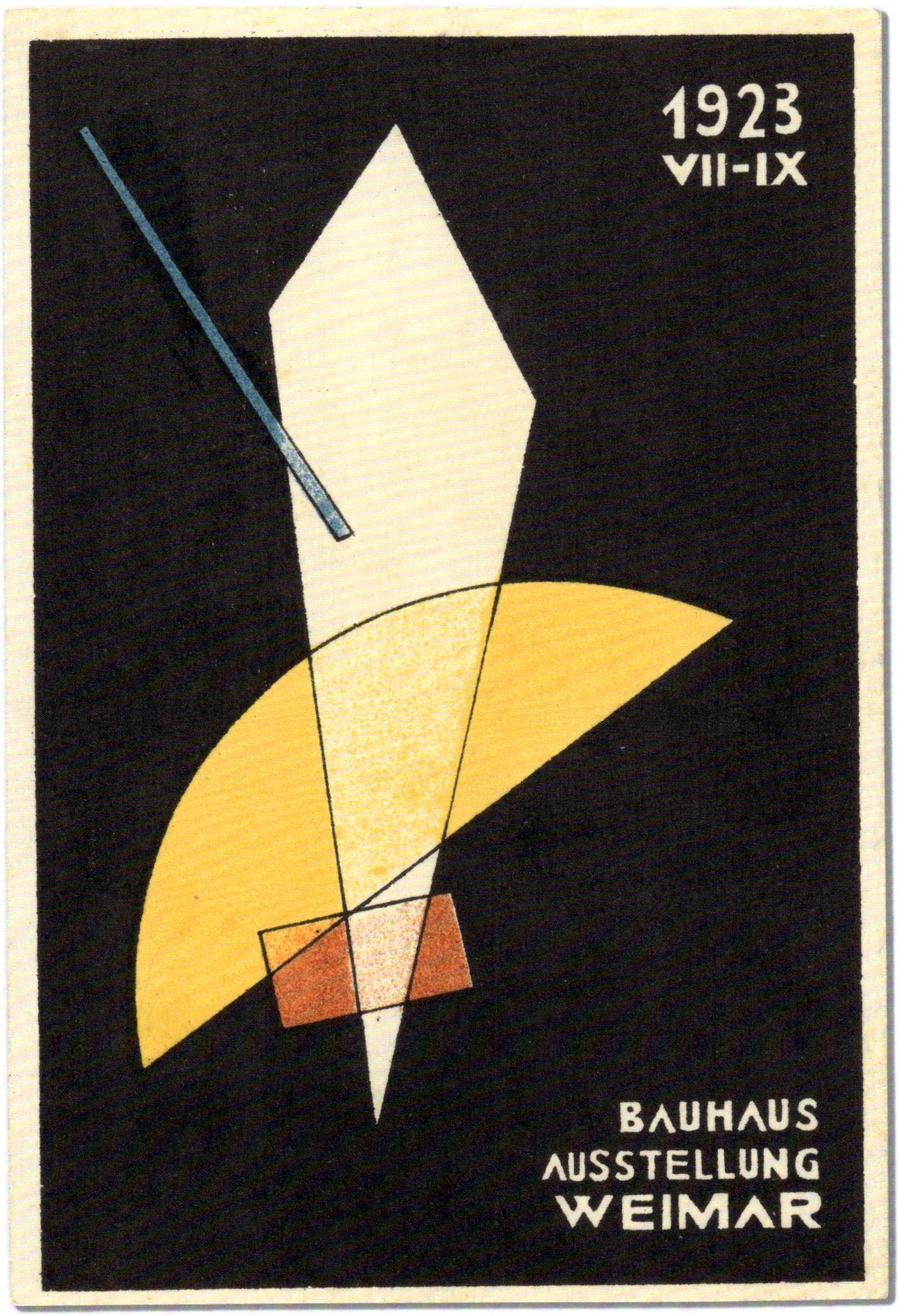
1923
VII-IX
BAUHAUS
AUSSTELLUNG
WEIMAR

proclaimed that the Bauhaus should not exist for the 'production of luxury goods for connoisseurs'.[26] The school was also facing mounting pressure from the Thuringia government to justify its funding. Gropius concluded that two things were required to secure economic independence: the interest of consumers and the interest of industry, thus the idea of an exhibition showcasing the work of the Bauhaus was born.

The rationale for the exhibition was simple—corral the workshops to build and furnish a model house that exemplified the guiding principles of the school and made a clear offer of its capabilities to industry as Gropius had articulated. As art historian Éva Forgács notes, this task 'constituted an immediate and symbolic goal for every student and master at the school'.[27]

Typically for the early Bauhaus environment, differing opinions were immediately voiced. Gropius had appointed Emil Lange as the first business manager of the newly established Production Department in 1922 in an effort to develop commercial opportunities. Lange expressed how drawing on the collective efforts of the workshops often resulted in 'refusals—counter-proposals—new concepts ... but no decision as to a practical course of action.'[28] Perhaps the scattered democracy of the school and its powerful nurturing of independent thought could hinder the realisation of its utopic aims. As Josef Albers recalled, 'At first the Bauhaus meant opposition for me. Naturally, the strongest opposition came from young people, and this was supported by the work and attitude of the masters, who also did not follow others nor repeat others.'[29]

Regardless of the convoluted negotiations and compromises it took to create and open the exhibition, it attracted 15,000 visitors over its three-month run and was praised as 'a triumph in public relations' by contemporary critics.[30] A comprehensive catalogue was produced for the exhibition, bringing the efforts of the workshops together, from printmaking and bookbinding to typography. Titled *Staatliches Bauhaus in Weimar 1919–1923*, it included an exegesis on the school by Gropius, colour reproductions of work by artists such as Josef Albers in the glass workshop and Benita Koch-Otte in the weaving workshop, as well as nine exquisite colour lithographs by masters and journeymen including Marcel Breuer, Herbert Bayer and Hirschfeld-Mack. Despite its public success, the exhibition largely failed to establish significant connections with manufacturers producing household objects.[31] As Josef Albers reflected in 1964, 'The greatest success of the Bauhaus was to win over and interest industry. We realised this aim only to a small degree. Time was too short and possibly not yet ready for it.'[32]

The year 1923 was also pedagogically significant as two new masters delivered the preliminary course: Josef Albers and László Moholy-Nagy. Albers was the first student of the Bauhaus to be promoted to the position of master and Hungarian constructivist Moholy-Nagy was brought on to breathe a new, mechanical spirit into the school. The pair aligned more closely than the first generation of masters had with Gropius's mission, spelt out in the title of the 1923 Bauhaus exhibition: 'Art and Technology: A New Unity'.[33]

Josef was the perfect fit to bridge the gap between craftsmanship and industry. From a young age he had developed a deep appreciation for the meticulous, skilled labour of the blacksmiths, cobblers and joiners in the workshops that dominated his neighbourhood in Bottrop.[34] Through observation he had learnt that a profound knowledge and experience of materials and processes was essential to making work of the highest quality, and he taught material studies in the preliminary course with an intensity that left little room for Itten's 'expressionistic tendencies'.[35] He began by asking his students to test the 'dormant possibilities' of a material such as paper, foil or wire, to explore both its external, aesthetic potential and its internal, structural potential.[36] This process allowed the students to build an acute sense of 'tactile scales'—between hard and soft, smooth and rough, or warm and cold. Josef also

26 Walter Gropius, quoted in Anna Rowland, 'Business management at the Weimar Bauhaus', *Journal of Design History*, vol 1, no 3/4, 1988, p 154.
27 Forgács, p 104.
28 Emil Lange, quoted in Forgács, p 109.
29 Josef Albers, 'Thirteen years at the Bauhaus', in Neumann, p 181.
30 Frank Whitford, quoted in Rowland, p 158.
31 Rowland, p 159.
32 Josef Albers, 1970, p 181.
33 Borchardt-Hume, p 68.
34 Liesbrock, 2018, p 56.
35 Barker, p 244.
36 Barker, p 245.

Top Herbert Bayer, Walter Gropius, László Moholy-Nagy, *Staatliches Bauhaus in Weimar 1919–1923* 1923, letterpress and lithograph, 25.1 × 25.5 cm

Bottom Ludwig Hirschfeld-Mack, Plate 2, from *Staatliches Bauhaus in Weimar 1919–1923* 1923, letterpress and lithograph, 25.1 × 25.5 cm

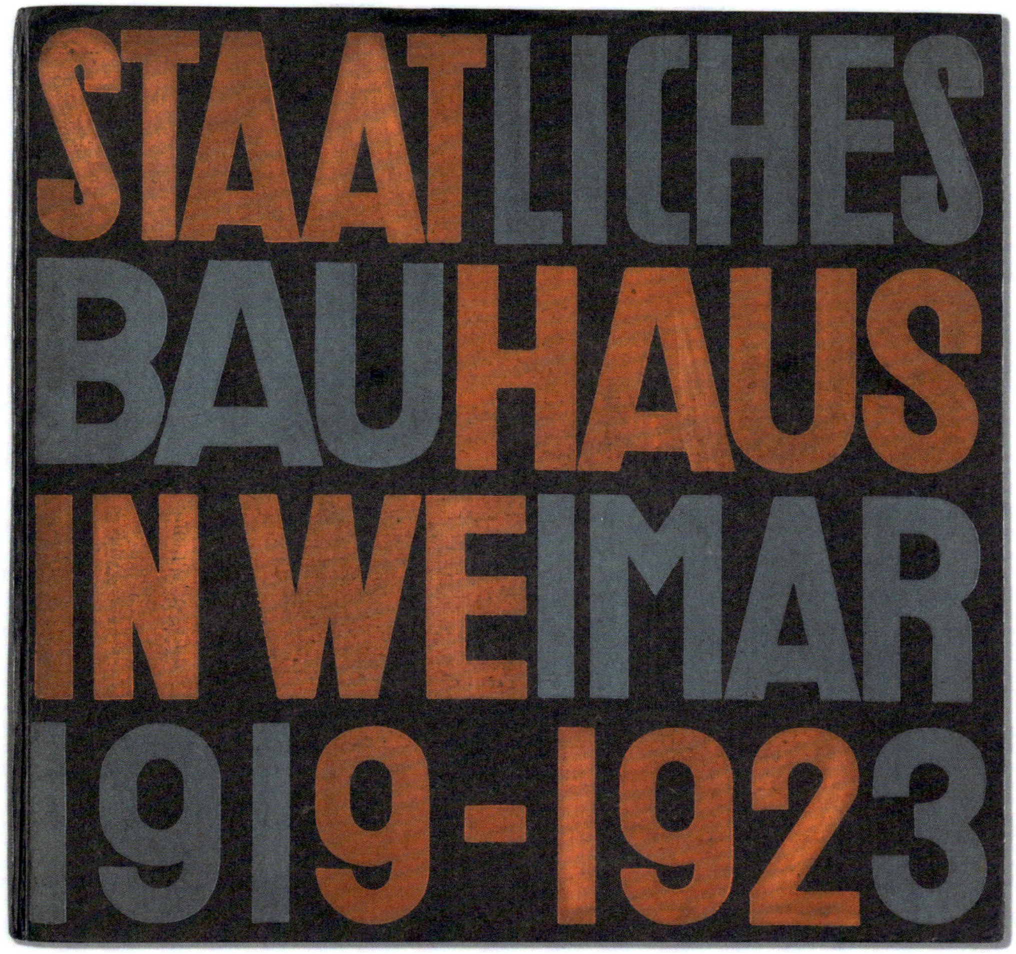

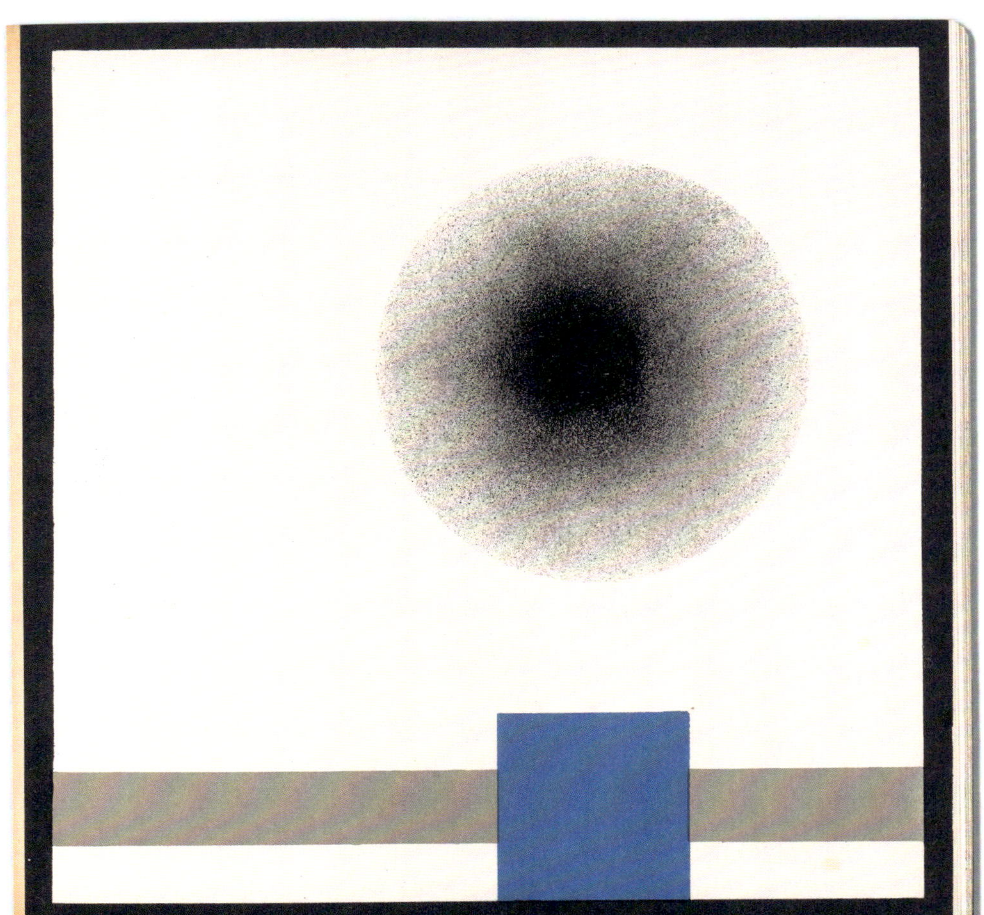

Below	Unidentified student, Bauhaus Dessau, Study executed in Paul Klee's course 1927, watercolour on paper, image 10.5 × 10.5 cm
Next left	Wari (Huari) people, central, south and north Peru, Tunic 500–800 CE, wool and cotton, 185 × 106.8 cm
Next right	Wari (Huari) people, central, south and north Peru, Band 600–1000 CE, wool and cotton, 49 × 7.6 cm

stressed the importance of economy, and set exercises that encouraged the minimisation of waste and an understanding of serial production that moved away from the 'snobbish interest in the unique work'.[37] This confluence of craftsmanship and industrial-minded design placed Josef's preliminary course at the centre of the Bauhaus's new orientation.

The activities of the weaving workshop also exemplified the redirection of the school, as energies shifted from the unification of art and craft to art and industry. The weaving workshop had been among the first to open in 1919, with Itten as its 'master of form', and Georg Muche joining as a master in 1921. A separate textile class run under the supervision of local artisan Helene Börner had merged with Itten's workshop in 1920. This early period is often referred to as the 'expressionist phase' because those who guided the workshop espoused handmade processes.[38] As Anni Albers recalled, 'in the early years there was a dabbling in a kind of romantic handicraft' fostered by Börner, who she described as 'a very inefficient old lady, sort of the needlework type'.[39] To the weaving students, Börner represented the stale decorative training of the academies and her reluctance to embrace experimental design on the loom led students to downplay her influence in the workshop.[40] Muche and Itten, on the other hand, embraced experimentation over instruction, helping to establish the workshop's creative approach. However, while students tested processes and patterns in an open-ended manner, the workshop's production remained somewhat incoherent. As Anni recounted, 'you knew nothing, you weren't taught anything, and you really dabbled around until something happened'.[41] There was particular concern over the weaving workshop's frequent inability to meet deadlines for commissions, especially given Lange saw it as having the most commercial potential.[42]

Perhaps this freedom inspired the strength of innovation from within the workshop itself, which contributed to a shift in direction towards industry. In 1922, students Gunta Stölzl and Benita Koch-Otte undertook a dyeing course in Krefeld and brought this expertise back, setting up a workshop that focused on dyeing with both natural fibres and chemicals. This gave students the skills to apply ideas circulating at the Bauhaus, such as colour theory, to their weaving. Muche was also committed to making the workshop more profitable. A Jacquard loom was purchased, which allowed complex patterns to be mechanically woven and offered at more reasonable prices.[43] In 1924 Stölzl and Koch-Otte returned to Krefeld to undertake a manufacturing course.

The changing aims of the Bauhaus were also reflected in the workshop's approach to using pre-Columbian textiles as source material. As art historian Virginia Gardner Troy writes, these materials offered 'an ideal alternative to the European tapestry tradition that many members of the Bauhaus Weaving Workshop sought to overthrow'.[44] While Itten's influential appropriation of the art of pre-Columbian and other ancient cultures had been focused on spiritual and symbolic qualities,[45] after 1923 interest among students in pre-Columbian textiles shifted towards technique and structure, a change that coincided with the Bauhaus moving towards industry-led working methods. Students such as Anni, with the goal of rationalising production techniques, started to apply the complex structures found in Andean weaving to their work on the loom.

Anni excelled in the successful application of techniques such as double and triple weaves, in textiles that drew their design from the process of weaving itself. Examples of multi-weave textiles, such as two bands created by unknown makers in the Wari (Huari) period (500–1000 CE) held in the National Gallery collection, provide an insight into the work of Andean weavers, who devised ways of incorporating up to four different planes of fabric in intricate geometric designs for ceremonial clothing. Similar examples were accessible to students of the weaving workshop in Germany's ethnographic museums, and had been described in archaeological reports by Wilhelm Reiss and Moritz Stübel.[46] Grasping the complexity of multi-weave constructions allowed Anni to experiment with colour patterning in new ways, as she

37 Josef Albers, quoted in Borchardt-Hume, p 74.
38 Virginia Gardner Troy, *Anni Albers and ancient American textiles: from Bauhaus to Black Mountain*, Ashgate Publishing Limited, Aldershot, 2002, p 40.
39 Anni Albers, quoted in Troy, p 40; p 42.
40 Troy, pp 42–43.
41 Anni Albers, quoted in Troy, p 47.
42 Rowland, p 154.
43 Troy, p 107.
44 Troy, p 44.
45 Troy, p 45.
46 Troy, p 50.

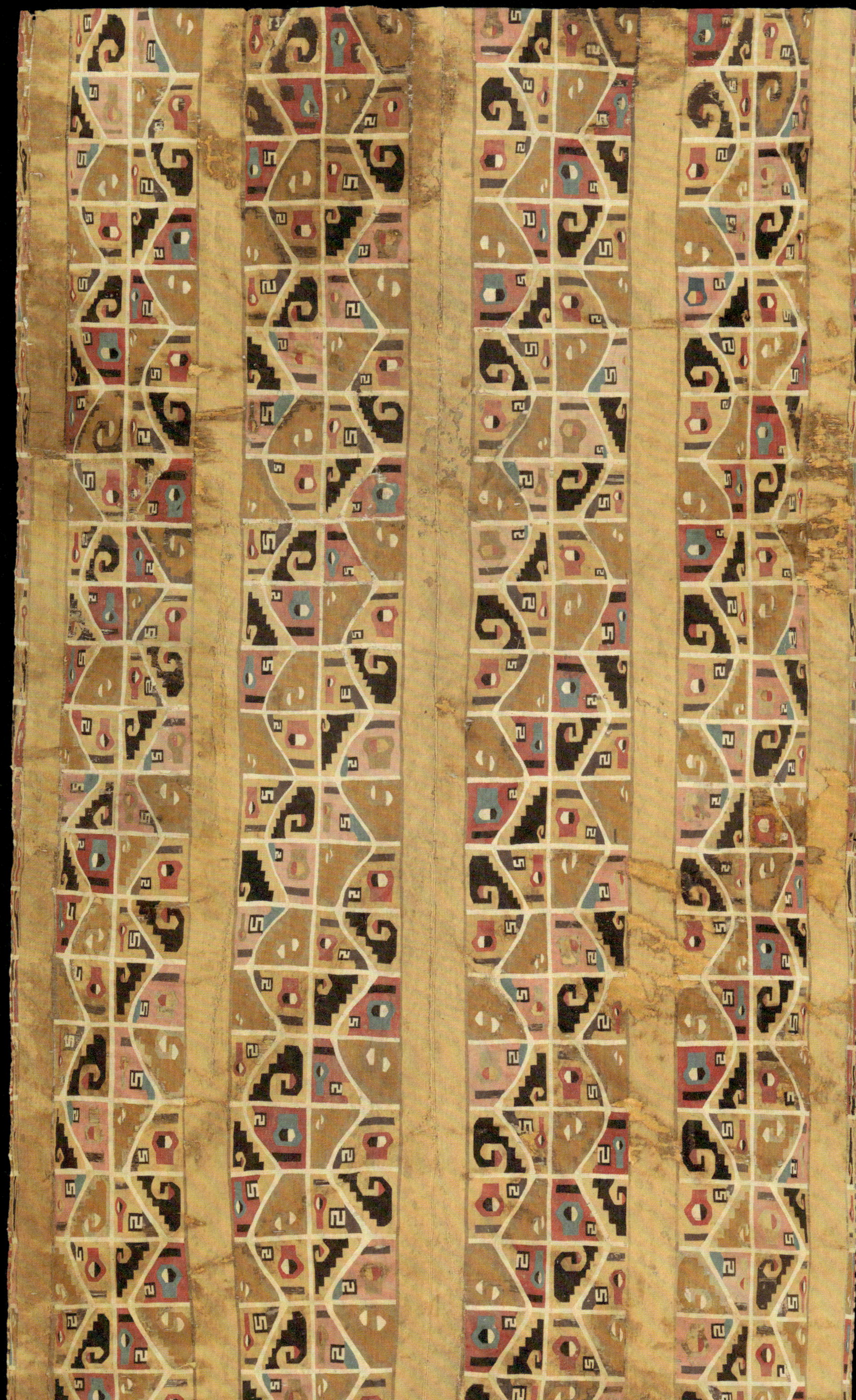

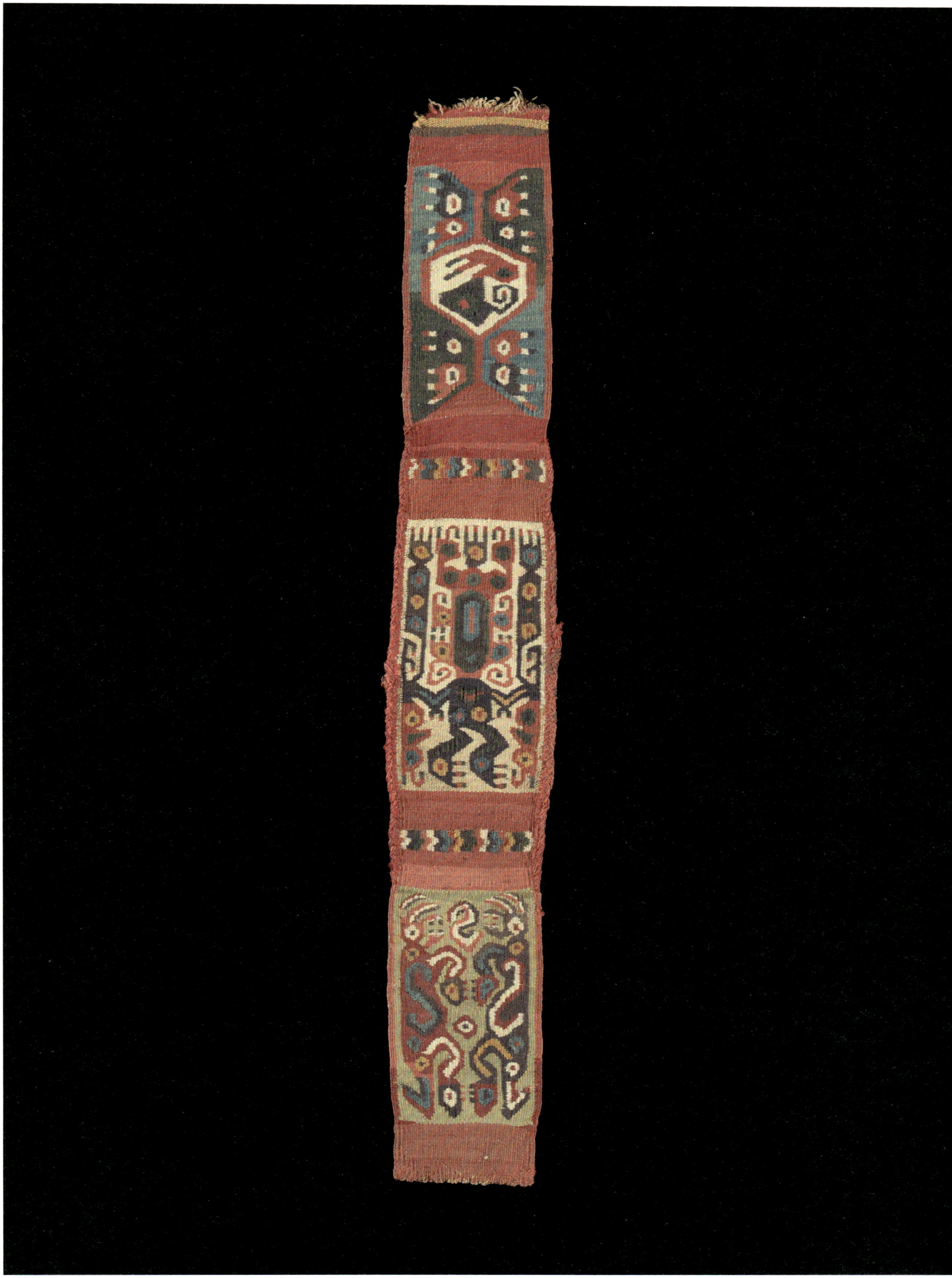

made multiple planes of fabric appear and recede.[47] These methods led to her famous wall-hangings produced at the Bauhaus, in which she played with the geometry of weaving to achieve non-symmetrical formal arrangements that appeared in unexpected and refreshing ways.

This geometry was mirrored in her husband's glass sculptures produced in the Dessau years of the Bauhaus (1925–32). Moving away from his early glass work, which on a technical level drew strongly from stained-glass traditions of assembling shards into compositions, Josef mastered the decidedly more mechanical processes of stencilling and sandblasting to arrive at flat geometric planes in arrangements that mimicked the burgeoning metropolis of the modern city. Decades later Josef produced the screenprint portfolio *Formulation : Articulation* 1972, an exercise in reflection and reinvention in which he revisited motifs from earlier works. He described a print that directly references his glass sculpture *Pillars* 1928, from Folio I, folder 22 and now in the National Gallery collection:

> Starting in the lower left corner with a tiny dark red square and continuing along the bottom edge with one light red line, we then follow a few small steps of the same light red as it leads up to a colossal building of many stories which ends broader than high at the top.[48]

The mechanical method of making glass, new to Josef, combined sandblasting and flashing techniques, and unlocked the potential for him to realise works in serial production.[49] It was the weaving workshop, however, which had a genuine market for its goods and was most suited to producing prototypes for manufacture. As weavers such as Anni mastered the marriage of material and technique with the functional applications of woven materials, they could move more smoothly between the hand and the machine:

> The desire to reach a larger group of consumers brought about a transition from handwork to machine-work: work by hand was for the laboratory only; work by machine was for mass production.[50]

For Anni, both craft and industry remained essential to her artistic endeavour. This is evident in her 1947 essay 'Constructing textiles', which takes the form of a thought experiment: she imagines herself as an Andean weaver witnessing the production of modern textiles. In so doing, she laments that these time-bending weavers would be horrified, not by the large machines used to produce textiles, but by the lack of experimentation performed by hand to produce prototypes that underpinned the meticulous construction of good design.[51]

New beginnings across the Atlantic

Anni and Josef's long tenure at the Bauhaus (Anni 1922–33; Josef 1920–33) saw the couple traverse a sea of shifting priorities, approaches and personalities that had come together under a common pursuit to cast off the shackles of the past and see things anew. When the Bauhaus closed its doors in 1933 facing insurmountable pressure from the National Socialist Party, the Alberses found themselves anchorless in Berlin. The loss of a steady income and access to the workshops saw Josef turn to woodblock printing for its economy and ease of production. Anni's Jewish heritage became an increasing concern as anti-Semitism rose across the country. In 1934, by chance, Anni ran into Philip Johnson from the Museum of Modern Art in New York. A strong admirer of Anni's work, Johnson saw an opportunity to bring her and Josef to the United States and suggested that Josef take up a teaching position at the newly established experimental Black Mountain College. Anni and Josef packed their bags once again and took up the invitation without hesitation. Arriving at the idyllic Black Mountain, the Alberses encountered new sources of inspiration, from the abundant nature that surrounded them to Mexico and its art, now in tantalising proximity. Josef reoriented his practice to painting, while Anni entered a new period of intense innovation in her weaving practice. Settling in to a familiar experimental

47 Troy, p 77.
48 Josef Albers, 'Statements of content: Portfolio I', *Formulation : Articulation*, Ives-Sillman, Inc, New Haven, 1972, unnumbered (p 3).
49 For the artist's description of the making process see Josef Albers in Liesbrock, 2018, p 88.
50 Anni Albers, 1927–28, in Bayer et al, p 144.
51 Anni Albers, 'Constructing textiles', 1947, republished in Nicholas Fox Weber and Pandora Tabatabai Asbaghi, *Anni Albers*, Guggenheim Museum, New York, 1999, pp 94–97.

Below Anni Albers, *Black-White-Red* 1926–27 (woven by Gunta Stölzl 1965), silk and cotton, plain weave double cloth of paired warps and wefts, 179.4 × 122.2 cm, the Art Institute of Chicago, 1970.343

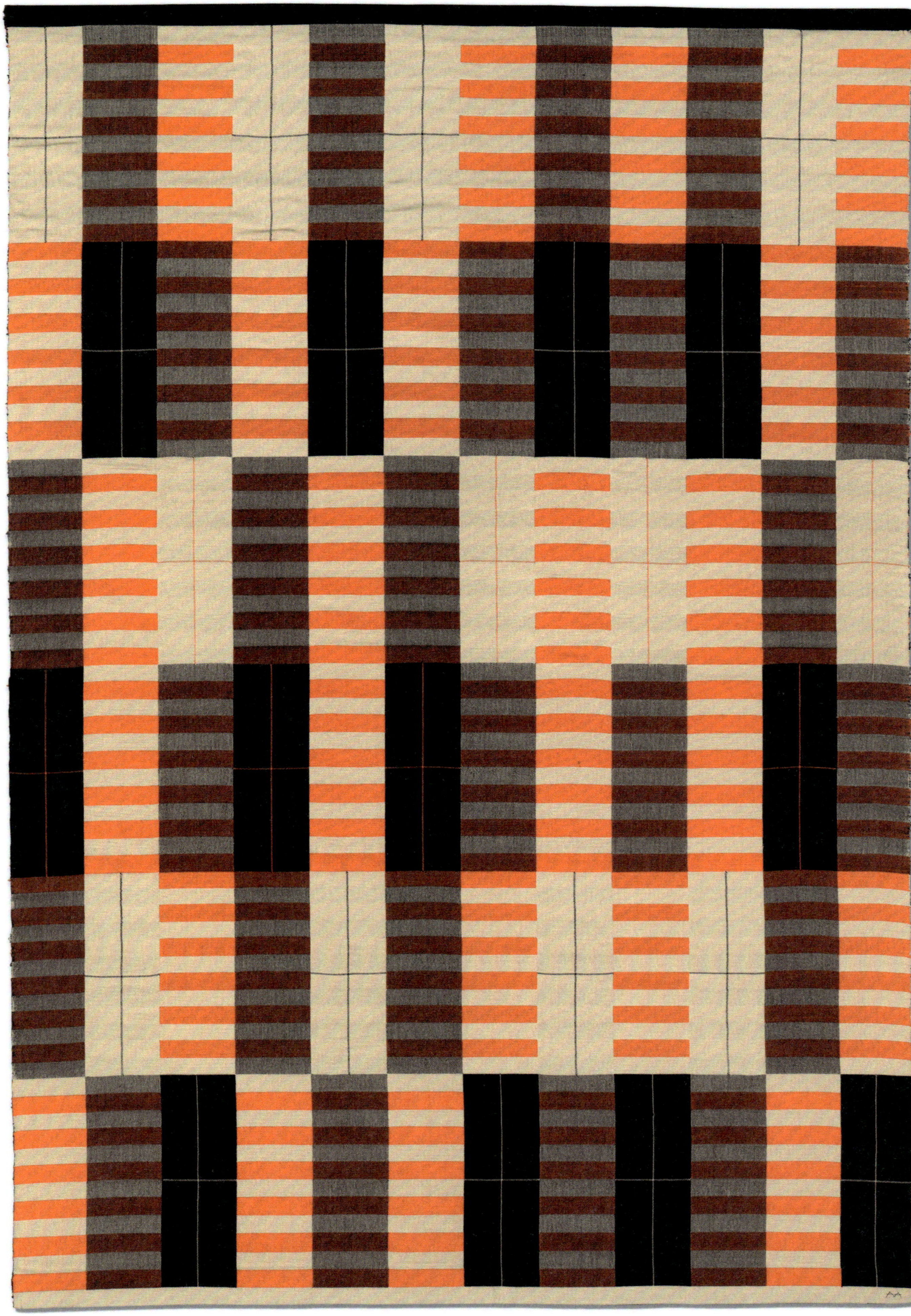

Below Josef Albers, Folio I, folder 22, from *Formulation : Articulation* 1972, screenprint, image 33.3 × 34.6 cm, sheet 38.2 × 50.7 cm

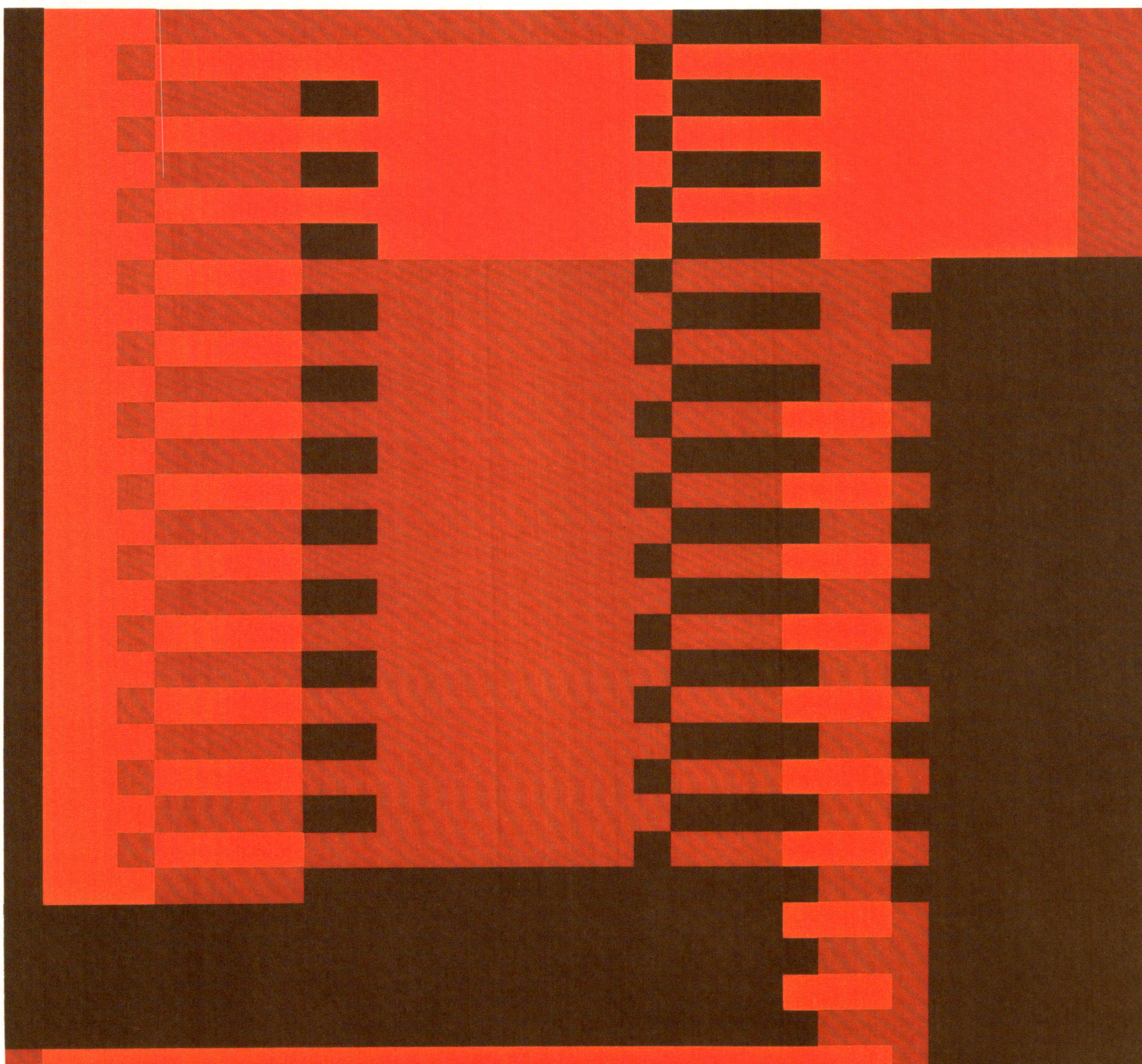

Below Josef Albers, *Pillars* 1928, sandblasted flashed glass, vitreous paint, metal and chipboard, 60.6 × 60.6 cm, the Metropolitan Museum of Art, New York, 1970.139

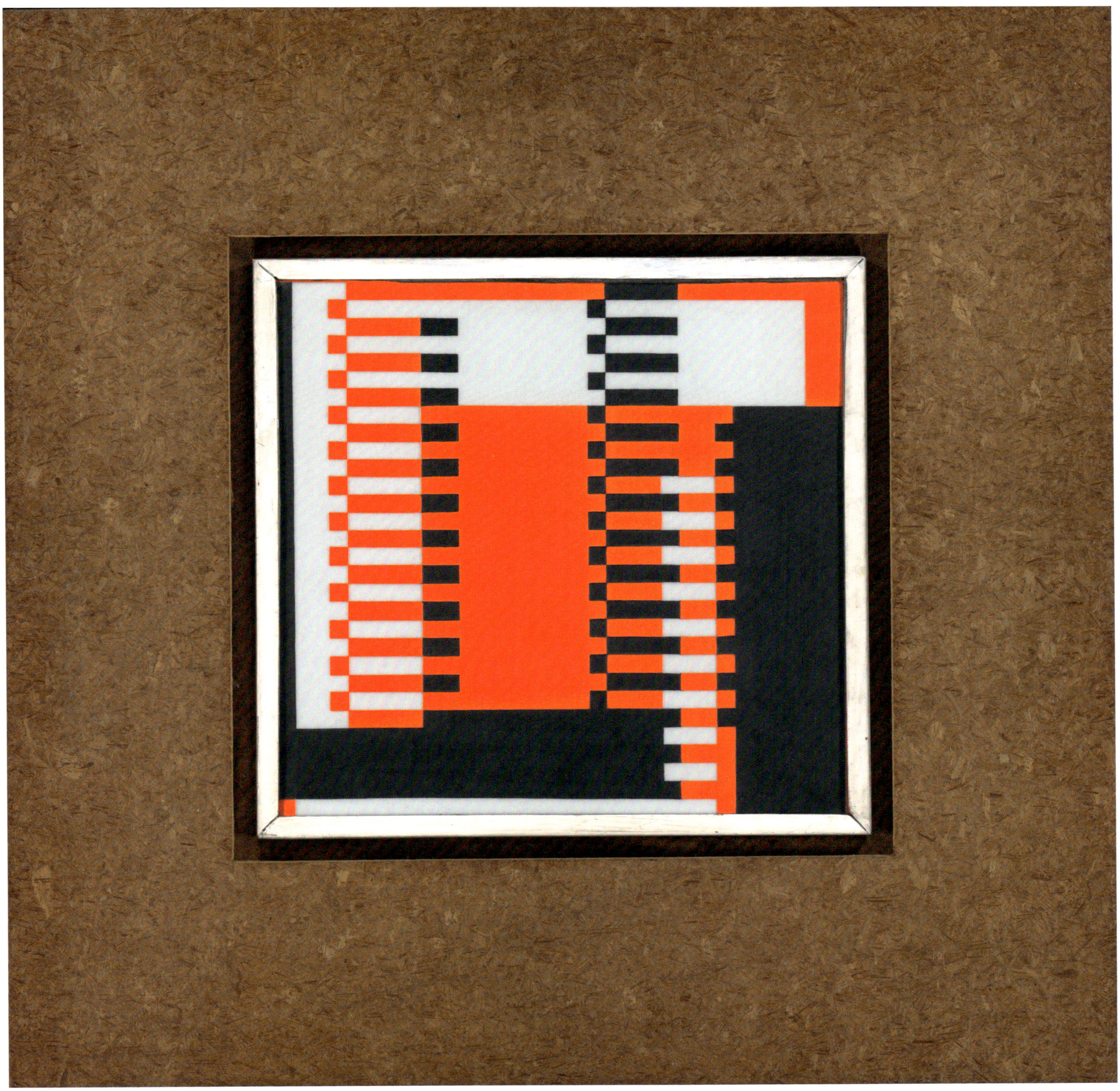

Below Lena Bergner, Weaving sample, swatch for clothing fabric 1930, handwoven cotton and rayon, 11.4 × 10.4 cm
Opposite Gunta Stölzl, Textile design c 1926, watercolour, gouache and pencil on paper, image 31 × 19 cm, sheet 35.8 × 25 cm

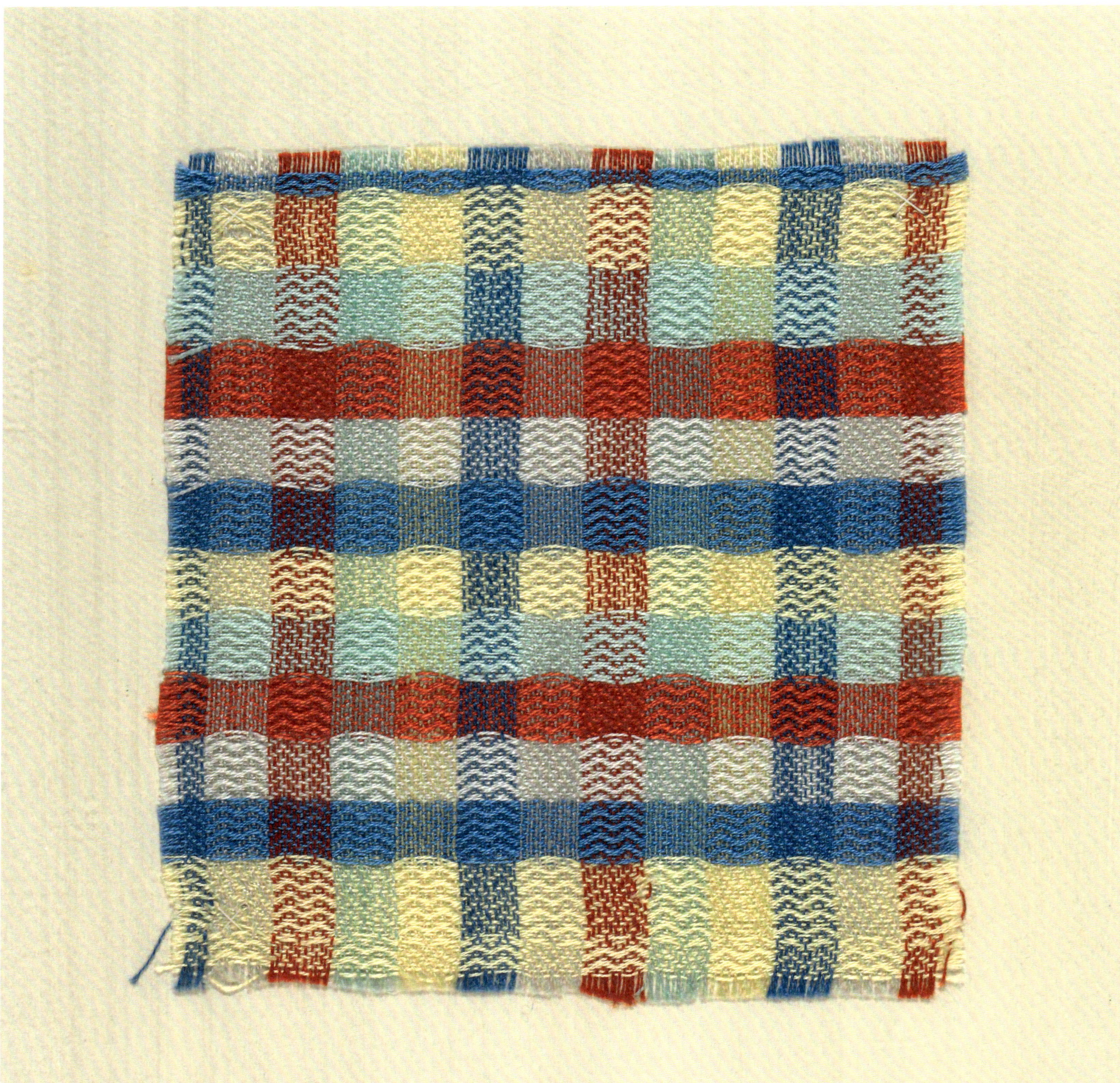

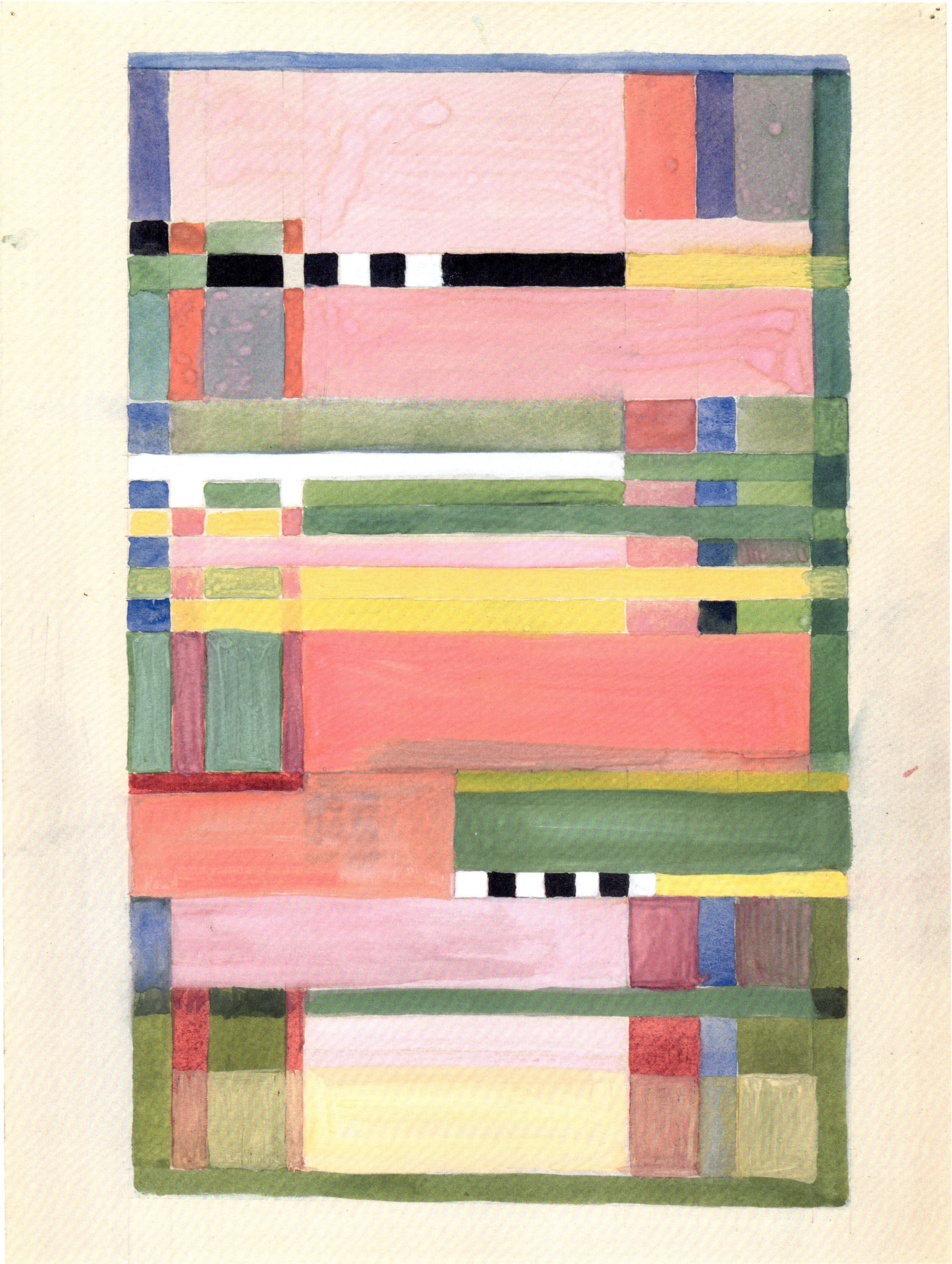

Below Josef Albers, *Zelte/Tents* 1933, woodcut, image 23.2 × 25.5 cm, sheet 29.2 × 31.9 cm
Next Josef Albers, Study for *Variant/Adobe* c 1947, oil on paper, 20.1 × 26.8 cm

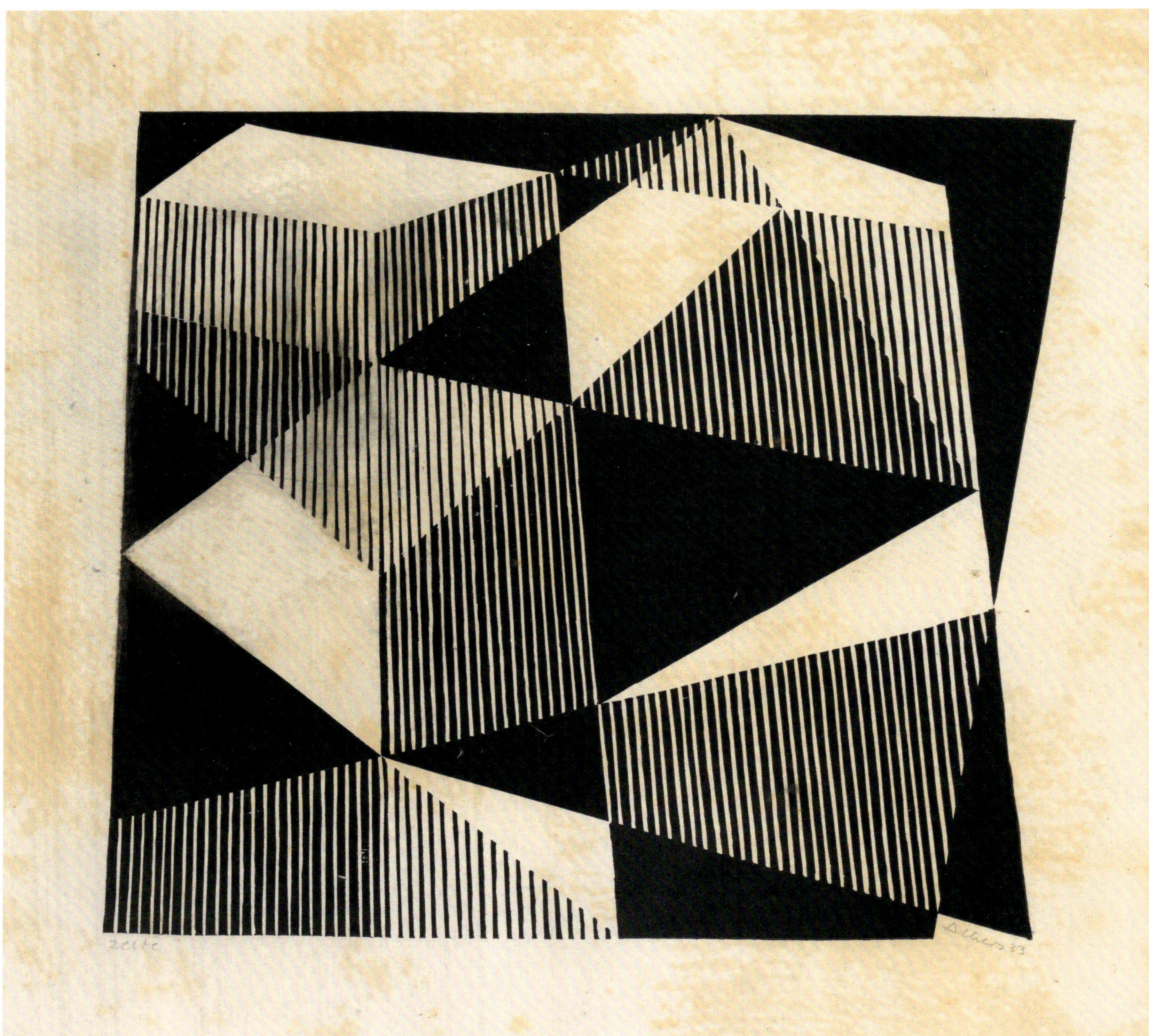

and collaborative environment at Black Mountain, the Alberses nonetheless expanded on the principles that had concerned them at the Bauhaus, taking their practices in exciting new directions. In 1950, they moved to Connecticut and continued to influence the development of modern art in America, with Josef heading up the department of design at Yale University and Anni continuing to weave and write, publishing her influential treatises *On designing* (1959) and *On weaving* (1965).[52]

After 30 years in the country, during a residency at Tamarind Lithography Workshop in Los Angeles, the Alberses came across a bright young printmaker who would coax out their Bauhaus beginnings. This relationship fostered the creation of exquisite prints that distilled the principles that each artist had inherited from their time at the school.

A revival of spirit: the Alberses and Kenneth Tyler

> He stirred my imagination, influenced me, and above all loved giving me a challenge and being there to cheer and praise me on. He was a very good friend, a teacher and an exceptional mentor.[53]

An extraordinary affinity can be drawn between the Bauhaus spirit that underwrote the Alberses' approach to art, and the youthful ambition of master printer Kenneth Tyler, who became the Alberses' greatest collaborator in the print workshop. Tyler was no stranger to Bauhaus concepts. It is significant that during his studies in the early 1950s he was close to students from the Institute of Design in Chicago (formerly the New Bauhaus), which embraced an interdisciplinary and holistic approach to design. He remarked in a recent interview, 'I was very familiar with the Bauhaus ... Don't forget where I came from, the Art Institute of Chicago.'[54] Josef gave him documents from the Bauhaus, including Gropius's early writings.[55] While Tyler has never been regarded as aligned with Bauhaus ideas, to the Alberses, the unique convergence of craftmanship, industry and experimentation that connected his interests to theirs had its roots in the Bauhaus.

Anni and Josef were united by a reverence for both craft and industry, resulting from their experience of the shifting instructional landscape of the Bauhaus. Embracing new technologies while remaining devoted to a firsthand knowledge of materials and processes lay at the heart of their practice. Anni remembered that students at the Bauhaus 'had felt the sterility of the art academies and their too great detachment from life. They believed that only manual work could help them back to solid ground and put them in touch with the problems of their time.'[56] Josef's upbringing had much to do with his receptiveness to these ideas. He grew up the son of a tradesman in the industrial town of Bottrop, an environment where the skilled application of a trade was central to a person's working life. Josef credited his father for teaching him how to paint a door, starting from the centre and working outwards to maintain a smooth appearance, catching any drips as he progressed across the surface.[57] This method became central to his painting, most significantly of his ongoing *Homage to the Square* series; Josef painted the crisp geometry of a successive arrangement of squares by hand, from the centre outwards. Josef also gained from these early experiences an understanding that 'every artistic activity is characterized by meticulousness, disciplined practice, and technical skill'.[58]

Tyler came from similar origins. Born in an industrial town in Indiana, his father was a steel worker and Tyler himself took up a job handling and processing the raw materials of manufacturing to help pay for his schooling.[59] He credits his father for inspiring in him a love of materials and labour: 'my love of stones, of the

52 Anni Albers, *On designing*, The Pellango Press, New Haven, 1959; Anni Albers, *On weaving*, Wesleyan University Press, Middletown, 1965.

53 Kenneth Tyler, in Pat Gilmour, *Ken Tyler, master printer, and the American print renaissance*, Hudson Hills Press, New York, & Australian National Gallery, Canberra, 1986, p 46.

54 David Greenhalgh, conversation with Kenneth Tyler, Lakeville, Connecticut, 9 September 2022, typed transcript, information management file 22/0013, National Gallery of Australia.

55 Judith Goldman, 'Kenneth Tyler: the artisan as artist', in *Tyler Graphics: the extended image*, Walker Art Center, Minneapolis, & Abbeville Publishers, New York, 1987, p 28.

56 Anni Albers, 1927–28, in Bayer et al, p 143.

57 Heinz Liesbrock, 'Movement in stillness: Josef Albers's ecstasy of colour', in Heinz Liesbrock and Michael Semff (eds), *Painting on paper: Josef Albers in America*, Hatje Cantz, Ostfildern, 2011, p 17.

58 Liesbrock, 2018, p 58.

59 Gilmour, p 33.

Below Josef Albers, *Homage to the Square: Impartial* 1966, oil on board, 121.9 × 121.9 cm

physicality of work comes from him'.[60] When he moved into sales for a steel manufacturer, he observed the importance of developing industrial techniques to the survival of a corporation.[61] His experience of, and receptivity to, a variety of practical jobs was a unique foundation that propelled him into the realm of innovation in his later work with artists. Following his art school studies, Tyler took up a fellowship at Tamarind Lithography Workshop in 1963 that helped set him on this path. Tamarind was instrumental in the burgeoning revival of printmaking occurring at the time, and while Tyler thought it did not push technological innovation far enough, the experience gave him clarity of purpose. He shared the pioneering spirit that had absorbed the Alberses at the Bauhaus, and wanted to create art for a modern society:

> By 1964 it became clear to me that most traditional methods, as well as some recent practices of the hand-printing crafts, were not compatible with the images of major contemporary artists. As a collaborator I left the ranks of this [print] revival to aid the major artist in his search for new graphic expression and new work environments.[62]

Tyler's work with Josef at Tamarind involved a great deal of problem-solving to achieve the specific requirements of the Alberses' vision. For *Midnight and Noon* 1964, this involved creative thinking around manipulating the density of ink in order to realise Josef's aims to give one colour 'three lives'.[63] Josef suggested to Tyler that 'we make all the prints so extremely thin, as nobody dared before ... it appears adventurous, thank heaven.'[64] This kind of thinking resonated strongly with his reverence for economy, which he had stressed so heavily in his preliminary course at the Bauhaus:

> Economy is the sense of thriftiness in labour and material and in the best possible use of them to achieve the effect that is desired. Economy of labour is as important as economy of material. It is fostered by the recognition of quick and easy methods, by the constant use of ready-made and easily procured means, that is to say, by the correct choice of tools, by the use of ingenious substitutes for missing implements, by the combination of several processes or by restricting oneself to a single implement.[65]

Art historian Riva Castleman outlines the ways in which Tyler achieved prints that resembled what artists produced in other mediums: he increased their size and developed larger and more precisely balanced presses; printed on larger, more rigid sheets of paper; and used lighter stones and processes that lessened the physical strain on the printer.[66] Possibly Tyler's greatest contribution to printmaking was the invention of his hydraulic press. Josef was particularly impressed by its registration, usually 'the poorest of all printing processes', which he described as 'terrific'. 'I would like to see sometime how your machines do it', he said to Tyler.[67]

The great innovation here was the ability to print flat surfaces of colour without marks, as the hydraulic press-bed and scraper-bar system facilitated a clean printing process. It resulted from ingenious thinking sparked by the demands of printing Josef's work to a standard not yet achieved by his other collaborators, one that more accurately reflected Josef's experiments with colour in painting. Tyler faced the challenge of printing each square of colour directly on to the page without overlapping other squares. The degree of stretch of the paper under pressure and the corresponding level of precise registration required to perfectly align two plates of colour (with the added challenge in the *White Line Squares* series of leaving a thin void between them) took Tyler two years to determine. He recalled that after 'months of experimenting with various systems for making printing plates that could meet this task, I finally developed a successful photographic method for controlling the registration problem'.[68] Tyler's appetite for a challenge, and his persistence,

60 Tyler, in Goldman, p 20.
61 Gilmour, p 33.
62 Tyler, in Gilmour, p 35.
63 Josef Albers, letter to Kenneth Tyler, June 1964, quoted in Gilmour, p 39.
64 Josef Albers, in Gilmour, p 39.
65 Josef Albers, 'Concerning fundamental design', in Bayer et al, p 118.
66 Riva Castleman, 'Technics and creativity', in *Technics and creativity*, Museum of Modern Art, New York, 1971, p 13.
67 Josef Albers, phone conversation with Kenneth Tyler and Henry Hopkins, c 1966, typed transcript, box 3, folder 5, Kenneth E Tyler Collection archive, National Gallery of Australia.
68 Kenneth Tyler, notes, typescript, not dated, box 71, folder 5, p 3, Kenneth E Tyler Collection archive, National Gallery of Australia.

intersected perfectly with his willingness to embrace the technology of the day, and resulted in an immaculate distillation of Josef's ideas. In her writing, Anni similarly welcomed new technology:

> The more we avoid standing in the way of the material and in the way of tools and machines, the better chance there is that our work will not be dated, will not bear the stamp of too limited a period of time and be old-fashioned some day ... and it will outlast fashions only if it embodies lasting, together with transitory, qualities.[69]

The workshops of the Bauhaus had also introduced the Alberses to interdisciplinary thinking. Fine art and applied art were not siloed according to elitist hierarchies, and the pair embraced industrial and mechanical means to realise artistic outcomes. Tyler did too—he was unafraid to look beyond artistic circles for solutions and was known for 'being willing to try anything to produce a print. He hired scientists, industrial designers, metal embossers, papermakers, foundries, commercial printers.'[70] In the same way that the Bauhaus found it difficult to engage industry, due to the fact that the resources required to invest in development were often incompatible with commercial scale and viability, Tyler often encountered dead ends trying to engage industry without the support of grants; as Castleman notes, 'until the possible return to industry can be envisioned in dollars, development of materials oriented toward the arts is low and subject to much experimentation'.[71] Tyler was successful, however, in developing a mechanical embossing process through a National Endowment for the Humanities grant. The forming press was used in the creation of Josef's series *Embossed Linear Constructions* 1969 and required a programmer to translate his drawings to a digital tape that could be read by an automatic engraving mill that would incise the drawings onto an aluminium plate.[72] The goal of the Bauhaus to arouse the interest of industry was shared by the two artists and their printer.

Tyler's ability to recognise the potential of a material was another point of connection for the collaborators. The close study of materials and their properties had dominated Josef's teachings at the Bauhaus and was likewise a guiding principle for Anni in the weaving workshop. Tyler exhibited his reverence for materiality and its importance to creative production in a story of sourcing stones from a defunct lithography workshop that were large enough to realise his ambitious projects:

> I didn't have any money, I was a student at the time, so we went back there with a Volkswagen with a broken spring, cos I decided there was one stone that was 52 inches and was grey ... and the sucker was so gorgeous, but I had to have that, even if I broke everything in the Volkswagen, it was worth more than the Volkswagen to me.[73]

Anni had likewise developed a keen sense for understanding and exploiting the properties of a material in the execution of an artwork. Her finishing work at the Bauhaus, for example, utilised the sound-absorbing quality of chenille and the light-reflecting quality of cellophane to design a wall covering for an auditorium, exquisite in its subtle perfection.[74] When she turned her attention solely to printmaking, she had to work across a variety of techniques and sought to understand each process in its entirety so she could make the most of its graphic potential. We can see this in Anni's transition from the dazzling gold embossing in *TR III* 1970 to her refined *Mountainous* series of 1978. In *TR III*, Anni used screenprinting to achieve a solid gold field of ink, which she then subjected to the forming process of embossing to create a print echoing the weight and shine of a block of metal. Eight years later, she returned to embossing, this time removing colour altogether and relying solely on the indentations to mark the contours of her geometric design. Inspired by sites such as Monte Albán in Oaxaca that she encountered with Josef on their trips to Mexico, Anni used embossing to create meandering peaks and troughs in the paper that carry across the formal logic of ruins being uncovered by a glut of contemporary archaeological digs. The way she achieved deep indentations by

69 Anni Albers, quoted by Nicholas Fox Weber in 'Anni Albers', in Gene Baro, *Anni Albers*, Brooklyn Museum, New York, 1977, p 11.

70 Goldman, p 14.

71 Castleman, p 14.

72 Castleman, p 14.

73 Kenneth Tyler, in *Reaching out: Ken Tyler / master printer*, 1976, film, Avery Tirce Productions, 28 mins 15 secs, in Kenneth Tyler E Collection archive, National Gallery of Australia.

74 T'ai Smith, 'Monumental: developing a wall covering', in Anne Coxon, Briony Fer and Maria Müller (eds), *Anni Albers*, Tate Publishing, London, 2018, p 61.

Below Anni Albers, *TR III* 1970, embossing on silkscreen, sheet 41.8 × 47 cm

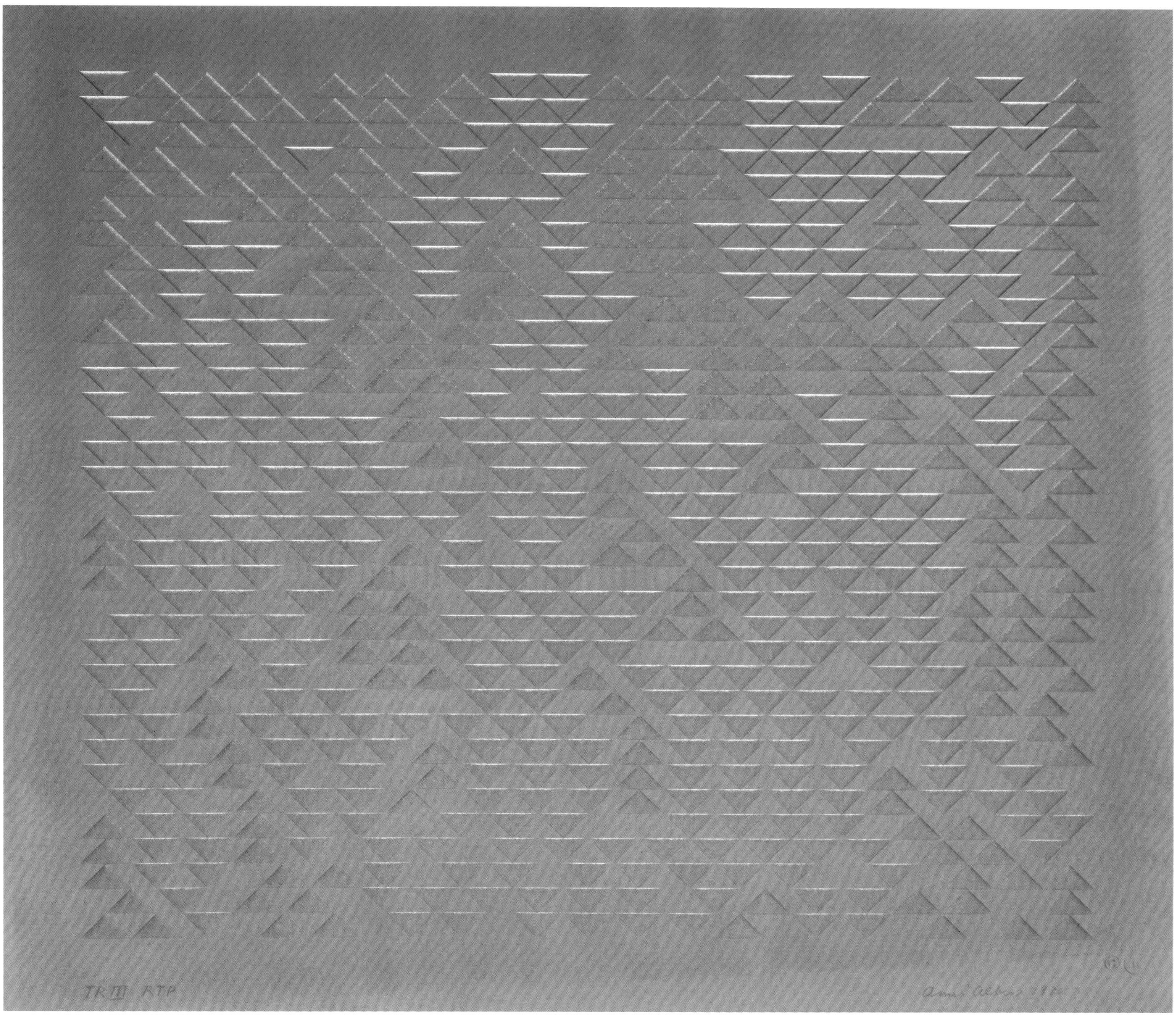

Below Anni Albers and Kenneth Tyler discussing the initial drawing for the *Mountainous* series of embossings, Tyler Graphics Ltd, Bedford Village, New York, 1978, digital file from colour photo print, photo by Lindsay Green, Kenneth E Tyler Collection archive, National Gallery of Australia

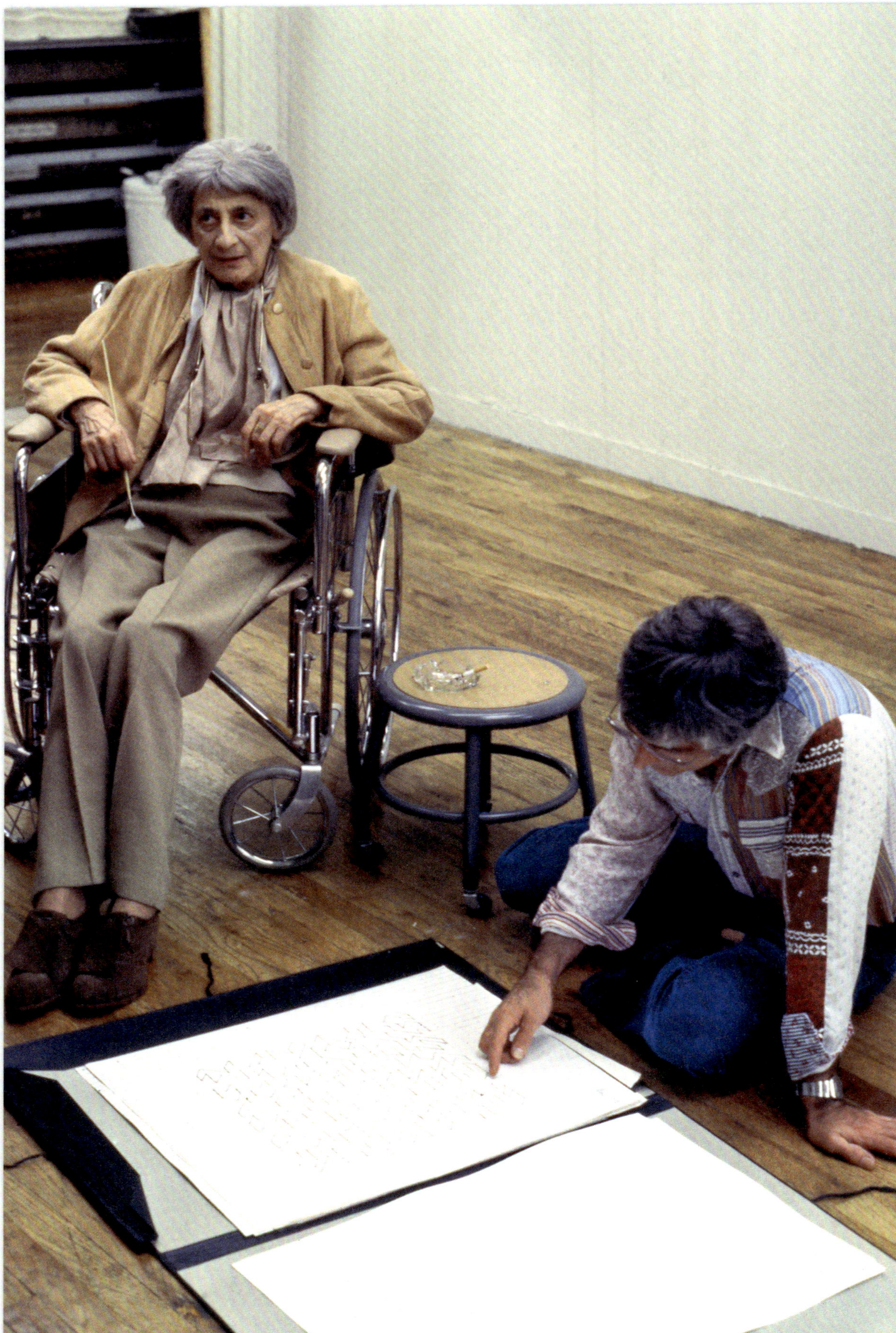

exploiting the materiality of paper handmade by Tyler Graphics Ltd reveals a genius for elegantly marrying material, process and form.

Tyler is often characterised as a brilliant marketer. He took the business of printmaking very seriously and ran a workshop with commercial efficiency, producing high-quality but affordable prints by some of the greatest artists of the twentieth century. Much as the Bauhaus had reoriented the workshops toward the production of well-designed goods for a modern society, Tyler took an entrepreneurial approach to the organisation of his studio. Aside from his embrace of industrial methods that allowed the production of more ambitious works and attracted high-profile artists with the promise of projects beyond what other printers offered, Tyler also ensured that the ingenuity and quality of the work being produced was evident to potential buyers. Even from the very beginning of Gemini Graphic Editions Ltd, Tyler had coordinated the production of catalogues to promote the groundbreaking work achieved at the studio—the first being for Josef's *White Line Squares*, with text written by curator Henry Hopkins. He also insisted on the creation of detailed documentation sheets—something also instigated within the Bauhaus weaving workshop—to explicate the process of making and assert the authenticity and ingenuity of what had been created.[75] His approach to the editioning of the *White Line Squares* series also balanced the need to turn a profit with creating work that was accessible to the intended audience. For this series, 50 editions were set aside to be sold only as complete sets, while 25 editions of each print were free to be sold as single artworks, allowing Josef's work to reach audiences with modest budgets, such as students and artists. Tyler kept Albers informed of sales in their regular phone conversations, noting that

> we have sold a great deal of singles and sets. We are selling mostly the sets to the collectors who want all of them, you see. To the professional students and the teachers who don't have a lot of money, they're buying the singles ... we did a very good thing by pre-publishing at a very reasonable price. See, many of the architectural students could only afford 100 dollars and many of the university art students, and the artists, too—many artists have bought your prints—which is about the highest compliment I can tell you about the single prints.[76]

The prints Tyler produced with Anni and Josef met their Bauhaus-driven aim to create high-quality, accessible art and reflected the printer's ability to respectfully realise their unpretentious work. Tyler recalled of Josef,

> In the thirteen years I worked with him, I never knew him not expressing his profound love for art, for craft, and for the work struggle that creative people are involved with. Money, success and power were not of concern to Josef.[77]

Over two decades, Anni and Josef dedicated their artistic efforts to the radical and utopian project that was unfolding in the workshops of the Bauhaus. In its aim to produce art for a modern society, the school fostered a unique pedagogy that encouraged independent and ambitious thought, grounded in a knowledge of material and form that could be learnt only through firsthand experience. While other concerns intensified for the Alberses as they settled in America, such as an obsessive experimentation with colour and use of pre-Columbian cultural artefacts as source material, the principles absorbed at the Bauhaus remained fundamental to their creative approaches. Concentrating more intently on the creation of prints later in life, the couple embraced the innovative and entrepreneurial spirit of master printer Kenneth Tyler to realise the translation of their ideas into print. Tyler's can-do attitude, which looked beyond traditional technologies of artistic production, resonated strongly with the two artists, who had spent the best part of their early careers thinking, testing and producing in a similarly experimental spirit. The thrill that stirred within the artists and printer when faced with a challenge to push materials and processes to their limits resulted in works that embodied the spirit of the new and opened the eyes of the viewer to novel visual experiences.

75 For reference to Tyler's workshop documentation, see Goldman, p 15. For reference to the Bauhaus weaving workshop documentation, see Rowland, p 156.

76 Kenneth Tyler, phone conversation with Josef Albers, c 1966, typed transcript, box 3, folder 5, p 3, Kenneth E Tyler Collection archive, National Gallery of Australia. Note that the added ellipsis registers the elision of a question from Albers.

77 Tyler, in Gilmour, p 46.

Below Lena Bergner, Textile design with yarn sample 1928, watercolour and pencil on paper with wool sample, 16.5 × 13 cm

Right Lena Bergner, Textile design for throw rug 1928, watercolour on paper, 30.1 × 20.2 cm

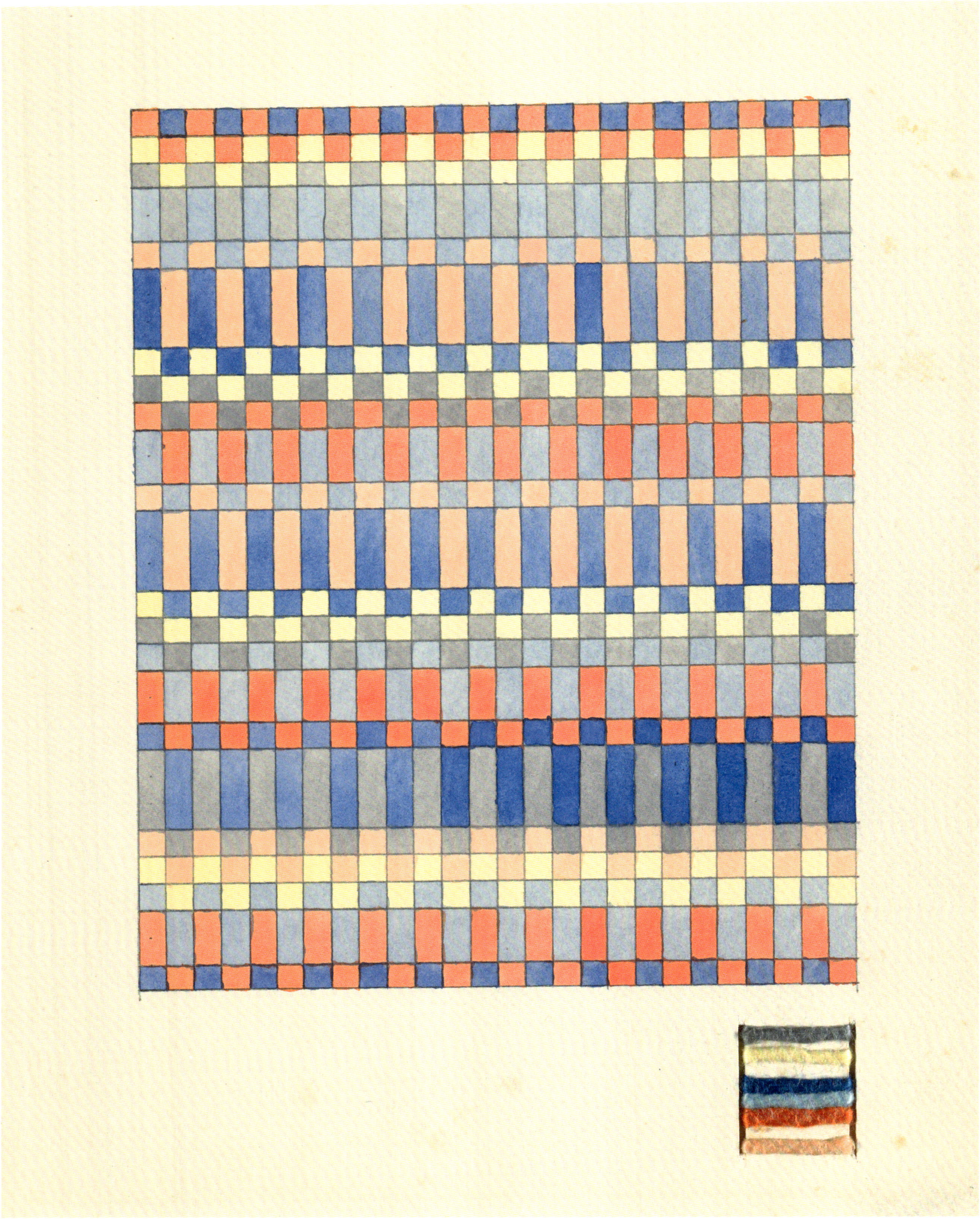

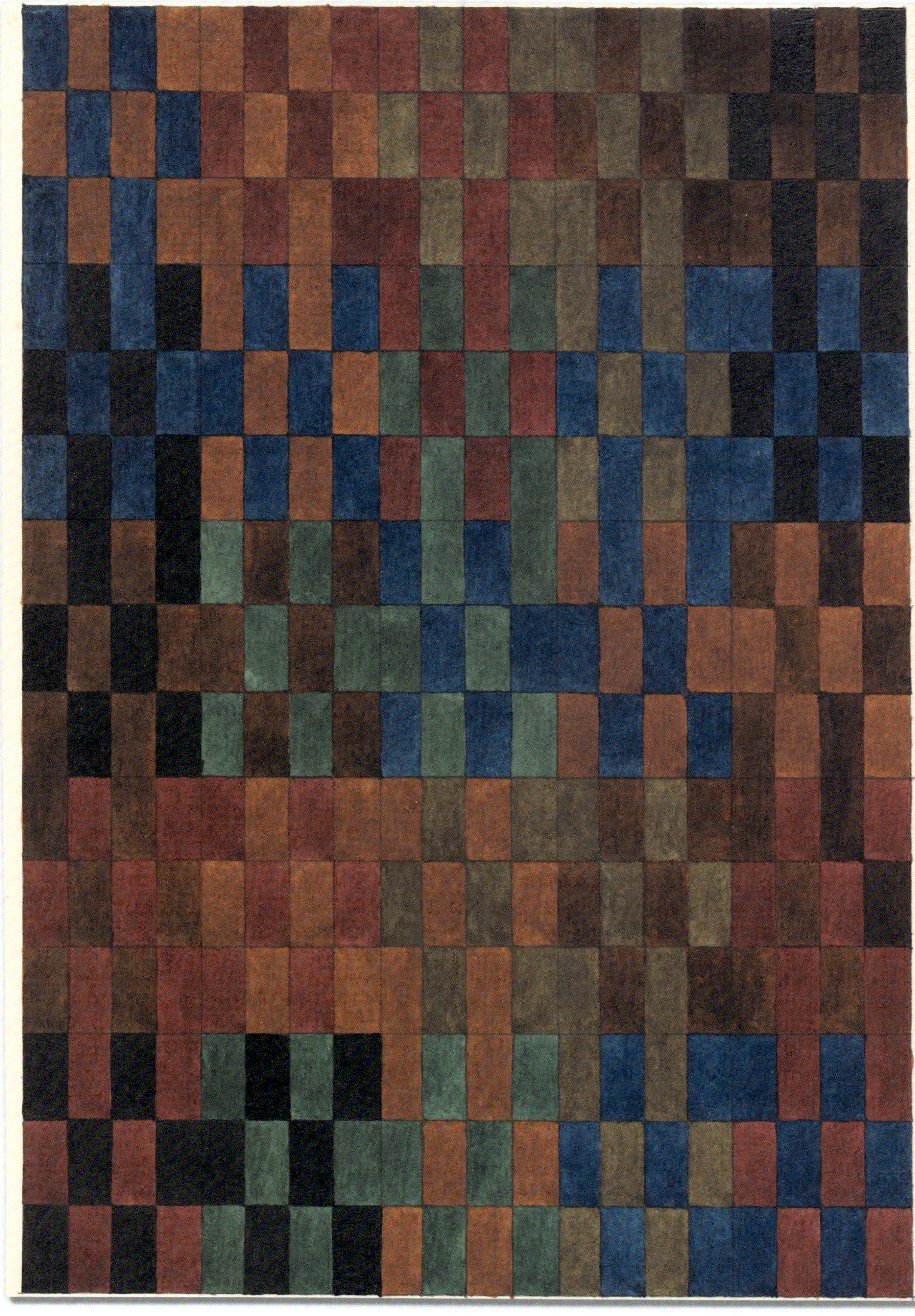

Below Bauhaus Dessau weaving workshop, Weaving study, furnishing fabric swatch c 1926, wool, cotton and rayon, 11.8 × 20.2 cm

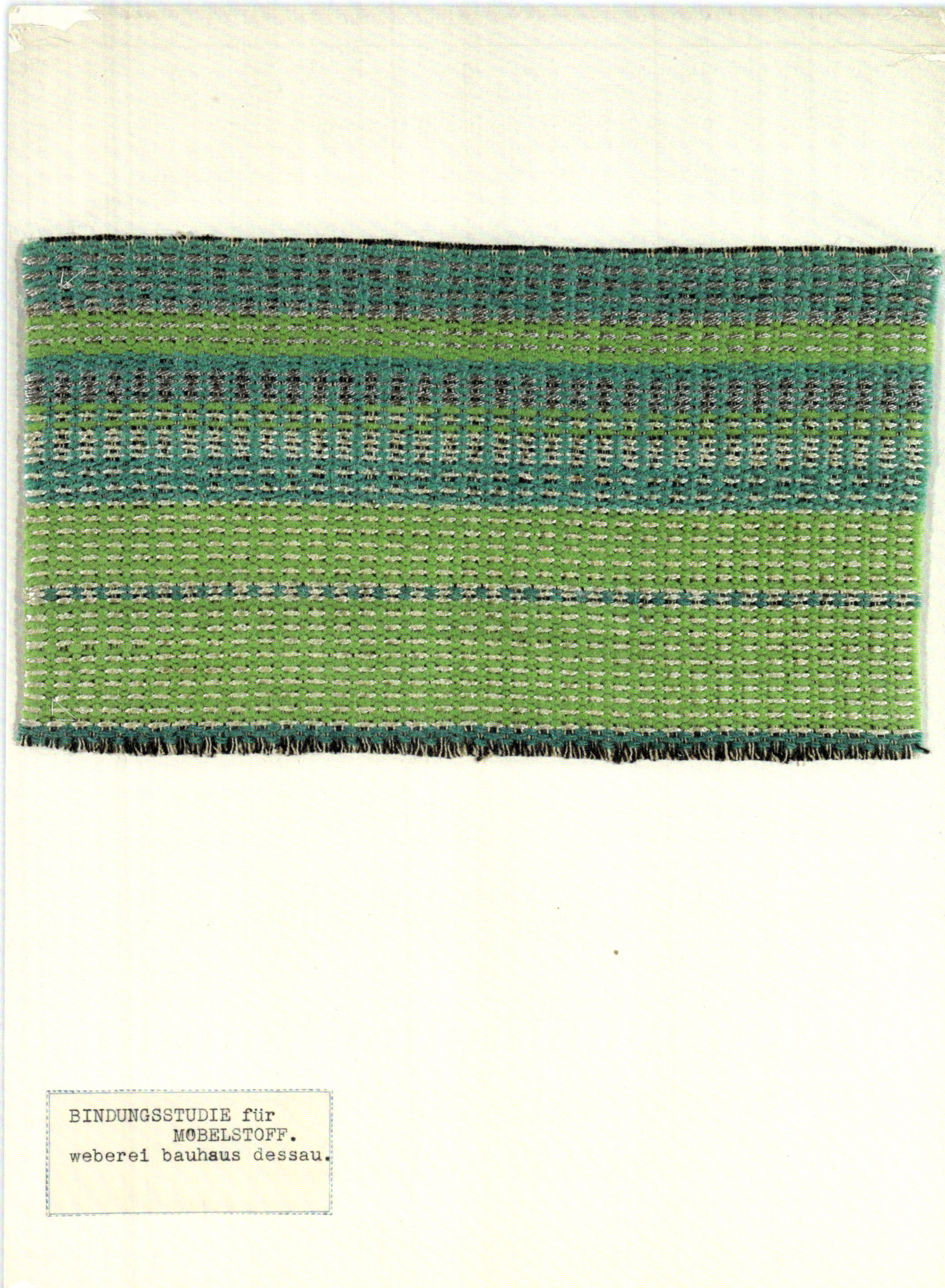

Below Lena Bergner, Weaving study, fabric swatch for divan cover 1930, handwoven wool, cotton and rayon, 14.6 × 8.6 cm

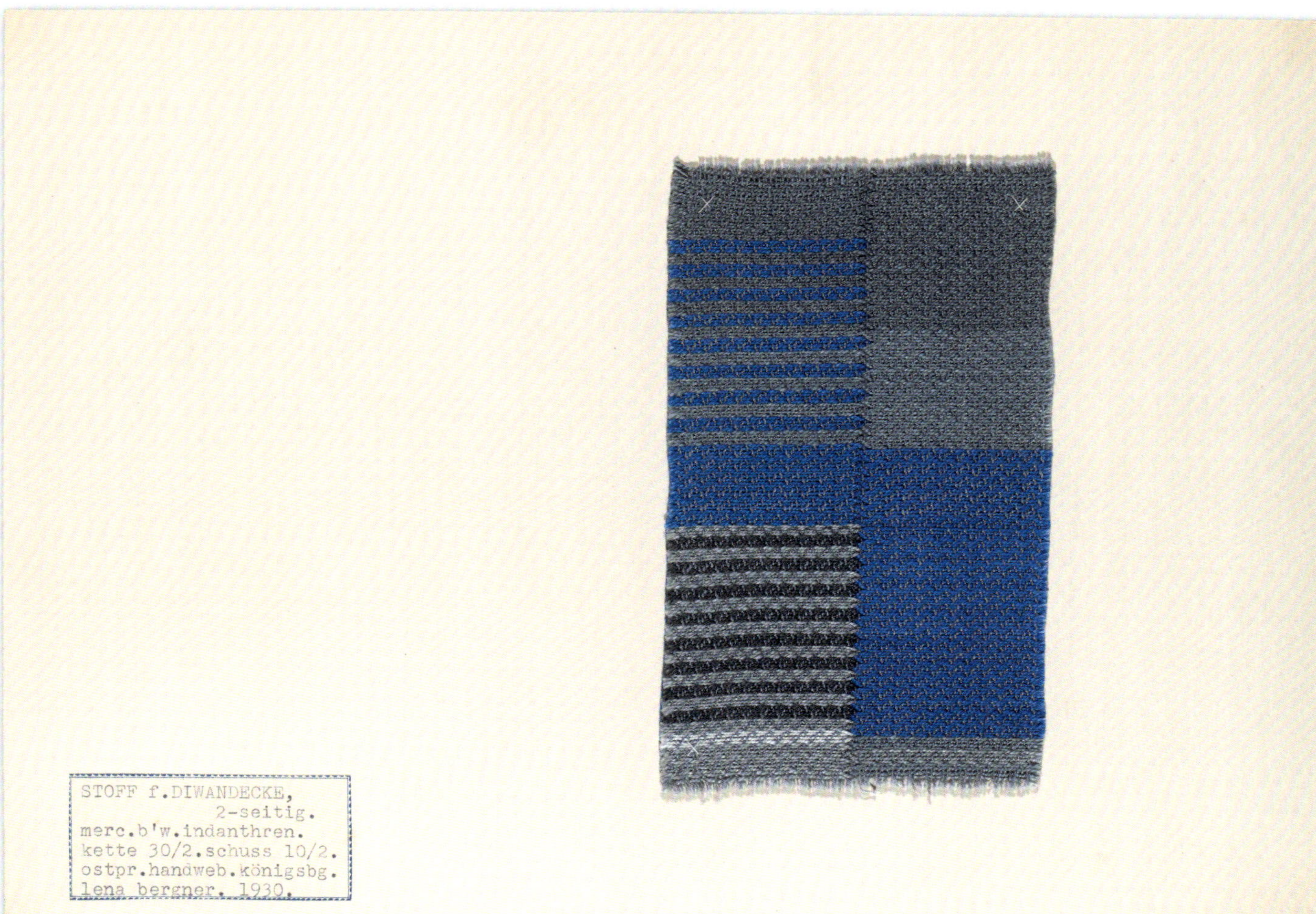

Below Hilde Reindl, Textile design c 1928, watercolour and pencil on paper, image 10 × 10 cm, sheet 13.8 × 13.6 cm

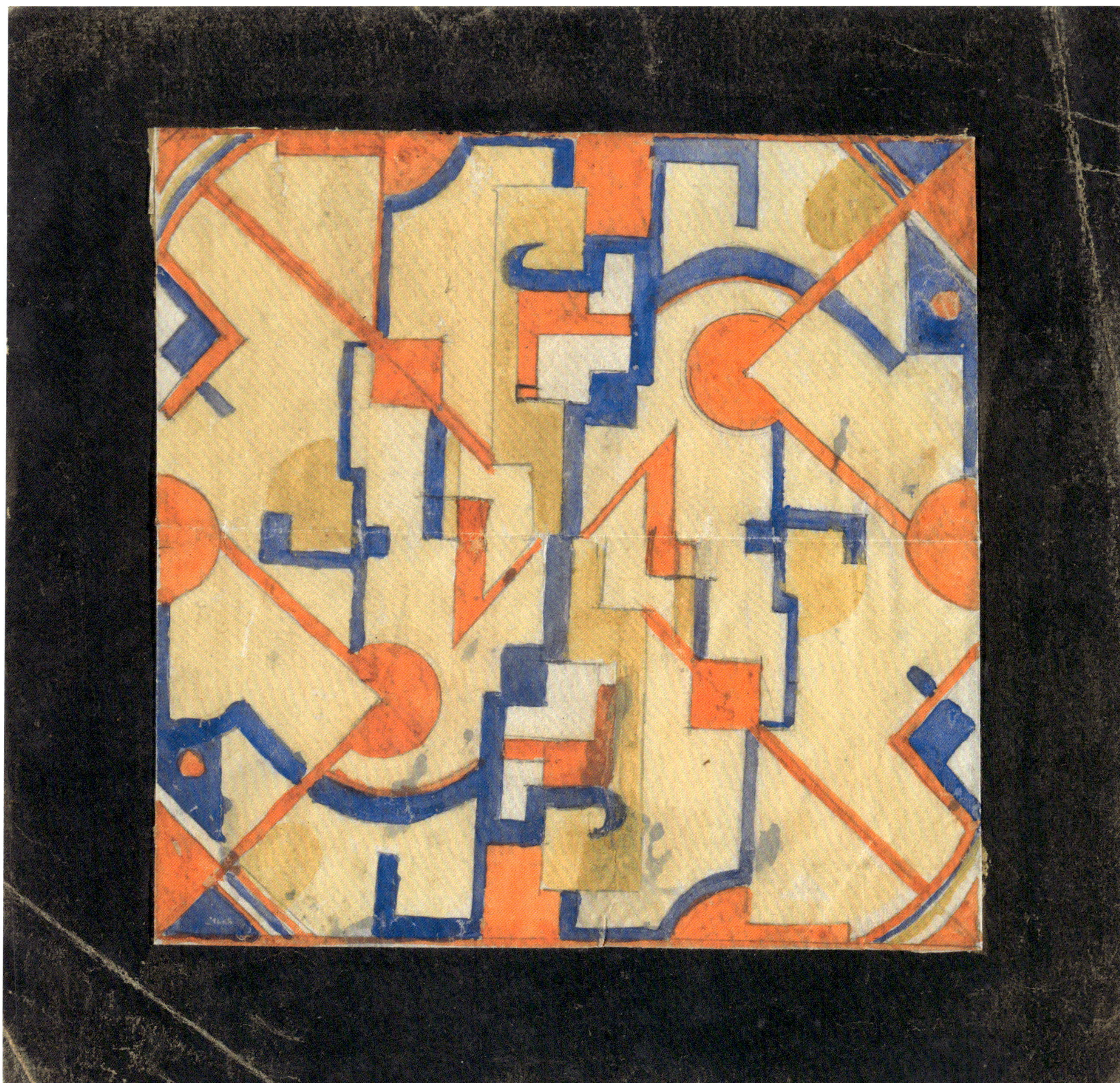

September 3, 1968
to JOSEF ALBERS

Hello, Anni.

Yea,

Ken, How are you?

Oh, glad to hear you. When are you coming?

Lets see, probably the end of September.

Oh, not earlier?

Perhaps earlier, Annie, I'm not sure yet.

Yea. Josef is out for a little walk. I'm sorry, but I can't call him for you.

Uh huh. Well, I can call back later then. Did he receive my two packages?

Let me see...

The Art News magazine?

Yes, and that was wonderful to have...

Uh huh.

And what was the other item?

The little sample of embossing. The white paper.

I'm not sure about that. He may not have shown that to me. So why don't you call in a little later then, or say we call you back.

No, why don't I call back within an hour.

Very good...

He'll be back by then.

I have been working on things because I prefer you would take over something for me...you know, of mine.

O.K., wonderful. Let's see...Norman was in

Yes

Uh huh...

Yes, I sent him there and his daughter Gracie was very impressed with your workshop.

Hu huh, beautiful. We had a nice visit, and it worked out very nicely.

Good, that's good, you'll see him probably when you come here.

Uh huh, good, yes, I expect to see him when I come back.

Fine. I sold my first silkscreen print

Beautiful!

to the Brooklyn Museum.

Beautiful!

Its a good start, isn't it?

That's a very good start.

Yes, so I'm all hopeful that you might be interested in doing one or another of mine.

Oh, certainly, and I think I told Norman several places to contack regarding that.

Regarding himself? or...

Oh no, regarding your silkscreens.

Oh, how wonderful!

So, what we'll probably do is we'll probably get a photograph of a couple of them.

Oh, that's marvelous!

And then we can talk to some of our people about them.

Oh, that's wonderful. Also i haven't got the museum of Modern Art yet, and...by the way, when the Brooklyn Museum asked me for the price of my print, I told them what you had told me, $100.

Um humm.

And they didn't think that was much at all.

Now, I told you that.

So, I was very grateful to you.

ha, ha...

But I don't want to hold you up with my affairs...

No...I'm very happy to hear about them.

Good.

Good, yes, well, you know, once some of the edition is sold out,

[illegible]

Good, that's good, you'll certainly [illegible], which [illegible]

[illegible], it's easier [illegible] back.

[illegible]

[illegible]

to the [illegible] Museum.

[illegible]

[illegible]

that's a very good start.

Yes, [illegible] that you might be interested in going to another [illegible]

Oh, certainly [illegible] places to [illegible]

[illegible]

and, regarding your [illegible]

Oh, wonderful.

[illegible]

[illegible]

And then we [illegible]

Oh, that's wonderful. [illegible] the [illegible] Brooklyn Museum [illegible] than what you had to [illegible]

[illegible]

And [illegible] think [illegible]

[illegible] you [illegible]

So, I was very [illegible]

Thanks.

[illegible]

[illegible]

Good.

[illegible]

then you raise the price a little bit.

Well, you have to teach me.

O.K. I'll teach you. Ha ha...it will be my pleasure, Anni.

Yes...and shall I ask Josef about your questions...if he received your two things?

Uh, yes, just that I want to talk to him about the embossings.

Oh yes, very good.

So I'll be talking to him in about an hour from now.

Awfully good.

Alright, wonderful, Anni. I'll call back later.

Yea.

Bye bye dear.

Below Josef Albers, Preliminary drawing for *White Line Square I* 1966, fibre-tipped pen, coloured pencil and ballpoint pen on graph paper, 35.6 × 43.2 cm

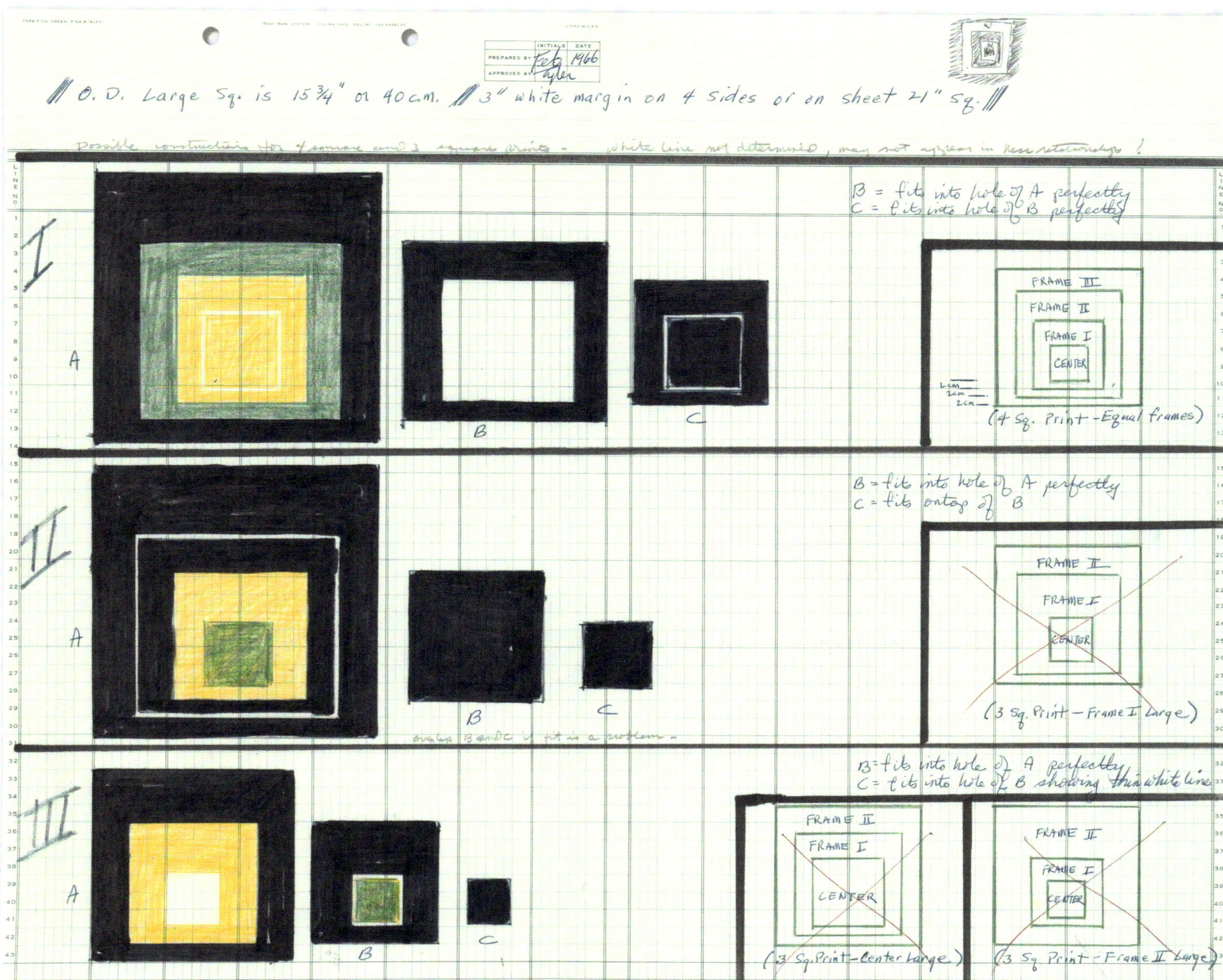

Below Josef Albers, Gouache studies for *White Line Square III* and *White Line Square IV* c 1966, gouache on paper, image (a) 30.2 x 15.2 cm, image (b) 30.5 × 15.2 cm (irreg)

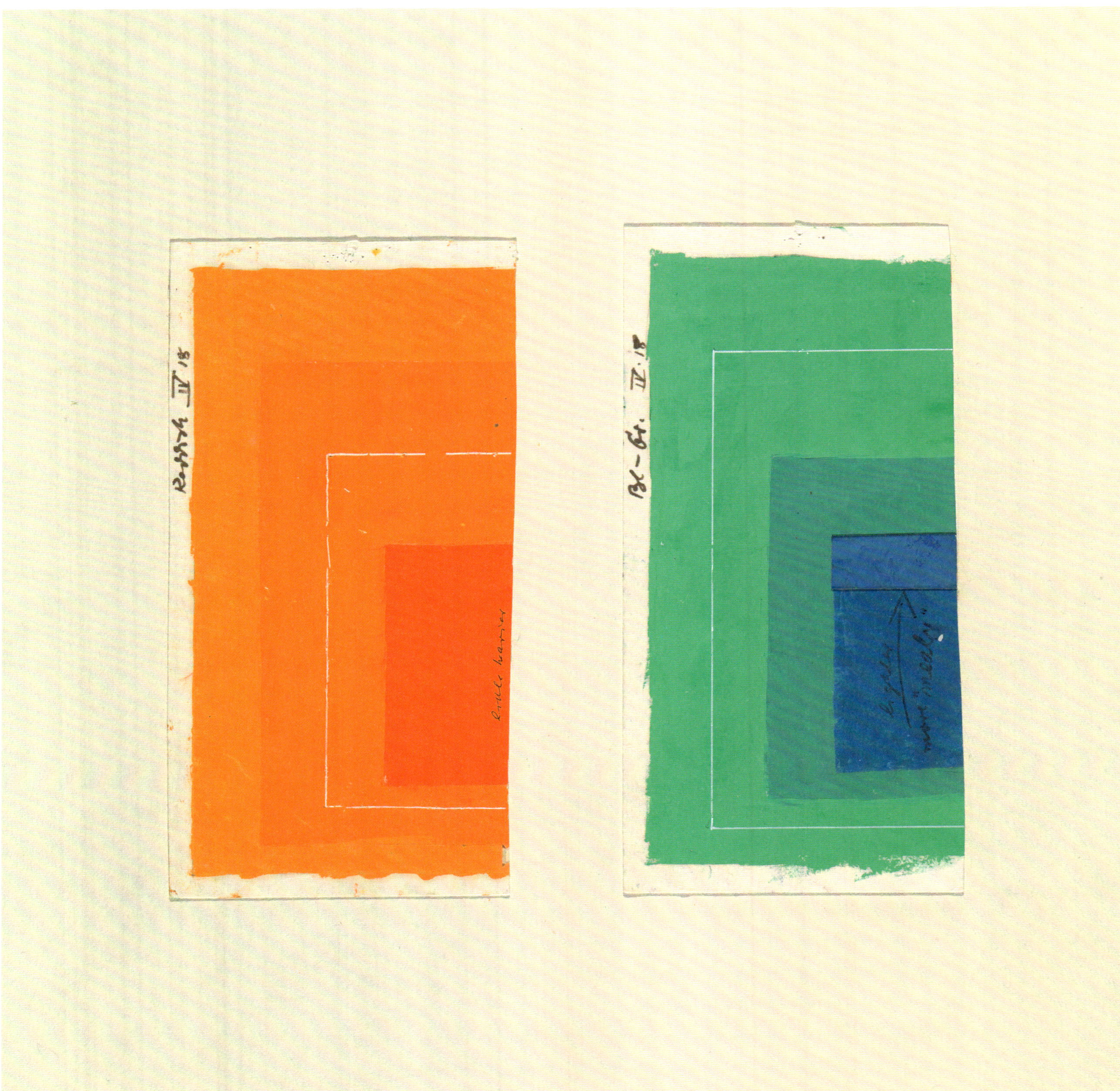

Below Josef Albers, Oil studies for *White Line Square XVI* and *White Line Square XII* 1966, oil on paper, image (a) 33.4 × 18.8 cm, image (b) 33.4 × 18.6 cm

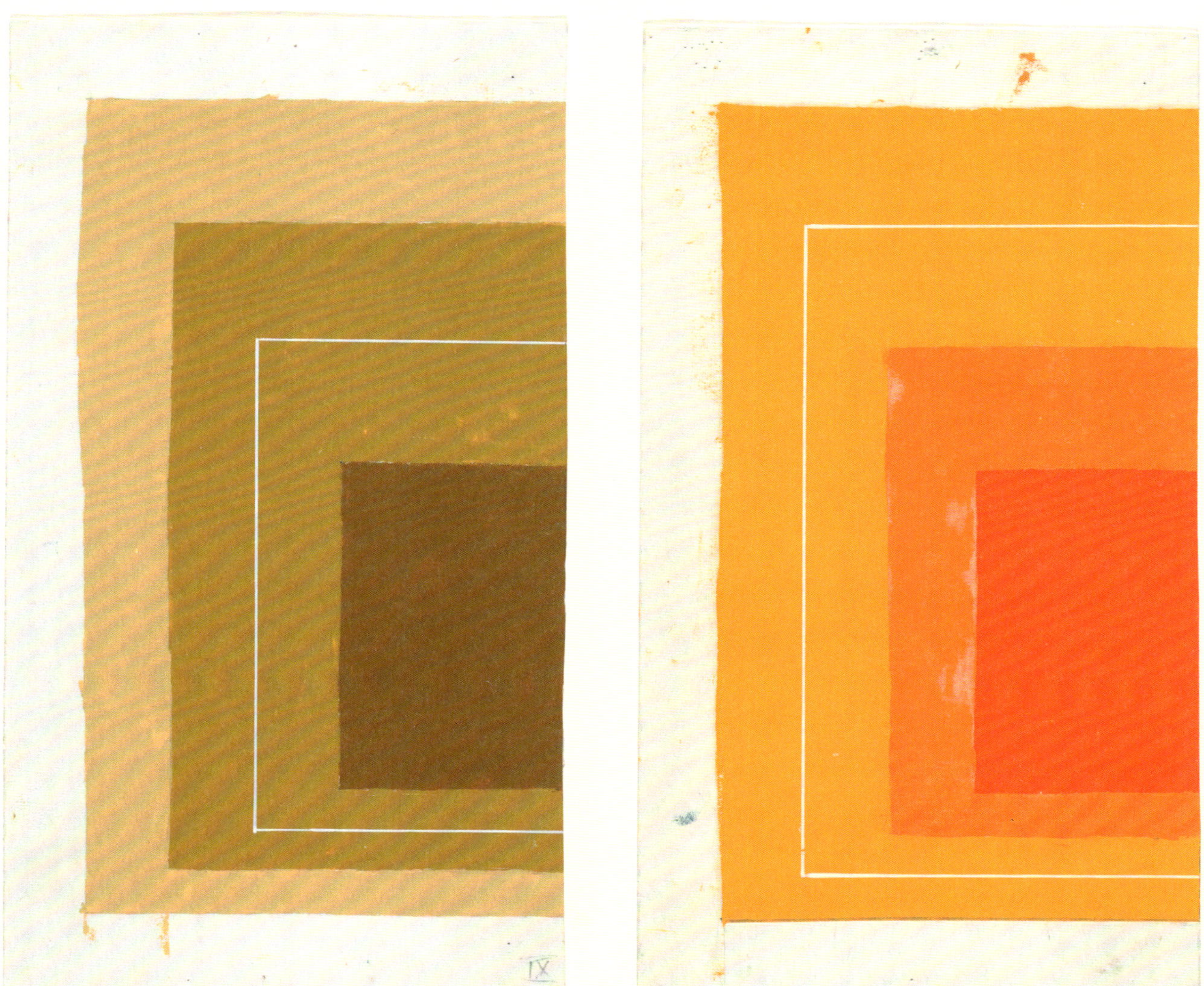

Below

Josef Albers, Oil studies for *White Line Square XIII* and *White Line Square XV* 1966, oil on paper, image (a) 33 × 18.8 cm, image (b) 33.6 × 18.6 cm (irreg)

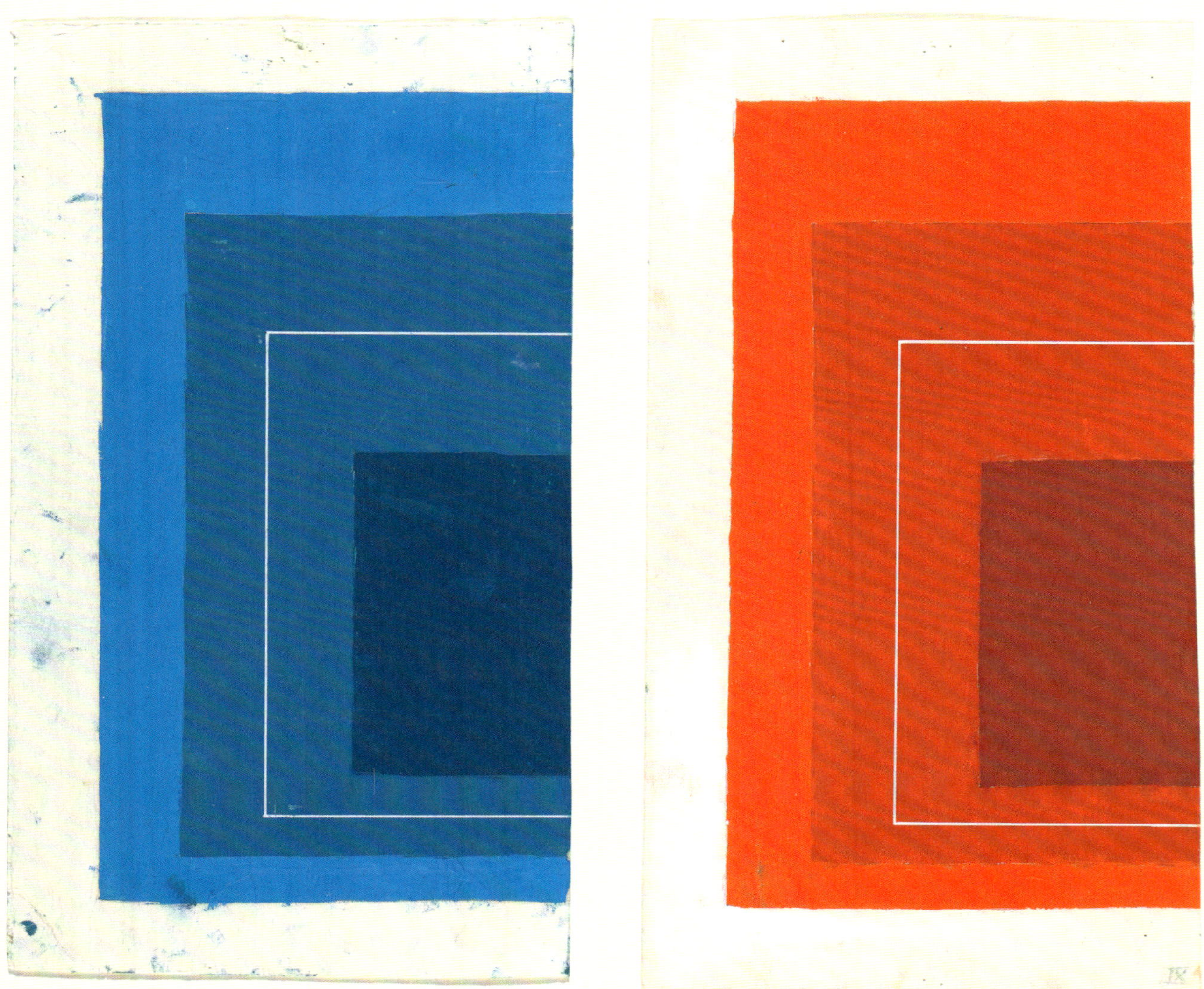

Below Josef Albers, Oil studies for *White Line Square XIV* and *White Line Square X* 1966, oil on paper, image (a) 33 × 18.2 cm, image (b) 30.4 × 17.8 cm (irreg)

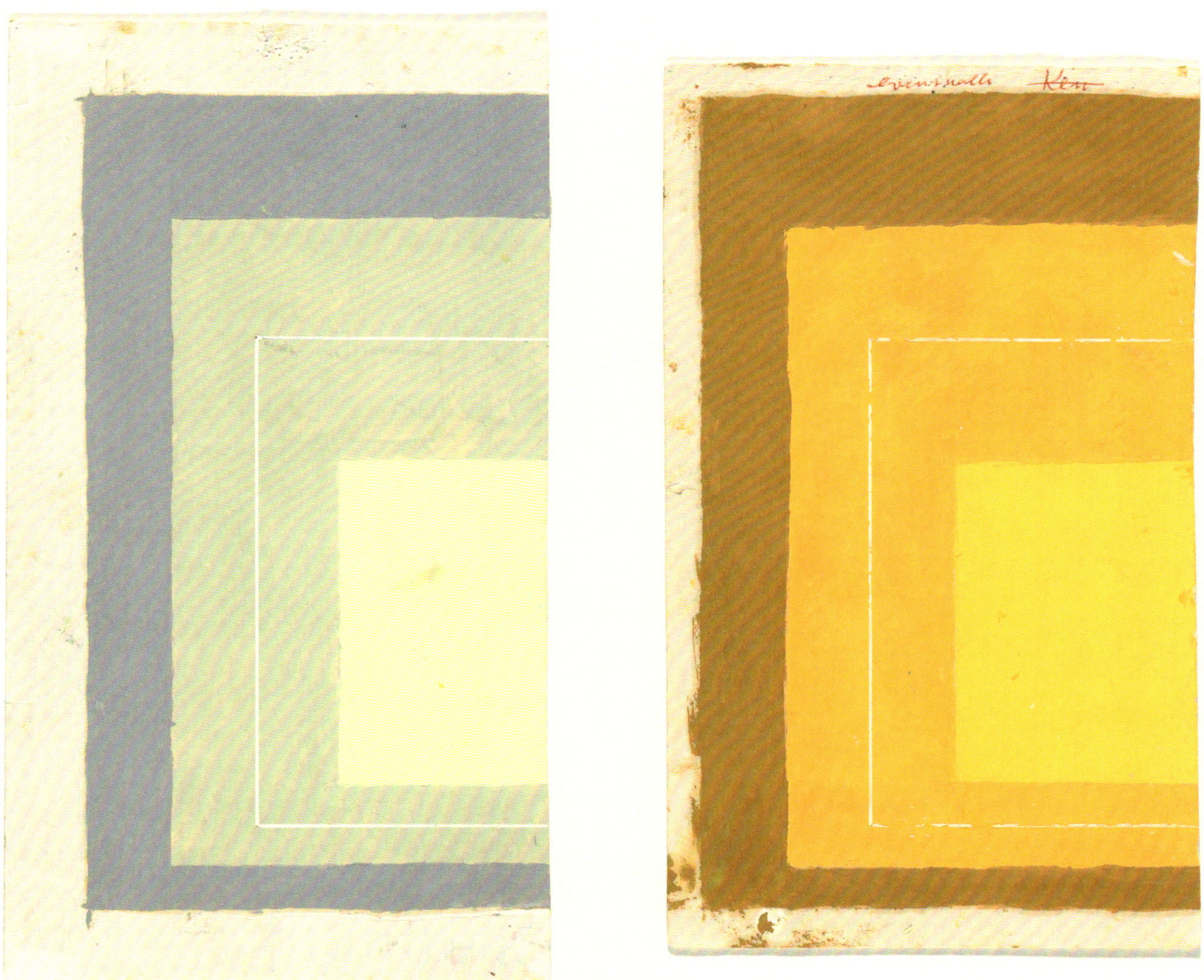

Below Josef Albers and Anni Albers in the Tyler Graphics Ltd workshop, Bedford Village, New York, 1976, digital file from black-and-white photo print, photo by Betty Fiske, Kenneth E Tyler Collection archive, National Gallery of Australia

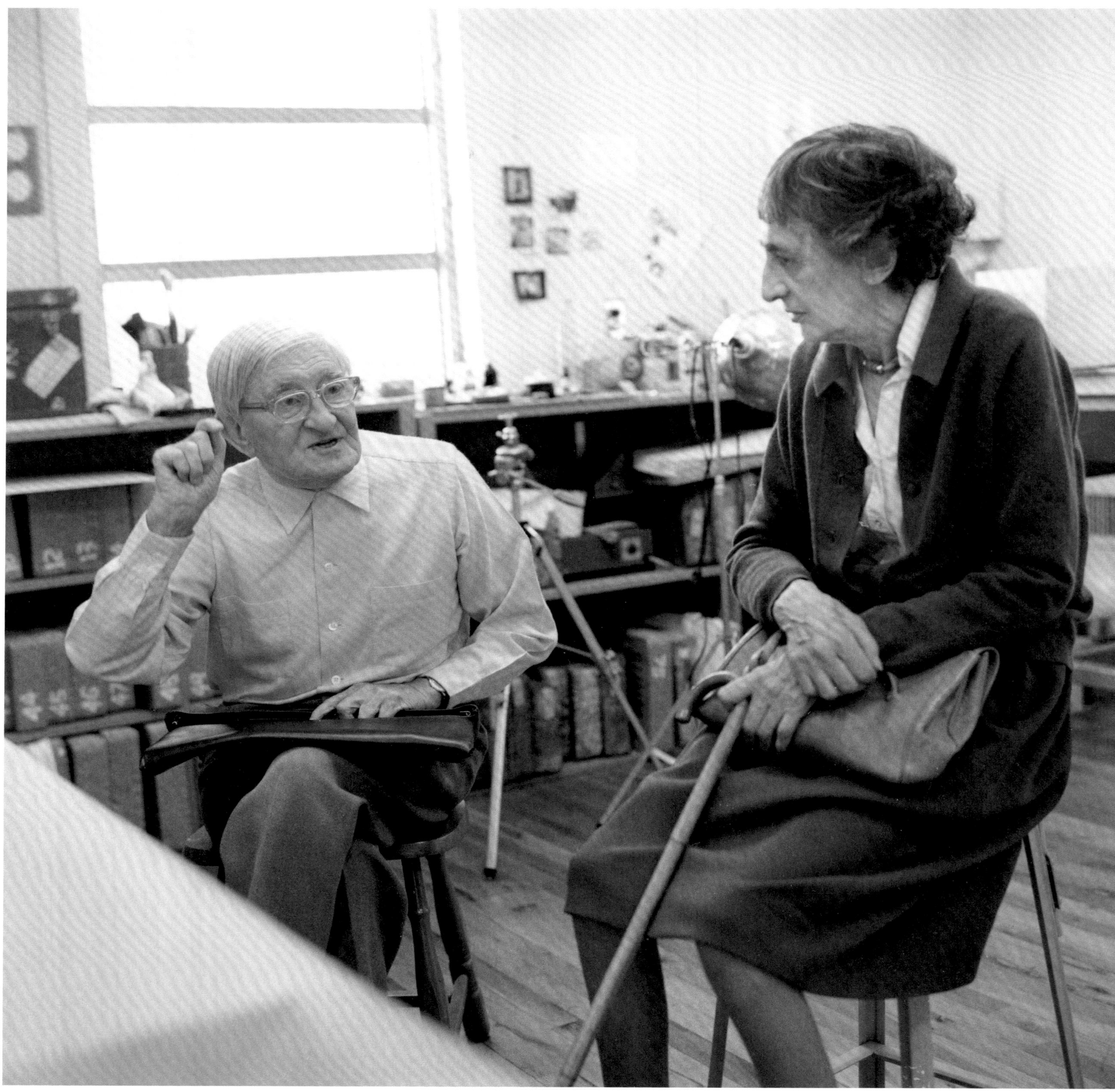

Josef Albers and Kenneth Tyler: a rare collaboration

Nicholas Fox Weber

If Josef Albers had a pantheon of artists, its gods were all craftsmen dedicated not to the expression of their private emotions or the perpetuation of their own egos but, rather, to further exploration of the possibilities of tools and materials. His father, Albers often announced with pride, had been a carpenter and painter and tinkerer—someone who might help build a house or fix the plumbing. He believed he could have come from no finer tradition. The elder Albers's trade suggested real knowledge and ability, the desired mixture of skill and honesty.

In the last years of their long-married life, Josef and Anni Albers—who had been together ever since they had met at the Bauhaus in 1922—would often extol the latest advances of modern technology. In preference to recent developments in the world of art, to the Abstract Expressionism they often deplored and the subsequent movements they deemed the decadent excesses of modern art, they sang the praises of Polaroid cameras, Sony televisions, and the Mercedes Benz that was one of the few out-and-out luxuries they permitted themselves in an otherwise austere way of living. And their saint among collaborators, the professional they seemed most to admire and who kept giving them a sense of the increasing possibilities of making art, was Kenneth Tyler.

When I first met the two Alberses in the early 1970s, their faces would light up at each mention of Tyler's name. (Just as Albers would refer to himself as 'Albers', and to 'Klee' and 'Kandinsky' as such, he opted invariably to use 'Tyler' rather than 'Ken'.) For one thing, the master printer was working with both of them—in very different manners, but in a way that made it exciting for them to go to Bedford Village together, and that gave each a sense both of personal progress and of contentment for his or her spouse. For another, Tyler was encouraging developments in new directions neither artist had ever thought of before—exactly the sort of stimulus people well along in years needed. And both Josef and Anni knew from the start that the end results would be as impeccable and elegant and meticulous as they desired. Tyler offered them the realm of invention, and at the same time perfection and fine-tuning they deemed indispensable to their art.

These were the years 1974 to 1976. Josef was in his mid 80s, Anni her mid 70s. It was often my privilege to drive them to the Tyler Graphics Workshop just over the border of New York State, about an hour from where the Alberses had retired in Orange, Connecticut. Josef and Anni freely admitted that they were happy to have someone else do the driving, but they also assured me that this was a splendid development for my education about art—far more useful than the sort of thing I had studied in art history at Yale. For now I would observe the real, mechanical issues that printmakers faced, the engagement with the tools, the inspiration that artists derived from process.

Moreover, since my family owned a commercial printing company, I would expand my knowledge of the trade in which I had been nurtured—a tradition that the Alberses deemed of pivotal importance.

What most excited Josef Albers in his work at that point with Tyler was one particular detail with regard to the creation of his *Homage to the Square* series. Albers explained this to me with a great beaming smile on his face. He had begun painting his Homages in 1950, when he was 62 years old. An essential factor in the technique of those paintings was that he always started with a white ground—applied in between six and ten coats of Liquitex to a masonite panel; for the first couple of years on the smooth side, but then on the rougher, canvas-like one—and then, using a painter's knife, put paints straight from the tube onto that white surface. He rarely over-painted. Yet even though no pigment was on top of another, all sorts of illusions occurred. It often seemed that one of the solid squares of colour had been painted on top of another: most often that the square in the middle was sitting atop the larger ones that surrounded it.

Albers delighted in his own chicanery. As he enjoyed explaining, he had always painted that middle square first; his father, with his training as a house painter, had taught him that when you paint a door you always start at the middle and then work outward toward the perimeters, so as to catch the drips and avoid getting your cuffs dirty.

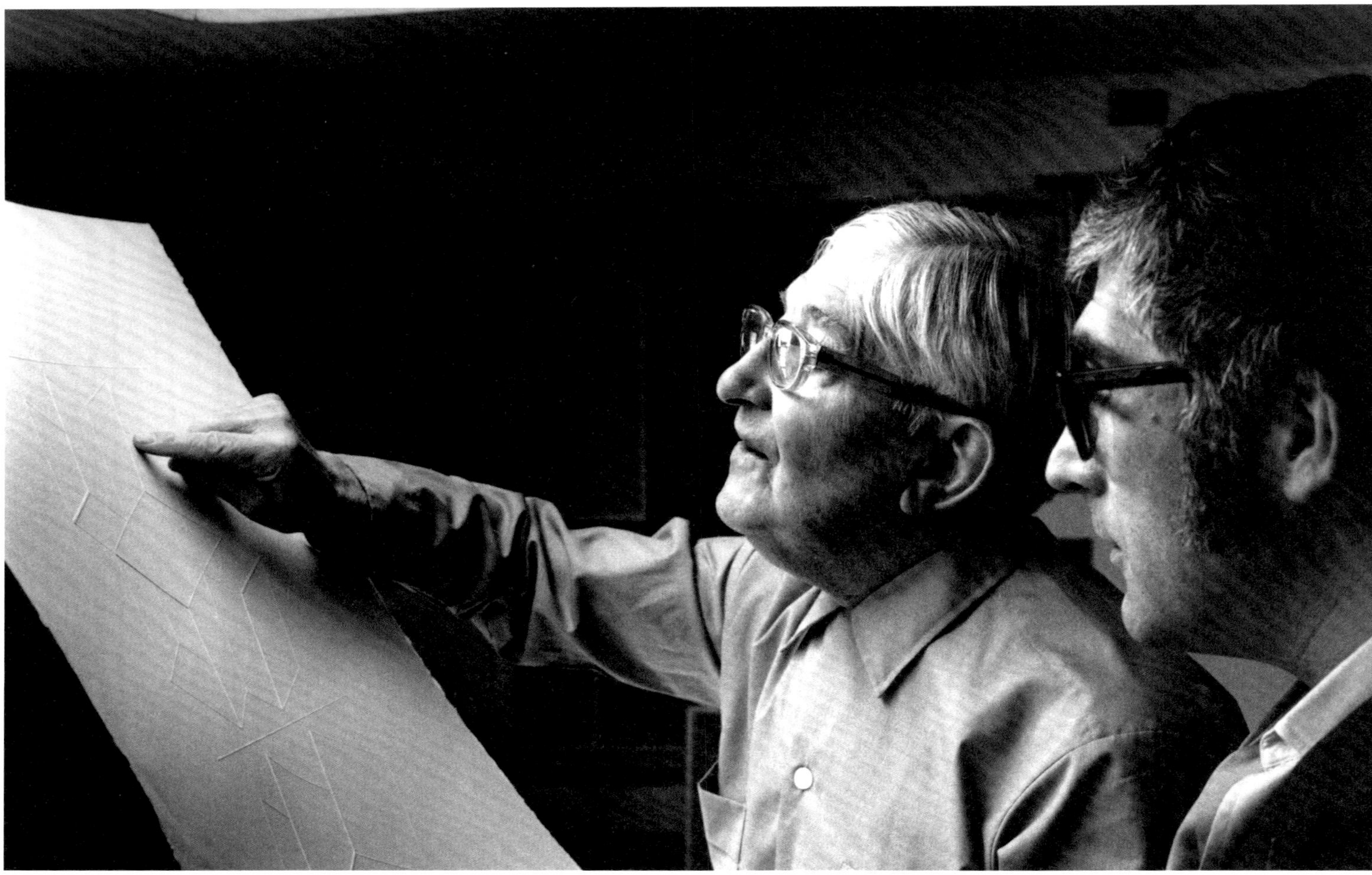

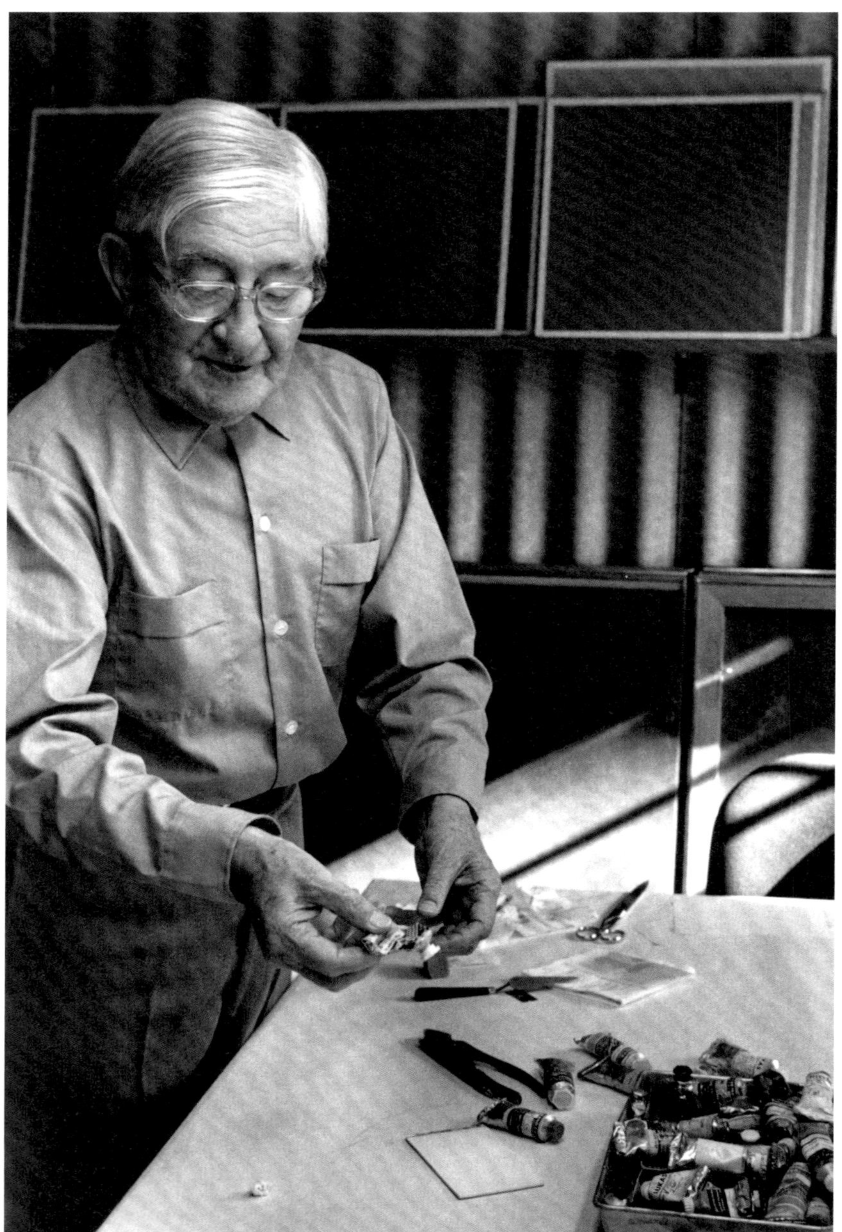

Left top — Josef Albers and Kenneth Tyler discussing embossed line quality on *Embossed Linear Constructions* proof in Albers's New Haven, Connecticut studio, 1969, digital file from black-and-white photo print, photo by William Crutchfield, Kenneth E Tyler Collection archive, National Gallery of Australia

Left bottom — Josef Albers in his New Haven, Connecticut studio, 1969, digital file from black-and-white photo print, photo by William Crutchfield, Kenneth E Tyler Collection archive, National Gallery of Australia

Below — Josef Albers, *Homage to the Square: On an Early Sky* 1964, oil on composition board, 122.2 × 122.2 cm

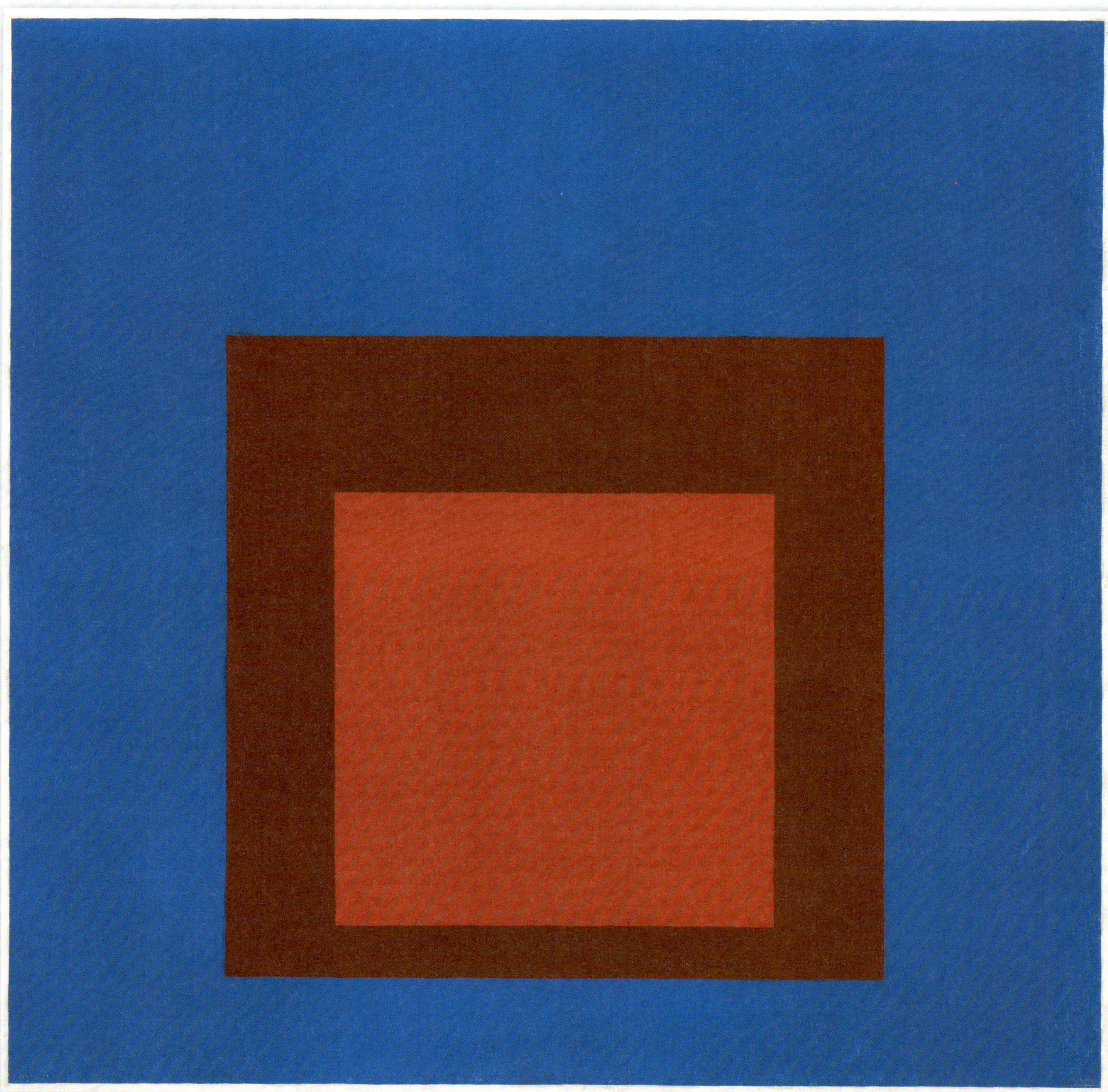

Yet, looking at Albers's paintings, most people found it impossible to believe that he had not painted that central square last, on top of the other two.

That method of applying each pigment to the white background also facilitated the maximum purity of luminosity of the individual hues. It helped avoid muddiness. And it permitted the splendid 'interaction of colour' that Albers craved and savoured: the way in which colours seem to penetrate one another, the way that one solid colour exerted a force on another so that illusory shadows and tonal changes would occur, the way that one plus one plus one could come to equal more than three. So art might exceed the possibilities of science.

But with his first forays in making these Homages as prints, alas, that recipe calling for each colour to exist only on top of white—and not on top of another colour—had been impossible. Albers had made a number of Homage screenprints with a very good firm near New Haven, and had been happy with the results, but here, indeed, the outermost square was printed first—as a solid colour—with the inner squares, either two or three of them, printed on top. The problem was that the printmaker could not get the registration precise enough, so that if each ink was printed on white paper only and not on top of another ink, the squares could abut one another, touching each other where edge met edge but not creating a slight and detrimental overlapping. This ghost line—where, if only for a minute fraction of an inch, colours muddied one another and imposed an unwelcome, alien element—was immensely disturbing and had to be avoided. The inks were sufficiently opaque in these Homage screenprints with colours on top of colours that the results could still be very beautiful, and Albers delighted in the expanded colour palette that printmaking afforded him, but he gave the impression that he felt a bit as if he had violated his own rules.

So he was very excited by the method Tyler had helped him develop first for the Homages he called *White Line Squares*, which had been printed in 1966, and now for some series of prints exclusively in an astounding range of greys. Josef explained this to me with palpable delight. Tyler had been able to perfect the process and hone the registration so that now, at last, each colour of ink could sit directly on white paper, and the boundaries between squares would have none of that undesirable overlapping. For Albers a dream had come true.

Albers had been engaged in the techniques of printmakers ever since he was a very young man. When he was still a figurative artist in his native Bottrop in the years 1915–17, he had made woodcuts and lithographs. In the 1930s he had made cork relief and wood-grain prints, as well as etchings. Periodically throughout his life, he had turned again to printmaking—exploring new techniques, delighted in the crisp straight lines invited by the process of zinc lithography, using etching for free and playful curves, allowing the impression made by the cross-section of a wooden plank to become sea or sky. He simultaneously learned from and utilised the various techniques.

His first encounter with Kenneth Tyler was at the Tamarind Lithography Workshop in 1963. There they worked together on *Day and Night*—a rich series of *Homage to the Square* lithographs in which Josef had used pure colour in the neutral, non-referential form of squares to create the warm brightness of daylight as well as the lush and mysterious darkness of the evening. This was well before the time when the artist and the printmaker would work to avoid overprinting; rather, in this earlier series, overprinting was the method by which the third colour of each of the Homages was achieved. Albers wanted that middle colour to have a certain transparency, and Tyler found that the means of achieving this was to blot the second colour right after he laid it down; the artist was impressed and delighted with the results.

Their next collaboration occurred the following year with another series of *Homage to the Square* lithographs for Tamarind, called *Midnight and Noon*. Like the previous series, these rich and velvety prints showed Albers's extraordinary ability to use the most seemingly rational, artificial form—the square—and a seemingly straightforward, scientific method (the printing of solid squares of colour, arranged in a precise pattern structured on a grid) to create art with humour, soul and romanticism. Artificial yellow became the light of the most joyous summer day at the beach, and black the deep and resonant pitch of the night sky without its stars. Characteristically, Albers had wanted to pare down his elements and adhere to a strict discipline.

Below Josef Albers and Kenneth Tyler discussing Tyler's registration device at the Tamarind Lithography Workshop, Los Angeles, California, 1963, digital file from black-and-white photo print, photographer unknown, Kenneth E Tyler Collection archive, National Gallery of Australia

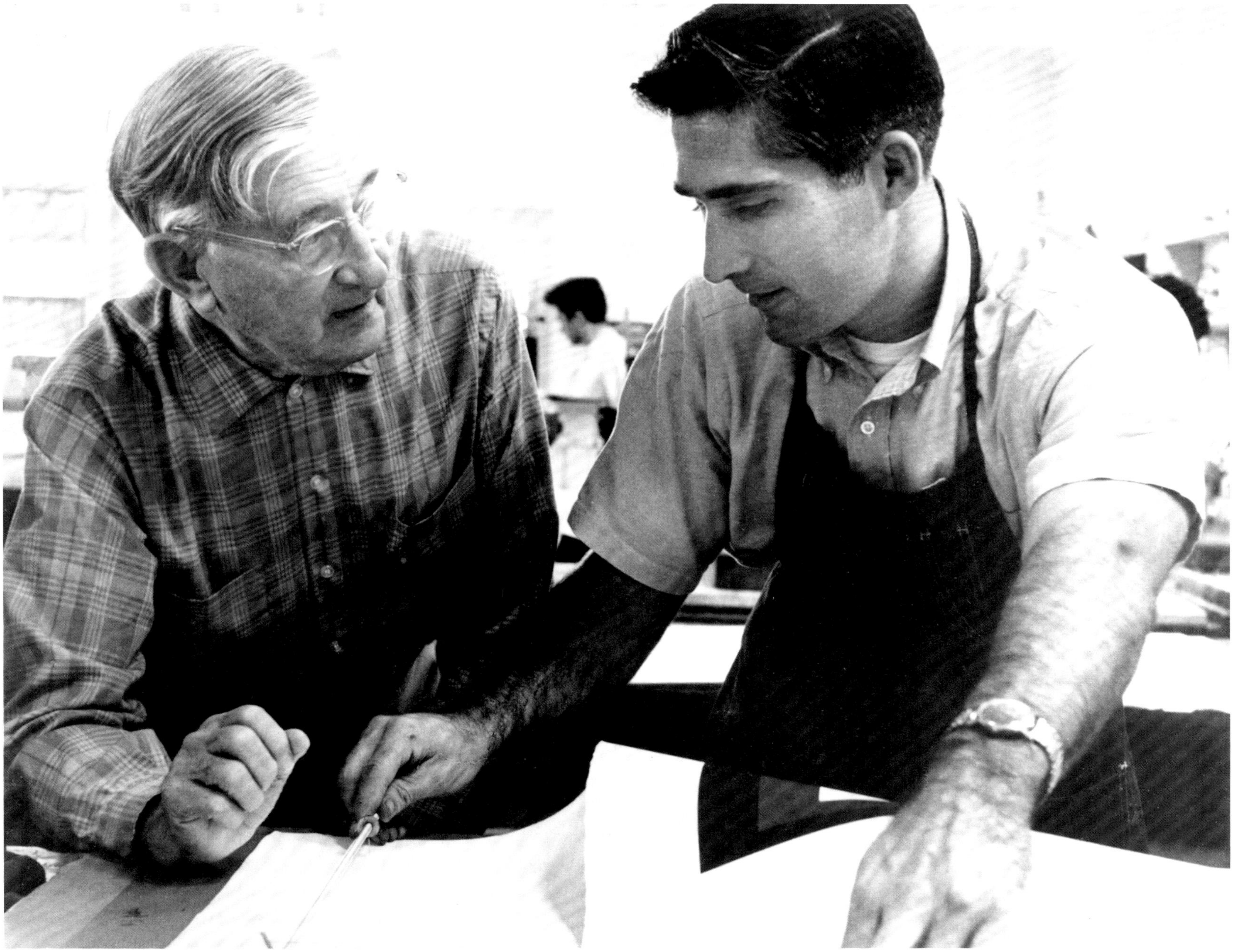

Below Josef Albers, Printing order showing format for prints inclusive of *White Line Square I* to *White Line Square XVI* 1966, fibre-tipped pen, coloured pencil and ballpoint pen on paper, 48.4 × 52.6 cm

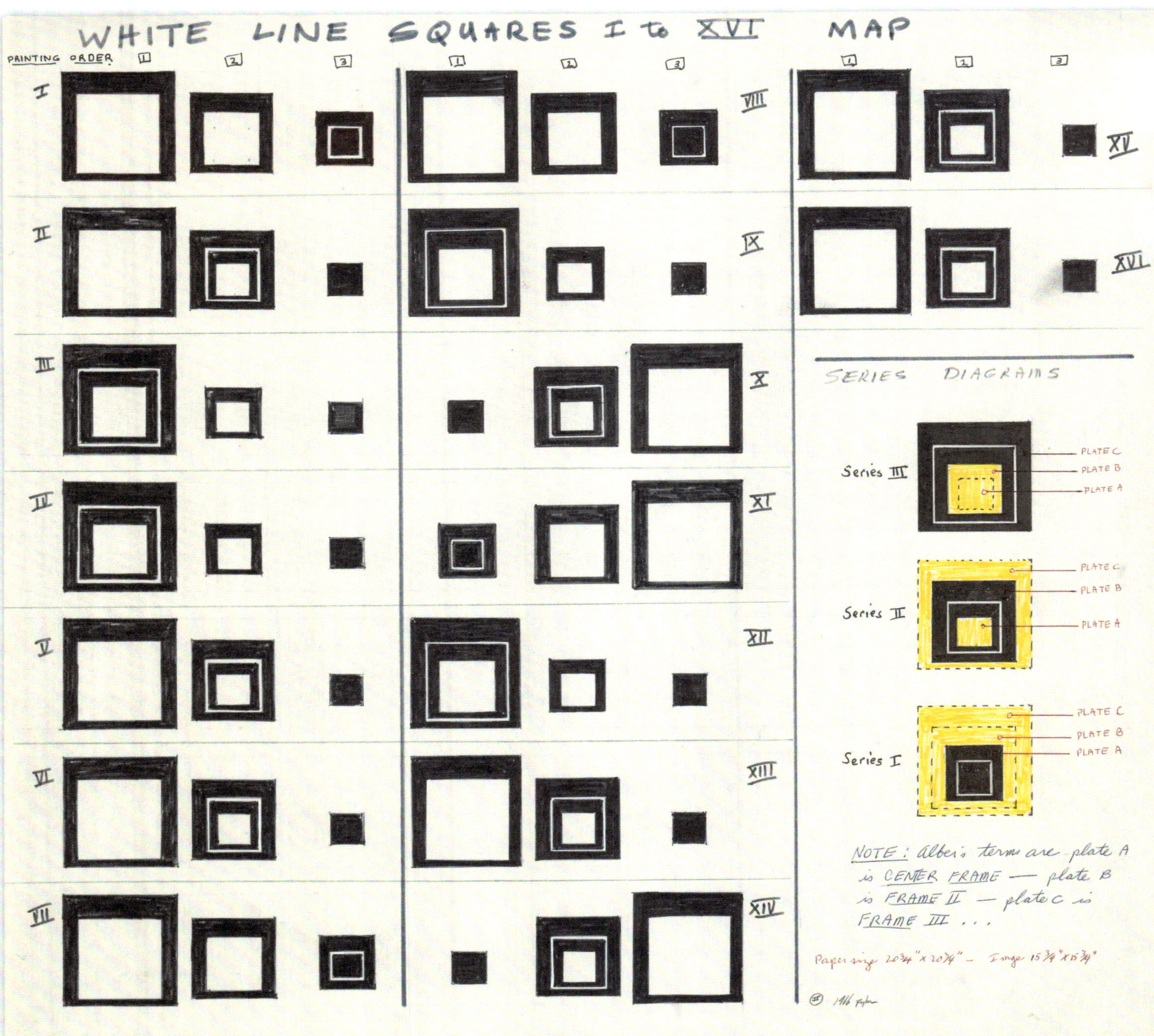

Below Josef Albers, Drawing for positioning of squares in printing of *White Line Squares* series c 1963, graphite pencil, coloured pencil on graph paper, 47.7 × 52.6 cm

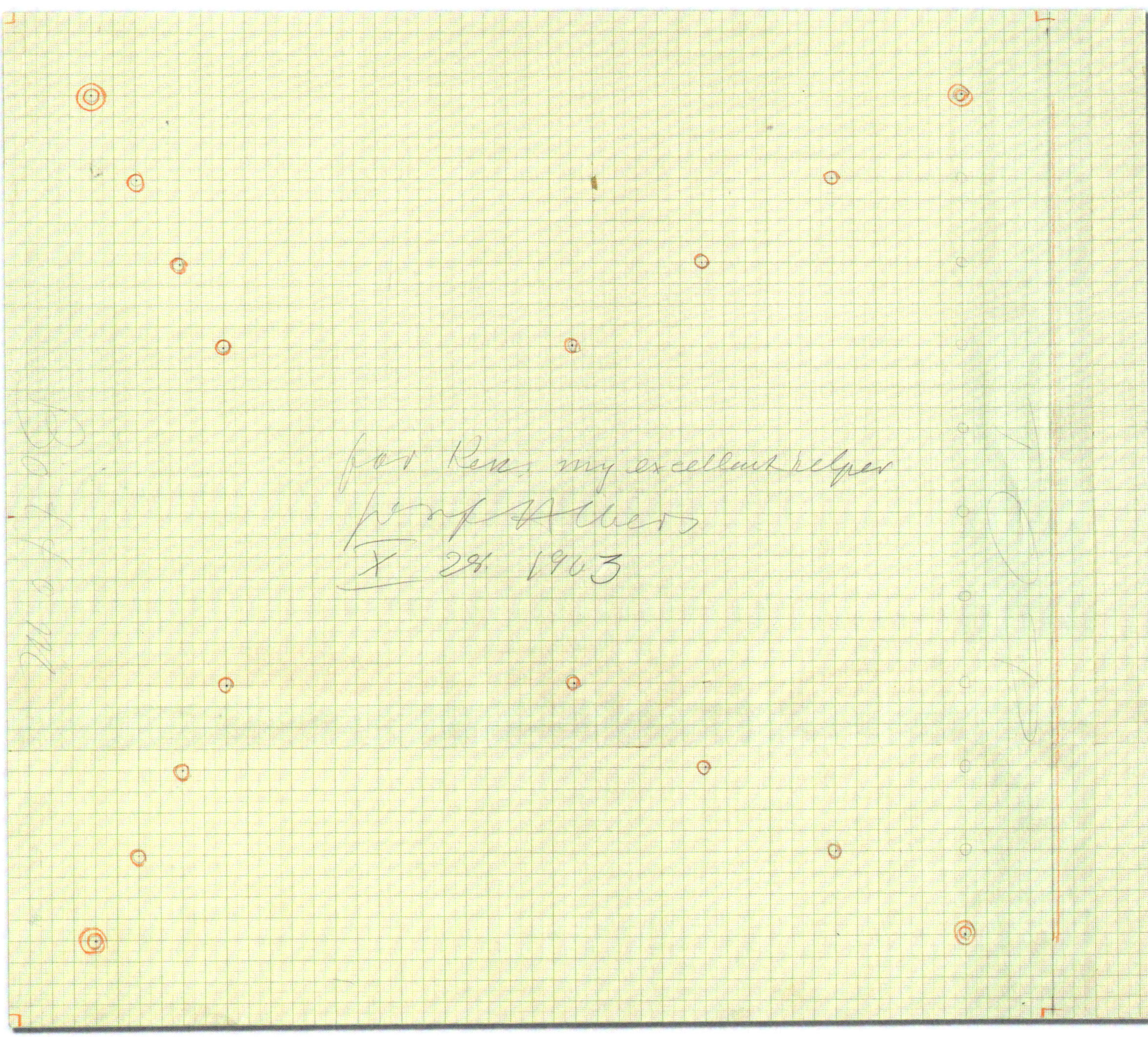

Below Josef Albers, *White Line Square I* 1966, lithograph, image 40 × 40 cm, sheet 52.7 × 52.7 cm

Below Josef Albers, *White Line Square III* 1966, lithograph, image 40 × 40 cm, sheet 52.7 × 52.7 cm

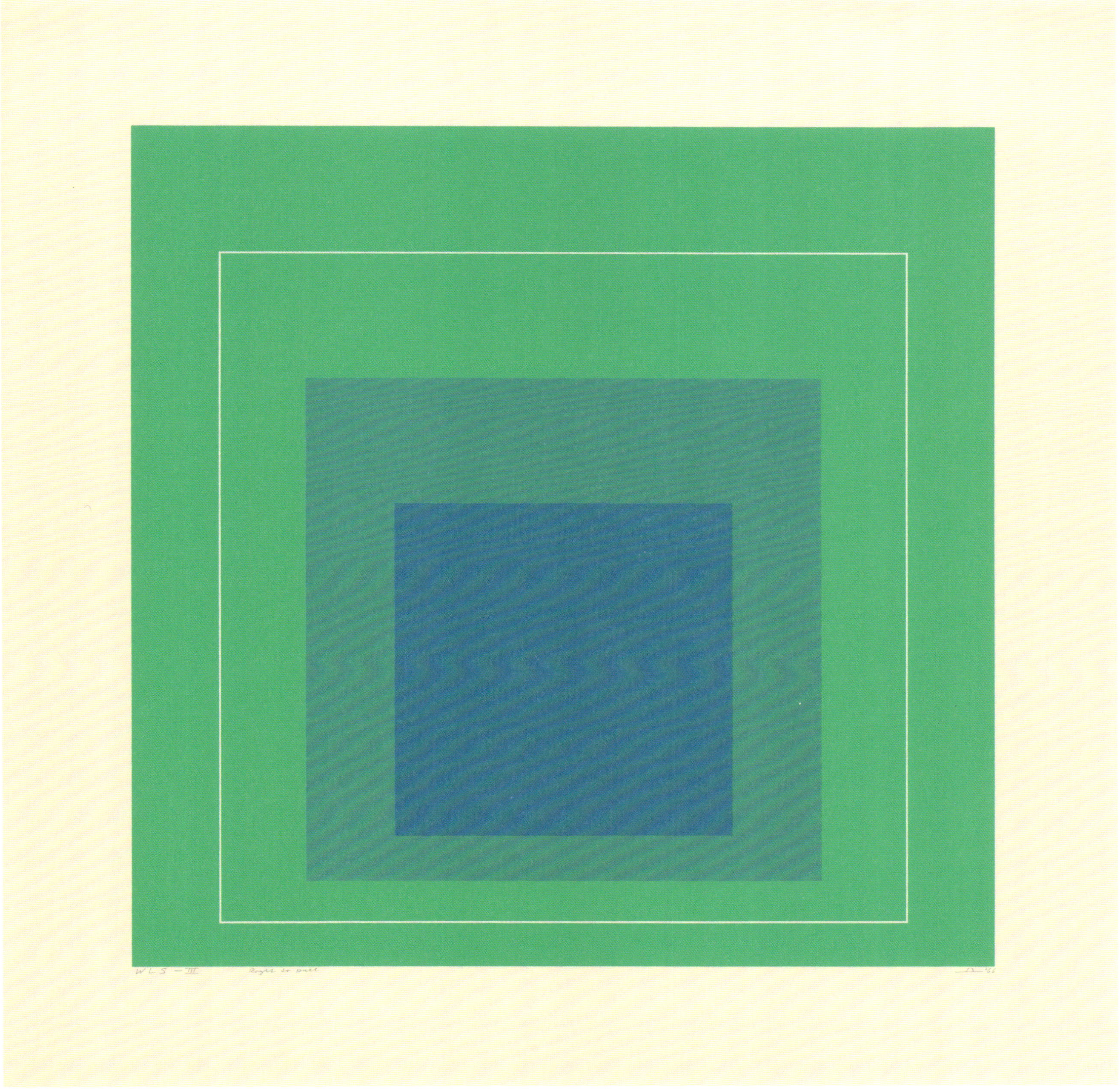

In each monochromatic print, a single ink was printed in different densities to achieve three different colours: one derived from the ink applied thickly, another from it thin, and a third from the overlap of the two. The process appealed to Tyler, who executed it imaginatively and meticulously and seemed never to mind Albers's tireless quest for perfection that meant trying colour after colour after colour and tone after tone after tone, until the pitch and rhythm and mood were everything the artist wanted them to be.

Then, in 1966, by which time Tyler had moved to Gemini GEL, the master printer helped Albers create two print series, each with eight *Homage to the Square* images, called *White Line Squares*. The collaboration was vital to the printmaker; it was his first series at his new workshop. For the first time, Albers used meticulously executed, narrow white lines to create linear squares within one of the three otherwise solid squares of colour in each Homage. The impression, therefore, is of four squares rather than three. Albers explained,

> A white line within a color area instead of its contours presents a newly discovered effect; it is placed within the middle of a color. Although very evenly applied, it makes this one color look like two different shades or tints of that color. To recognize these often minute differences we need sensitive eyes. Such white lines dividing intersecting colors are presented for the first time in the WLS lithos.[1]

This was the first occasion of the process about which Albers spoke to me with such delight—the printing of Homages in which each colour was fit against the other, side by side, without overlapping. To achieve this, Tyler cut, by hand, master stencils for the squares which were, in turn, transferred to aluminium plates. According to Pat Gilmour,

> Tyler had to achieve this immaculate precision necessary with papers that stretched in the press and with colored inks that each had a differing capacity for expansion. His brilliant solution was to minutely shrink or enlarge his rubylith stencils of the basic shapes by the way he differentially burned them into the photolitho plates.[2]

It was from these plates that the printing was done on handmade French Arches paper that had a rich texture and quality of absorption that suited the artist, but only after Tyler had devoted nine months to working out the printing and coming up with colour proofs that corresponded to the sample Albers had painted for him and that satisfied the artist.

For some, it was a painful process. The printers working for Gemini found it a struggle to work day after day to achieve the perfect, unmodulated flatness the artist craved. But Tyler and Albers meshed perfectly in their craving for precision and agreed as to the beauty achievable through mechanical means. Albers, who could be as generous and gracious as he could be didactic and tyrannical, responded by donating four-fifths of his profits from this print series to Gemini, which at that point was only in its second year.

Albers soon took his printmaking into yet another new territory. In 1969, he worked with Tyler at Gemini GEL to produce a series of eight inkless embossings called *Embossed Linear Constructions*. As Tyler explained in a brochure devoted to the series, these prints represented 'a new technical achievement for contemporary graphics'. Previously Albers had done inkless intaglios by more traditional means, pressing 'wet paper into the etched furrow of the metal plate with the use of an etching press'.[3]

Now, however, Albers had higher goals. The new prints were to be based on linear structural constellation drawings of a type that had come to obsess him. These refined compositions, made of carefully worked-out lines suggestive of geometric forms that fluctuate between appearance and disappearance, all had certain fundamentals in common. Shapes that are open and inviting become impenetrable. Paper-thin surfaces show both of their sides at once. Flat planes bend. Straight lines curve. Parallel lines appear to be at oblique angles. Parallelograms flip-flop and twist as we look at them.

1 Josef Albers, *Josef Albers: White Line Squares, a series of eight lithographs*, Gemini GEL, Los Angeles, 1966.

2 Pat Gilmour, *Ken Tyler, master printer, and the American print renaissance*, Hudson Hills Press, New York, & Australian National Gallery, Canberra, 1986, p 40.

3 Kenneth Tyler, quoted in *Josef Albers: Embossed Linear Constructions*, brochure, Gemini GEL, Los Angeles, 1969, unpag, Josef Albers artist file, National Gallery of Australia Research Library and Archives.

Top Kenneth Tyler and Anni Albers at Josef and Anni Albers's New Haven, Connecticut home, 1969, digital file from black-and-white photo print, photo by Malcolm Lubliner, Kenneth E Tyler Collection archive, National Gallery of Australia

Bottom Kenneth Tyler and Anni Albers review proofs for *TR I* at Josef and Anni Albers's New Haven, Connecticut home, 1969, digital file from black-and-white photo print, photo by Malcolm Lubliner, Kenneth E Tyler Collection archive, National Gallery of Australia

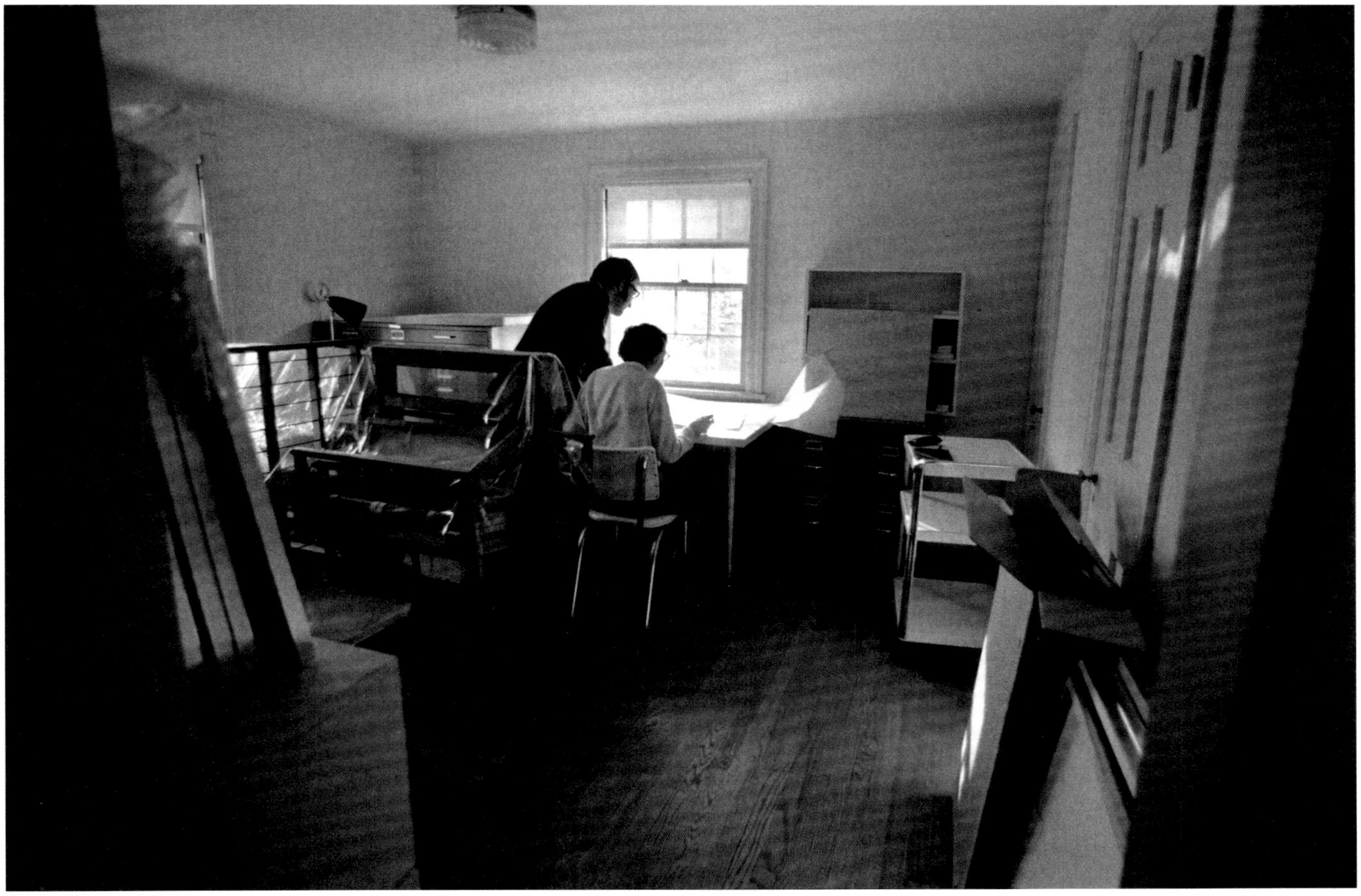

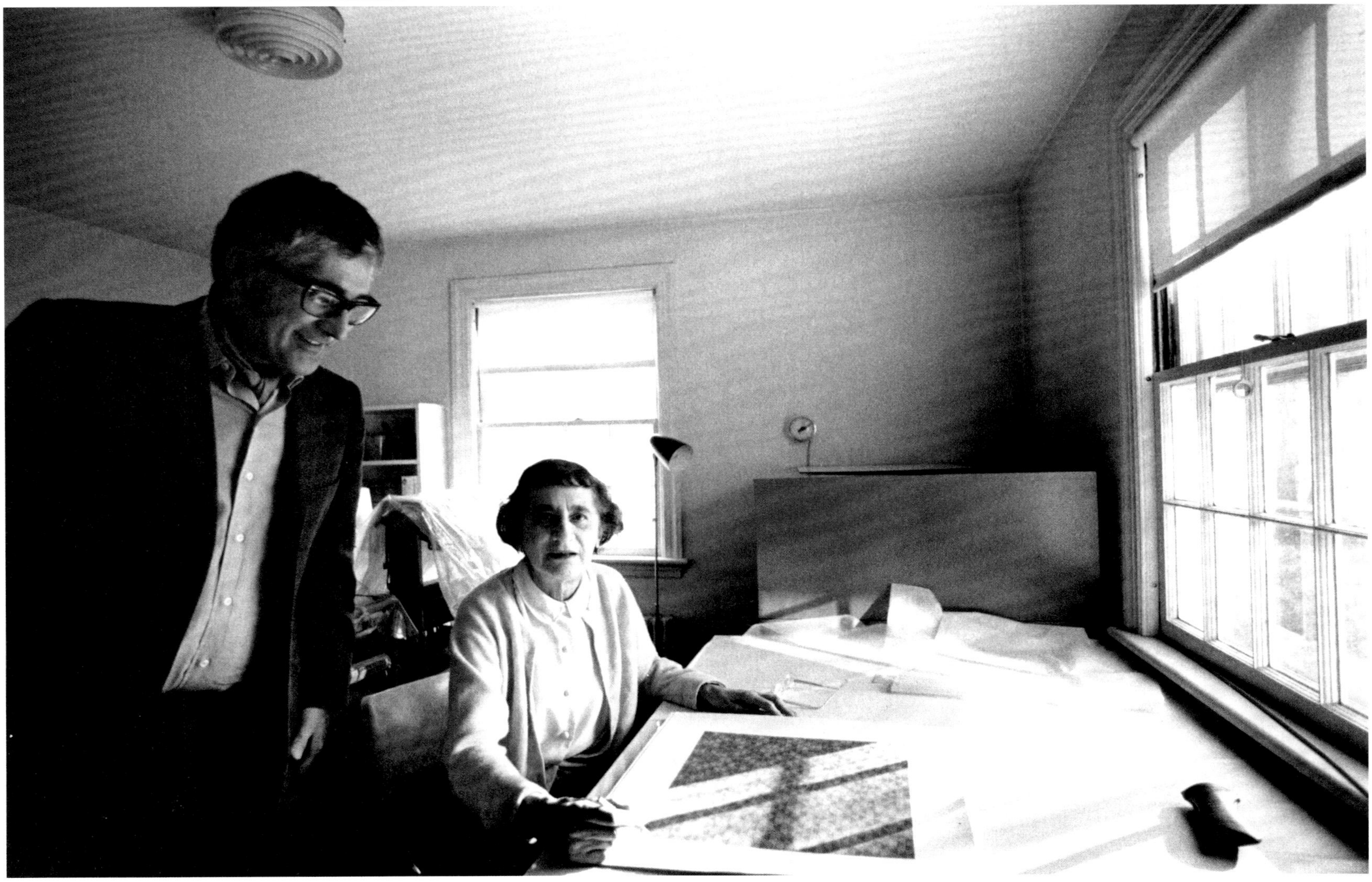

The result of this visual activity is that the action diverts us and takes us outside of ourselves. We feel secure, on a course that has been precisely premeditated—and at the same time adventurous, as we perceive an unimagined yet pleasing reality and irreality. We learn to maintain our faith in the face of ever-changing situations.

As with the Homages, the mood is calm and controlled, the quiet activity constant. The means are always mechanical, and the purpose resonates. The results of a relentless, uncompromising pursuit are objects for serene contemplation.

To ensure all of this, and to be true to Albers's precise line drawings, Tyler developed the necessary means.

> Investigations led to a system of programmed tape engraving. Collaboration between the artist, myself, and an engineering programmer established the exact profiles for each line and the proper thickness of paper. The engineering programmer translated the original artist's drawing to a digital mylar tape. The tape then directed an automatic engraving mill with specially designed cutting heads which cut into the printing plates the mirror image of the original drawings. Embossing the one hundred forty pound [300 gsm] weight Arches Watercolour paper was executed in a hydraulic forming machine. The use of heat and excessive pressure secured the image permanently into the mould made paper fibers.[4]

The results of this precision paid off gloriously. For all its appearance of austerity and purity, the work that was produced in such a deliberately mechanical way, devoid of any mark of the artist's hand, is vibrant and mysterious. The calm is not shallow and stagnant; rather, there is a natural complexity, humour as well as drama. Just as the *Midnight and Noon* prints permitted the darkness of night to coexist with the brightness of day, these embossings allowed what Albers called 'north light and south light' to shine simultaneously and moved us in opposite directions at once. They are courageous, airy, and playful and serious at the same time. Seemingly divorced from the natural world, in fact they extend its possibilities.

The same was true of Albers's next collaboration with Tyler, the 10 *White Embossings on Gray* they produced together at Gemini GEL in 1971. Also based on the *Structural Constellation* drawings, these combined colour print with embossing. Here Gemini developed a new all rag paper with the necessary 'uniform ink absorption and embossing properties'.[5]

Albers wrote that the drawings for prints of this sort

> Change
> in motion: from coming to going,
> in extension: from inward to outward,
> in grouping: from together to separated,
> in volume: from full to empty,
> or reversed.[6]

All these phenomena, and more, occur in these precisely produced double-image prints.

Once Tyler moved to Bedford Village, New York, and set up the Tyler Workshop, Albers was delighted to have his favourite collaborator nearby. Anni, too, had made prints at Tamarind and Gemini, and although husband and wife were proud of their independence from one another, and worked in very different veins, each now had a beloved workshop nearby. When I would make those drives down the Merritt Parkway with them, I sensed that the experience was not so different from what it must have felt like, half a century earlier, to go into the workshop of the Bauhaus. Engaging with the latest and best technology, they could pursue the art of which they endlessly dreamed. There was always a feeling of excitement, and productivity, on those journeys.

In 1974 and 1975, Josef produced *Gray Instrumentation I* and *Gray Instrumentation II*, as well as a few related individual images. This was his deepest excursion to date into his beloved territory of the black-white-grey spectrum. The effect of those two series, each with 12 hand-printed silkscreen prints, is quite unbelievable. Going from Homage to Homage, mood and rhythm and tempo constantly change. The variables achieved through limited means suggest Mozart's solo piano sonatas;

4 Tyler, quoted in *Josef Albers: Embossed Linear Constructions*, unpag.

5 Kenneth Tyler, quoted in *Josef Albers: White Embossings on Gray*, brochure, Gemini GEL, Los Angeles, 1971, unpag.

6 This statement by Josef Albers has appeared in various publications; it is reprinted in Nicholas Fox Weber, *The drawings of Josef Albers*, Yale University Press, New Haven, 1983, p 44.

Below

Josef Albers, *Never Before f* 1976, 5-colour screenprint printed from 5 screens in light pink, medium grey-pink, medium blue-violet, medium grey-yellow, and dark grey-orange, image 28 × 30.6 cm, sheet 48.2 × 50.8 cm, National Gallery of Australia, 77.879.6

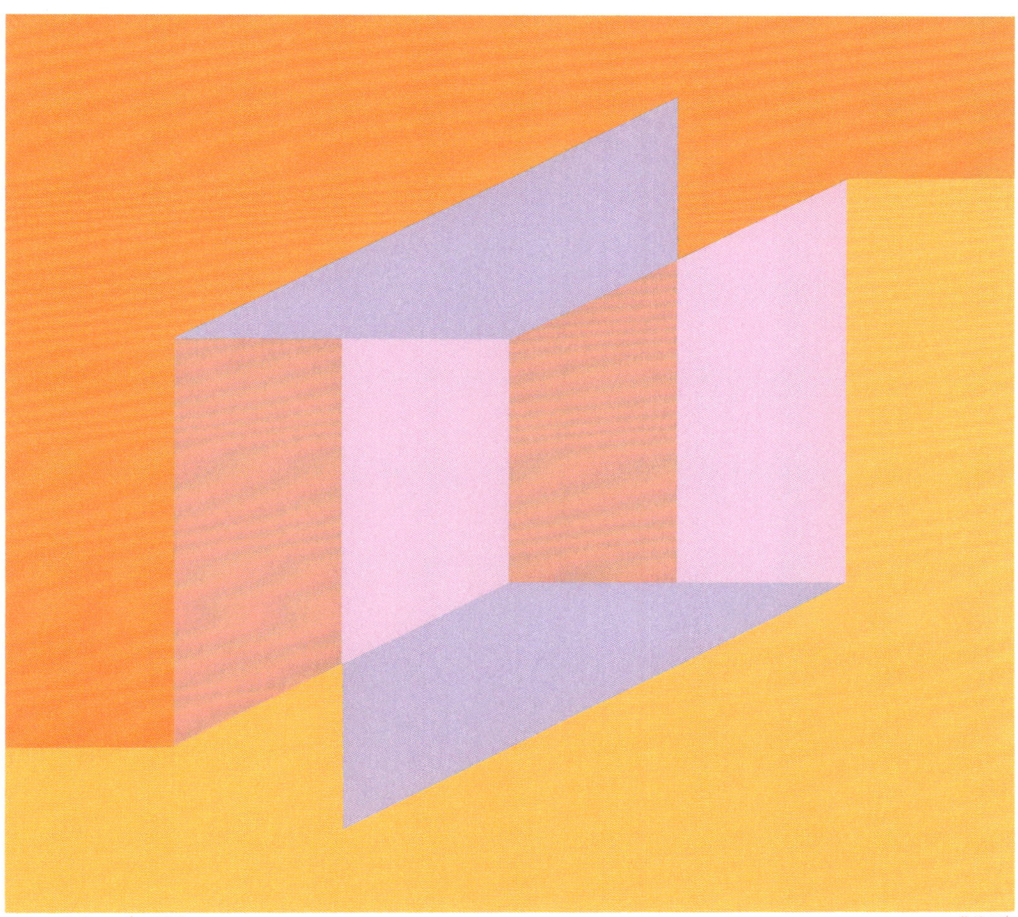

a few notes struck properly create poetry, and music, of unfathomable power. In single notes as well as in chords, the exquisitely selected range of greys alters the mood, even the breathing, of the viewer. We feel subdued and then elated, diverted and then brought closer to ourselves. It is calming and invigorating at the same time. And by fitting the colours side by side in the way that so delighted Albers, printing each ink directly on the white and achieving the meticulous registration necessary to make that process work, Tyler enabled the artist who had devoted much of his lifetime to the exploration of colour to further his search in the manner he wanted.

Then in 1976 came the *Mitered Squares*—an elegant variation of the usual Homages with new possibilities of rhythm and spatial flow opened up by variations within the squares and the angled lines stemming outward from the four corners of the central square. And finally, in the same year, Albers undertook a series he called *Never Before*. This last group of 12 images was based on a theme Albers had first taken up in the 1949 painting *Indicating Solids*. Painter and printer collaborated happily. Tyler made cut-outs in numerous sample inks, always following the design of Albers's painting. Albers then juxtaposed the cut-outs, creating over 100 collages before coming up with his 12 solutions.

The series showed clearly Albers's intent: to have colours interact, and to use colour to alter direction and make the lines and forms of the same format look entirely different from print to print. The mood, although varied, is consistently light and cheerful. Art, after all, offered the chance to invoke what one wanted: to counter the vagaries of life. Albers was 87 years old, but the art he was producing showed him at his most youthfully spirited and vital.

On 25 March 1976, the artist died—a week after his 88th birthday—before he had been able to finish signing the edition, but at least he had approved all 12 images. The *Never Before* prints leap—physically and spiritually. Precise technique, the wonders of the machine and the collaboration of a great technician made possible an art that soars, and that will continue always to do so.

Nicholas Fox Weber
Executive Director
The Josef and Anni Albers Foundation

This essay first appeared in *Josef Albers: autonomous color*, published in 1996 by the Center for Contemporary Graphic Art and Tyler Graphic Archive Collection, Japan, and has been minimally edited to align with National Gallery style.

Below Josef Albers, *White Line Square VI* 1966, lithograph, image 40 × 40 cm, sheet 52.7 × 52.7 cm

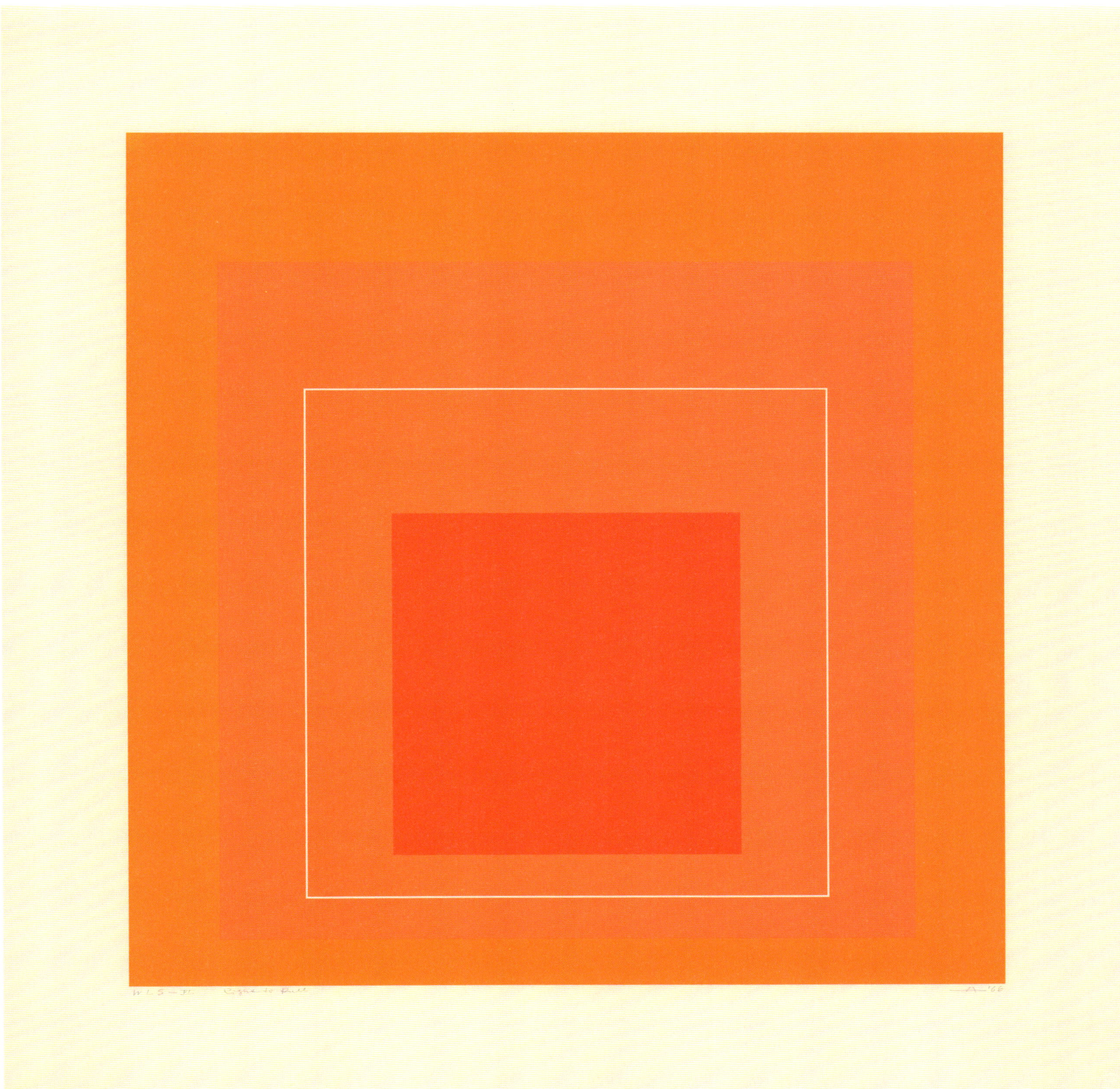

Below Josef Albers, *White Line Square XI* 1966, lithograph, image 40 × 40 cm, sheet 52.7 × 52.7 cm

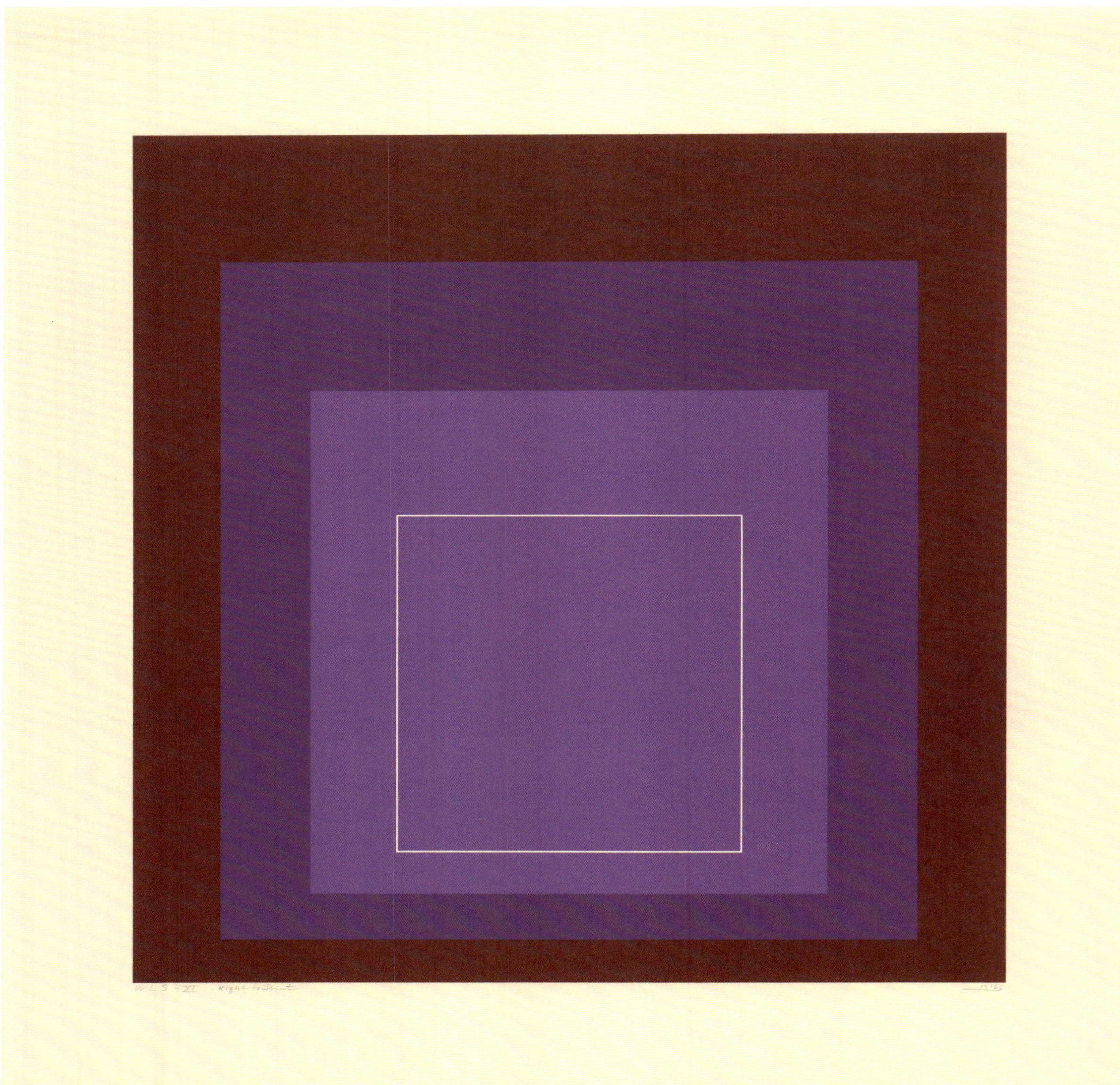

Below Josef Albers, *White Line Square XIII* 1966, lithograph, image 40 × 40 cm, sheet 52.7 × 52.7 cm

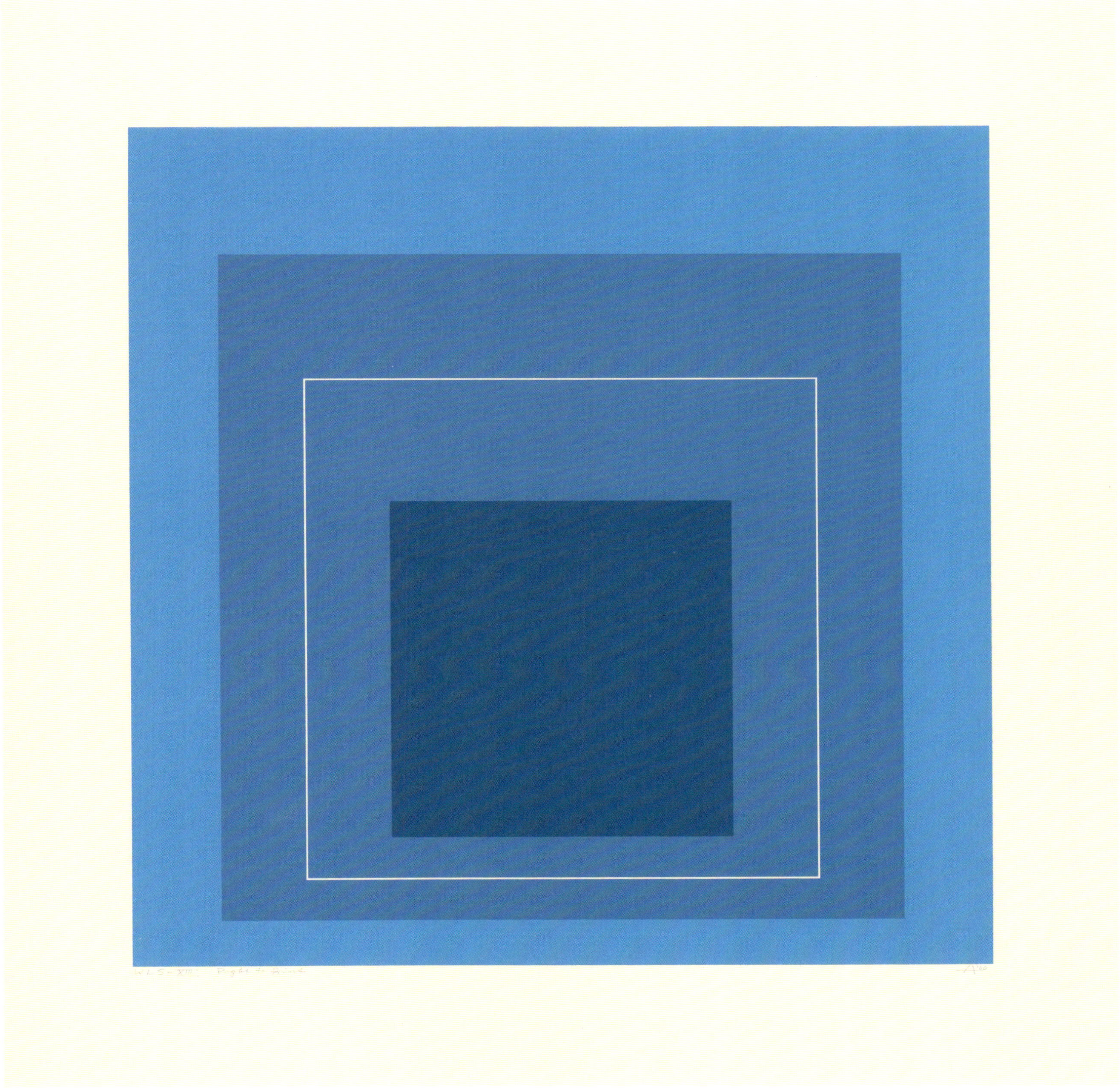

Below Josef Albers, *White Line Square XV* 1966, lithograph, image 40 × 40 cm, sheet 52.7 × 52.7 cm

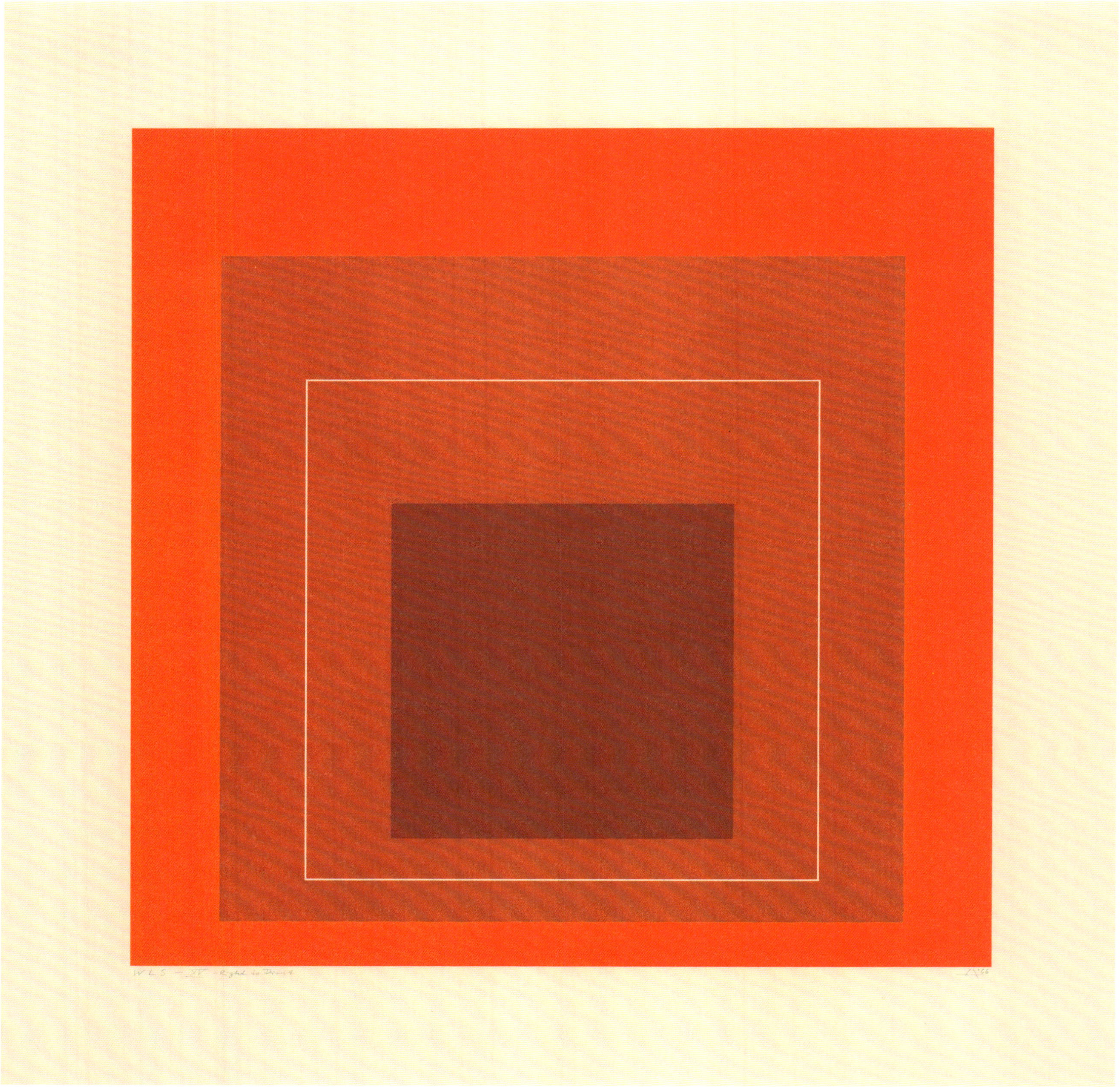

September 3, 1968
To Josef Albers

Hello Anni...

Yes.

This is Ken.

Yes, he's back.

O.K.

I also wanted to mention to you ... did you see in Vogue Magazine the write up about you?

Yes, uh huh.

Good. I cut it out...we can send it to you, or give it to you for an additional one.

alright...

O.K. Here's Josef.

Ken, good to hear you.

Hello, Josef, how are you?

Oh, seems alright.

Great! Great.

Now, you have something new in doing?

Yes, I...the little package with the white paper that I sent you...did you receive that?

No, you see, you send me sometime the very heavy paper with the ....and the lines, and you said you wouldn't choose that paper.

No, no, but what I wanted, what I wanted to talk to you about... does the straightness of that line look good to you?

Oh, yea.

O.K. Now what we are going to do is work on the depth of getting the embossing deeper and much richer looking.

Yea...

But, we wanted to first check if that straightness was fine. Now, that was done on an automatic machine from the tracing that I made from your drawing.

Uh huh.

And it's run electronically from the tape.

Yea.

And it's much more accurate than what a person can do by engraving by hand.

Yea, yea...

So, what we will do then is take one of the original tracings now and do a full one and make this complete die and then we will start sampling the better papers.

You have noticed that the lines when they meet sometimes when they overlap they really have a rounded ending...

Uh huh.

You have noticed that?

Yes.

Well, you see that is, that is the center of the construction . The soul of each line meet others again within the line.

Um hummm.

Let's say the abstract idea of the line.

Um hummm.

Is central core, the spine of the line. They meet everywhere within a line and in a corner, but when this line has width for visual reasons, then the ends round off. See

Uh huh.

So you must watch how the things overlap each other, sometimes with little rounded endings.

Uh huh...you would prefer that if they were ~~w~~ square.

Yea...you see, then you, let's say and thick line meets perpendicular, or somewhat perpendicularly, and other line so that a T shape arrives. Then the one line that goes into another one overlaps it with a little rounding. Have you noticed it?

Yes.

You see..

Ah ha.

That is mathematically right, otherwise the lines are not really constructed...then they are painted.

I see..

So I must...I give you...I must send you a little sample where that is explained.

That would be excellent. We're stopping it inside of the T, we don't let it go over. And you want it to...

Yea, it must go over the top line of the T because that is the continuation of the line and...

I see...

and I must send you a sample how that is understood.

O.K. well, when I receive that sample, then I'll study that and then we'll go ahead and make the first one.

Yea, now, then you send me the heavy paper, you said you wouldn't choose that one. You sent me another sample?

Yes, we ...no...when I make the new die, I'll try the heavier paper.

Yea.

I couldn't do it with the present die we have.

Yea.

That was just like a little sample.

Now, I want to thank you also very much for the Art New s you sent me.

Ah ha, good.

One came out of your own possession...thefirst one. And the other one you found? How do you call these stores that have these left over,...how do you call?

Well, we got that from the publisher of Art News.

From the publisher himself, I wouldn't have wanted....

What we did is we called them up and we told them that it was very, very essential that we get several copies, and they said they didn't have them.

Yea, but they sent you two.

No, no, then they told us all the places we could contact throughout the country that they thought might have some.

Ah yea ....how they call such bookstores which have the leftover issues of magazines?

Any of the Antiquarians would have it.... these are the people who deal with out of print books.

Out of print magazines...

[illegible] there?

So I must [illegible] ... I [illegible] you [illegible] [illegible]
[illegible] that's [illegible].

[illegible] ... We're going to [illegible] of [illegible]
[illegible] it [illegible]. And [illegible] it to.

[illegible] the [illegible] on the [illegible] because [illegible]
[illegible] of [illegible].

[illegible]

[illegible] ... [illegible] [illegible] [illegible] [illegible] [illegible]
and [illegible] and make the first one.

[illegible] and [illegible] you [illegible] [illegible]
[illegible] [illegible] [illegible].

[illegible] ... [illegible] [illegible] the [illegible] [illegible] [illegible] [illegible]
[illegible].

[illegible]

I [illegible] [illegible] [illegible] you have.

[illegible] ... [illegible] little thing.

You [illegible] want [illegible] you [illegible] [illegible] [illegible] just
[illegible].

[illegible]

[illegible] your [illegible] ... the [illegible] [illegible] [illegible]
[illegible] ... [illegible] that [illegible]
[illegible] [illegible] [illegible].

[illegible] ... that from the [illegible] of [illegible].

[illegible] the [illegible] ... [illegible] [illegible] [illegible].

What [illegible] ... [illegible] and [illegible] [illegible]
[illegible] [illegible] [illegible] [illegible] [illegible] [illegible]
[illegible] [illegible] [illegible].

[illegible] they [illegible] [illegible].

[illegible] ... [illegible] [illegible] [illegible] [illegible]
[illegible] [illegible] [illegible] [illegible].

[illegible] ... [illegible] [illegible] [illegible] [illegible] [illegible]
[illegible]
[illegible]
[illegible] ... [illegible] [illegible] [illegible] [illegible] [illegible]
[illegible] [illegible] [illegible].

[illegible] not necessary.

Yes

Yea

Um Humm

O.K.

And do then we went back and we told the publisher we couldn't find any. You see, they keep 20 copies of everything they print. They keep it in their files.

Yea, yea.

So what happened here is they wanted then to know why we wanted those two copies...

Yea...

And we told them that Mr. Albers needed them desperately

Yea...

To show someone in Europe for a publication, and that he had no copies, and that they had told him previously that they didn't have any copies and I thought that that issue was very worthwhile to Mr. Albers...

Yea...

And would they please release two of them.

Yea..

So they said alright, they would release two of them. So those are brand new, you see, they've never been used.

Now, two other things. You sent me also a very large white line square in red.

Yes.

Very large. But the center was not in it.

Well that was the one...No , I didn't send that to you...that was the one I left with you.

And you left it with me.

Yes, when I was there.

Doesn't, that doesn't help me if the scale is not full.

Ah hah...

Then, then I have in the center a great white hole, doesn't tell me

any interaction, you see. I must see the thing completed, then its only speaking when every place is filled out.

Ah hah.

Now, then I was very pleased to get the, that orange back. Are these the only two you worked?

No, I have the pencil and ink ~~and~~ drawings~~x~~

Ah, you have still more.

Yes , I have the pencil...

That's what I thought. Now, the best way to protect them ~~xx~~ is that acetate where you put them each in an envelope that has in front acetate.

Yes. They are that way.

A marvelous idea, and I want to copy that...I want to have ~~my~~x all my drawings instead of exposing them to the fingers of exhibitors, to have them in such envelopes, and I'm going to have such envelopes made which suit my portfolios I have for drawings.

Um humm.

I was very please d ~~to~~ with these things.

Well, if you, if you send me the sizes you need, we'll have them made up. They make them next door.

I can, I can have them made here too.

Uh huh.

Now you said once you have three more complete sets of my White Line Squares. Didn't you say it last time?

Gosh, I don't remember how many we have, Josef.

O.K._____, if there are ...

I thought we, I thought we sent all those to Yuro; to your wharehouse, didn't we?

No, I got only eight, eight of them.

O.K., I will, I will check that out and...

Check that and let me know how, how many are still available.

O.K.

Yea/

Um hmm.

I...heard from Anni you are coming end of September.

That's my plans, now, yes...

Yea?

Uh, huh.

Bring some samples of those English intaglios, you know...

Fine...

White on white. I'm very interested to see how that works.

Good. Well, I think by that time we will have some full ones completed ...

Yea...

And we'll move very fast on that now.

Let us know in advance when you come.

I will. So you get me a little sample of the intersecting line...

I do that...

And that way I'll be able to know exactly how to do it.

Yea, very good.

Wonderful.

Lot's of good luck.

O.k. Josef, I'll be talking...

You let us know when you come.

I will...I'll be talking to you later.

Yea...

Alright.

Thank you very much.

Bye bye

Bye.

Below Ica-Chincha people, south coast, Peru, Tabard c 1300 CE, feathers and cotton, 142 × 80.2 cm

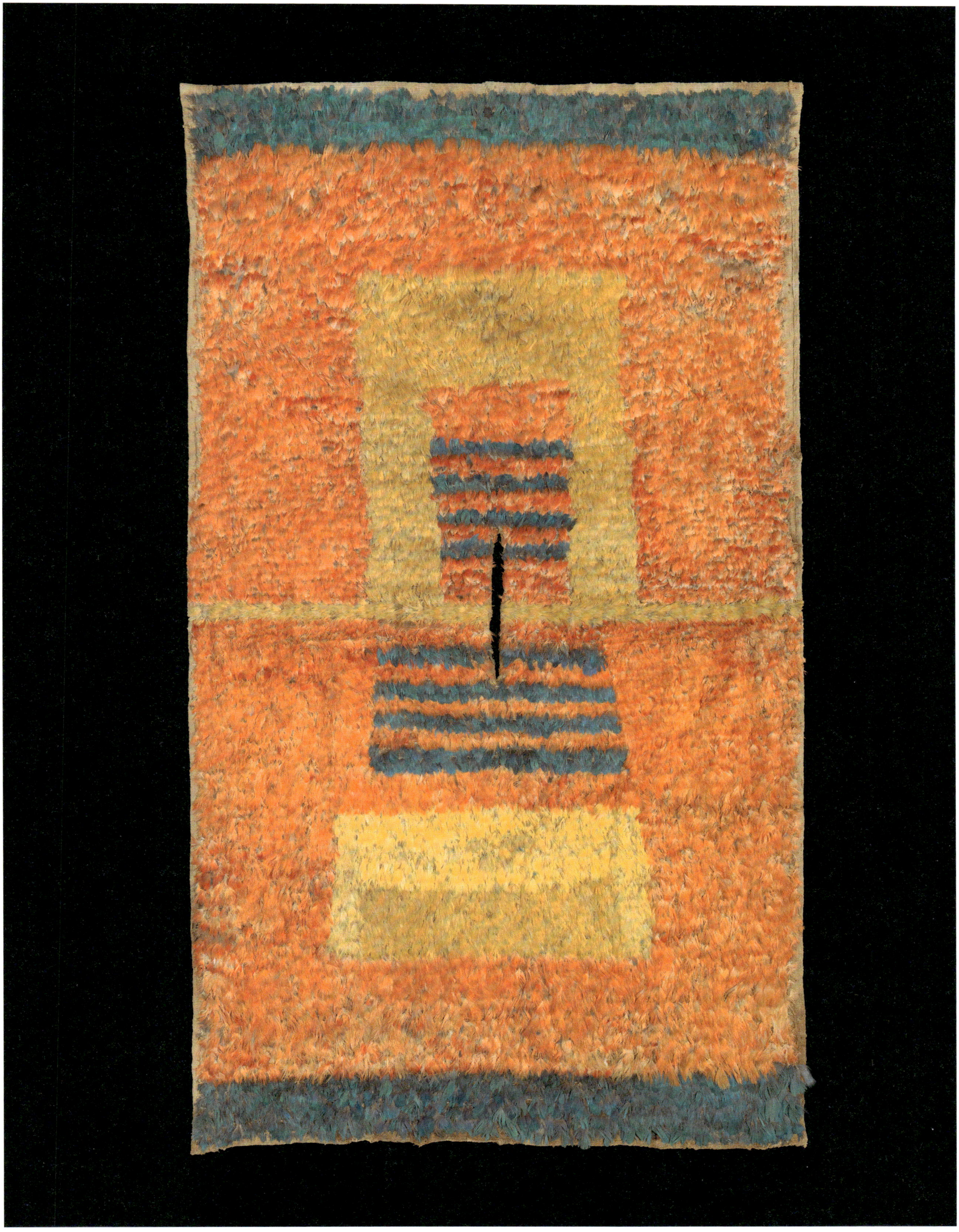

Below Sicán-Lambayeque people, north coast, Peru, Beaker 900–1100 CE, gold (hammered, embossed, annealing and repoussé), 13.2 × 10 (diam) cm

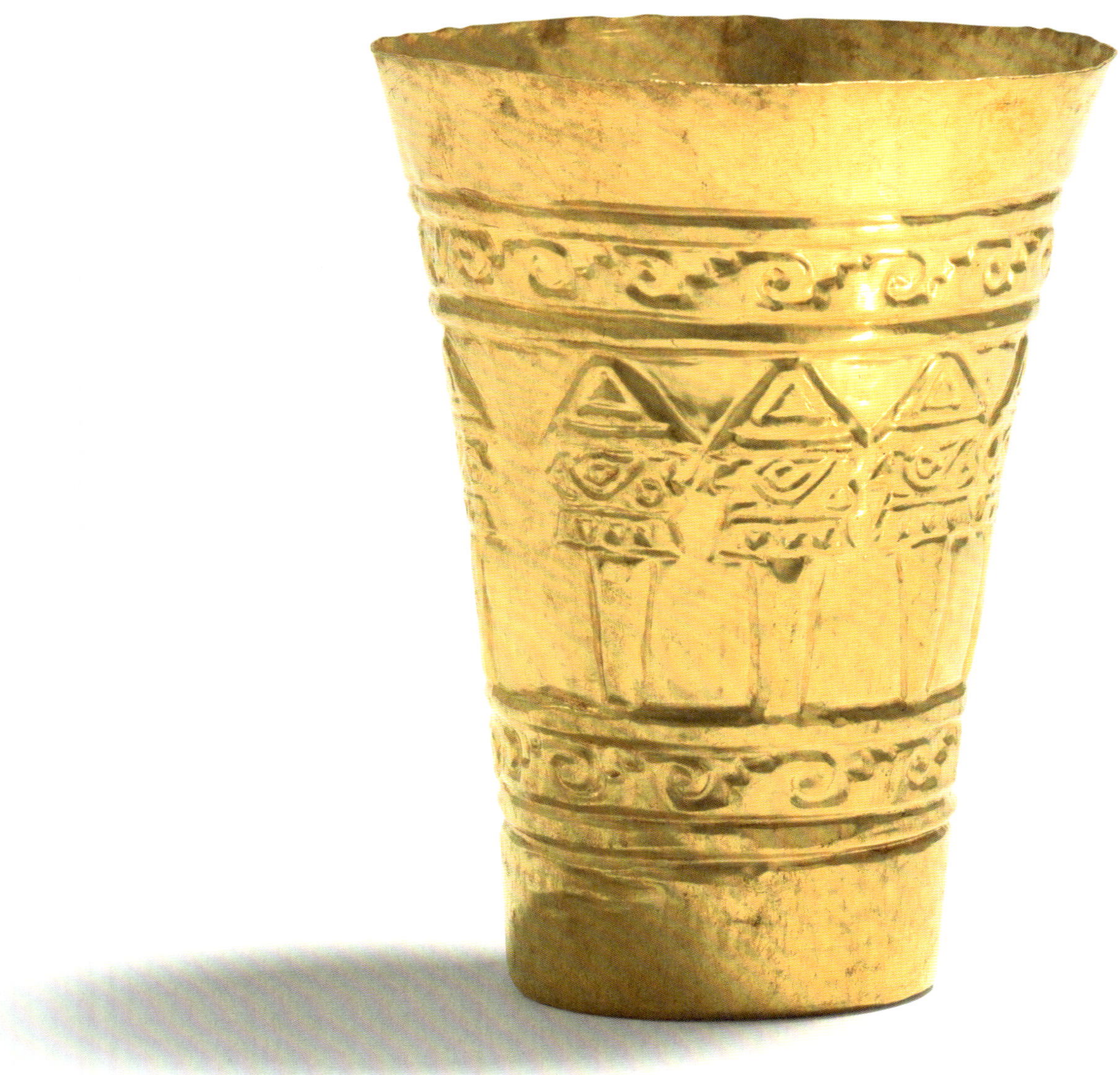

Below Moche people, north coast, Peru, Stirrup vessel with a geometric design c 600 CE, ceramic, 24 × 14.5 (diam) cm

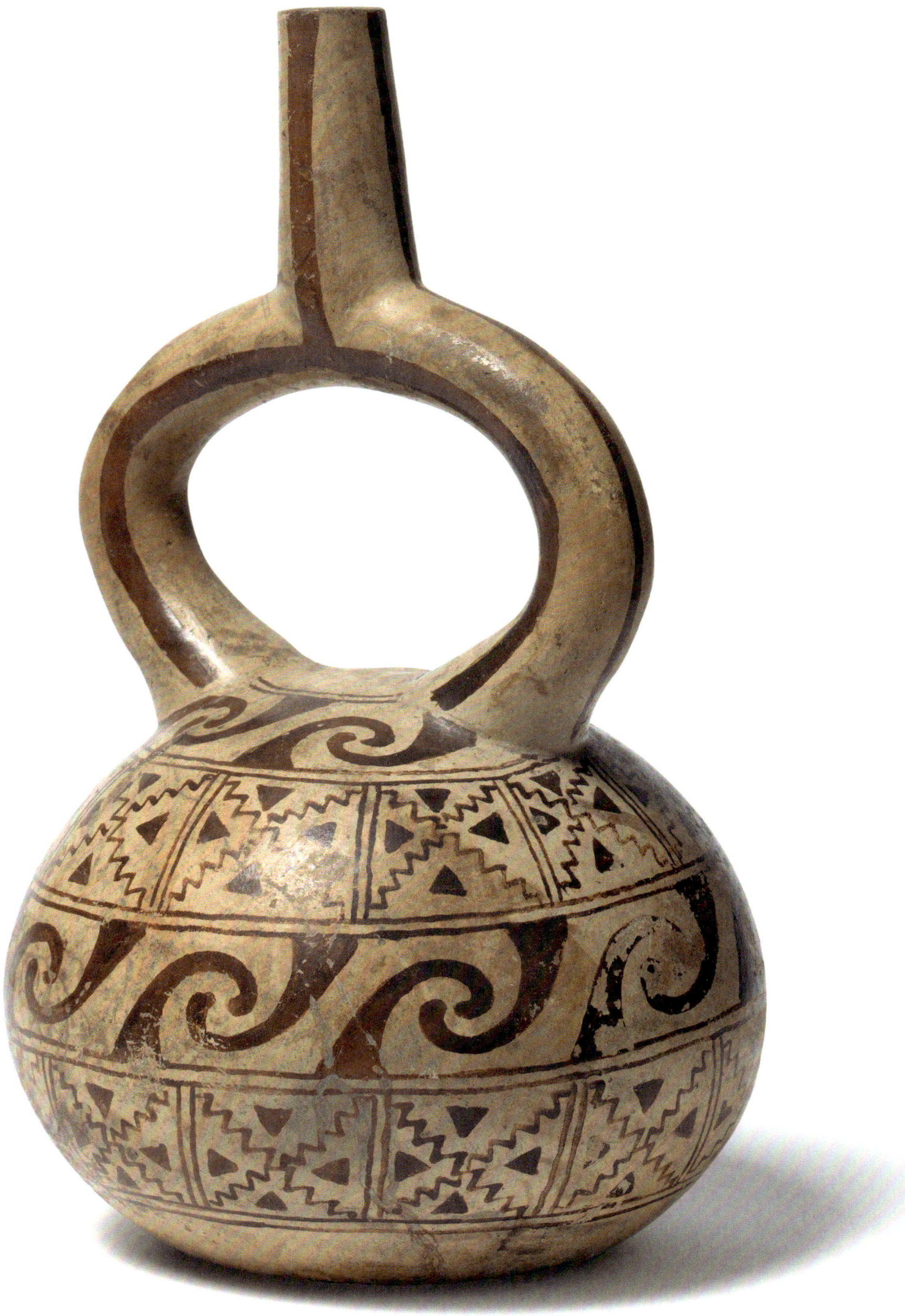

Below Anni Albers, Study for *Camino Real* c 1967, gouache and diazotype on paper, sheet 44.8 × 40.3 cm, photo by Tim Nighswander / Imaging4Art, the Josef and Anni Albers Foundation, 94.10.21

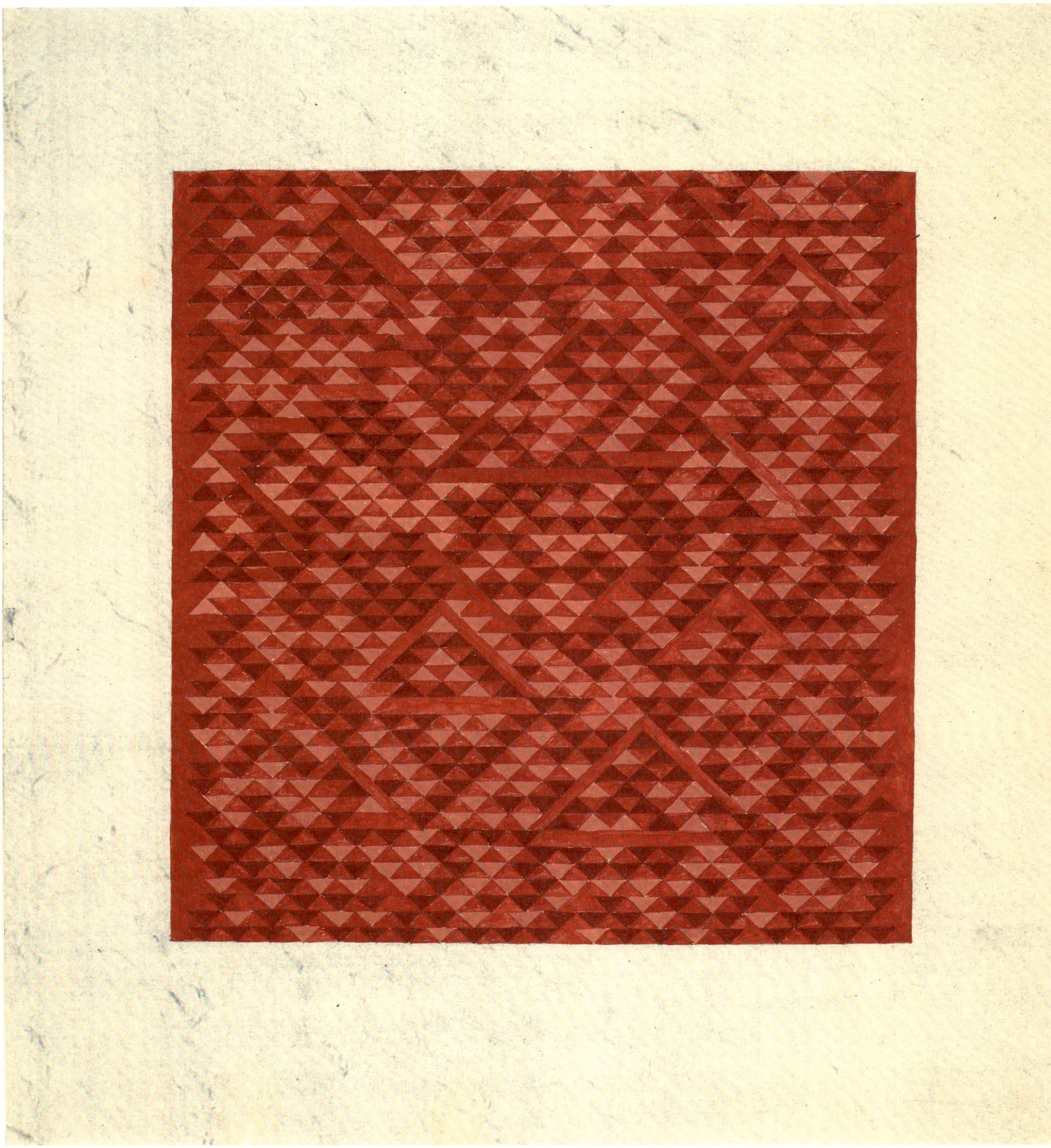

The permutations of Camino Real: Anni Albers and textile intermediality c1970

Jordan Troeller

Around 1967, Anni Albers began designing what would be her last large-scale wall-hanging: a 3-metre-high appliqué textile destined for the interior of a hotel in Mexico City. Mimicking the name of the hotel itself, *Camino Real* 1968 was as much in dialogue with its architectural environment as it was with textile construction and printmaking. Indeed, the work came at a pivotal moment in her career. In 1966, Albers created her last woven textile; afterwards, she sold off her looms and devoted herself to printmaking, both on paper and with fibres.[1] For the next two decades, well into the 1980s, she experimented with a range of printmaking workshops and technologies, including silkscreen, photo-offset, embossing, aquatint and etching, reinventing herself as an artist devoted to mechanical reproducibility.

Though diverse in appearance and materials, a surprising number of these prints share a common feature: all redeploy—in various ways—the geometric patterns of the 1968 wall-hanging. Take, for instance, one of the most overt examples, Study for *Camino Real* c 1967, where she has employed the technique of diazotype. Initially developed as an alternative to the blueprint, diazotype became a standard method of reproducing maps, architectural plans and other technical drawings. It is made by treating paper with diazonium salts so that it becomes photosensitive, which then allows an image to be projected on the surface and developed through photographic chemicals. Albers very likely saw the potential of such a technique in generating a matrix on which she could devise a complex, triangular design, trying first this combination of reds and that pattern of repeated shapes until she arrived at the rhythm she desired.

This is the topic that I explore in what follows: the degree to which *Camino Real* initiated a series of permutations in Albers's thinking about form, materials and technique in printmaking. To date, *Camino Real* has not been viewed as pivotal in Albers's development as an artist, nor has it been regarded as initiating a series of prints (including one in the series *TR*, produced at Gemini GEL in 1970 in her first collaboration with Kenneth Tyler). *Camino Real* is difficult to categorise in that it departs from Albers's usual way of working out a design through the warp and weft of the loom itself. Instead of being woven, it was assembled from variegated red felt triangles applied to a felt background, allowing for a degree of repetition particularly suited to printmaking. My interest in this work lies in how it registers Albers's transition from textiles to prints, from a medium typically associated with fibre and craft to one of mechanical reproduction.

Instead of a screenprint, a wall-hanging

First, some background on the origins of *Camino Real* as an architectural commission: in February 1967, the architects of the Hotel Camino Real in Mexico City, Luis Barragán and Ricardo Legorreta, and German-Mexican sculptor Mathias Goeritz, arrived at the Alberses' house in New Haven. As head architect of the hotel, Ricardo Legorreta had enlisted Barragán and Goeritz as consultants on the building's art program, which would eventually include work by Alexander Calder and Rufino Tamayo, among others. It was Barragán who seems to have suggested the visit to the Alberses. He had first met Anni and Josef on one of their many visits to Mexico. Barragán had a special interest in Josef Albers's work on colour, and the integration of colour into the hotel's interior spaces was one of the defining features of his—as well as his protégé Legorreta's—vision of a modern Mexican architecture in dialogue with its vernacular past. This work on colour was transmitted to Barragán through a copy of Albers's book and portfolio *Interaction of Color* (published in 1963), which was a feat of silkscreen printing. Barragán had even bought a reproduction on cloth of one of the *Homage to the Square* paintings, which he had likely purchased on a visit to the United States and had framed for his Mexico City home. As Sheila Hicks recalls, although the framed Homage was a

1 Marion L Buzzard's notes, quoted in Brenda Danilowitz and T'ai Smith, *Anni Albers: Camino Real*, David Zwirner, New York, 2020, p 14.

Below Anni Albers's wall-hanging *Camino Real* 1968. Lobby bar of Hotel Camino Real, Mexico City, 1968, photo by Jon Naar, the Josef and Anni Albers Foundation

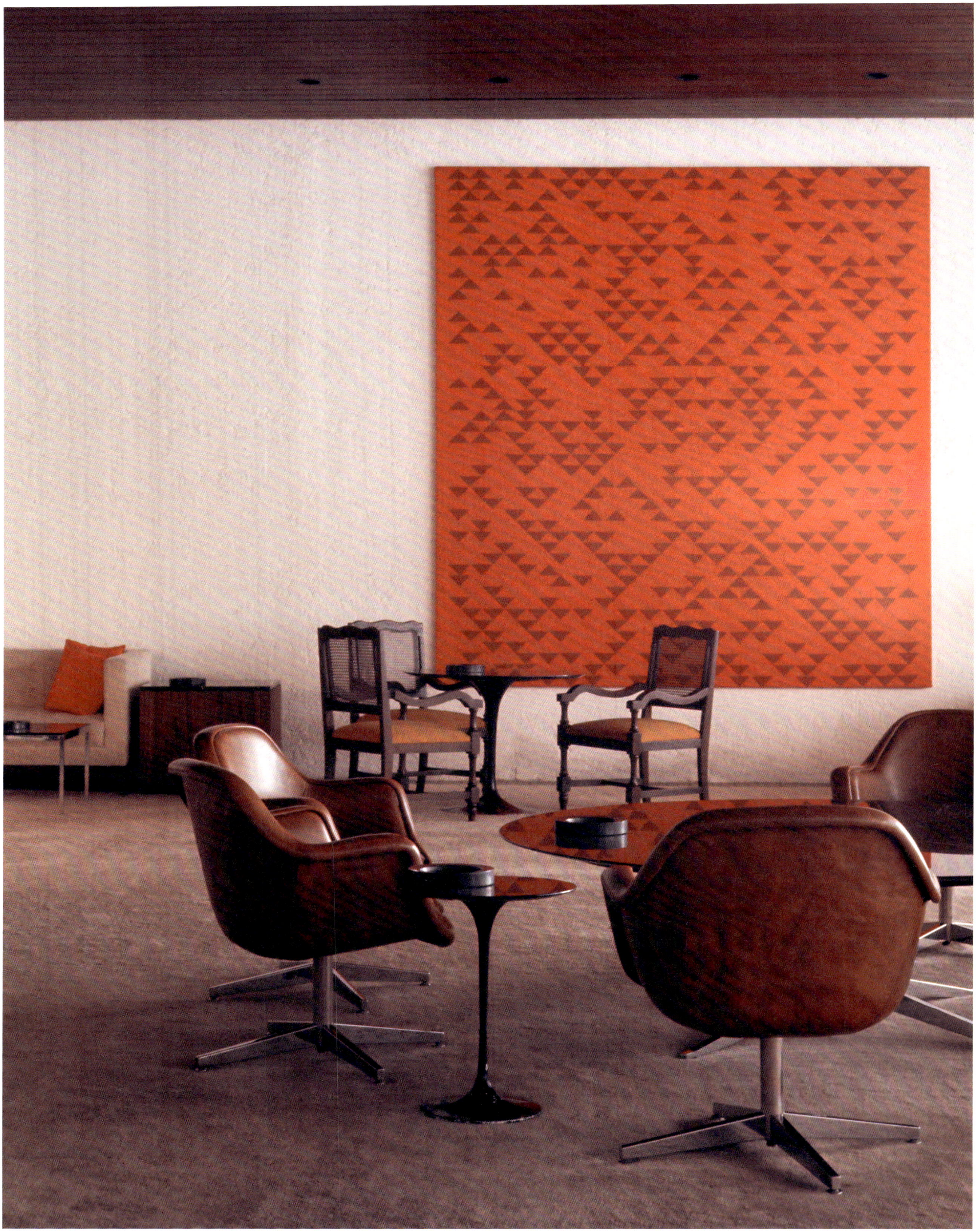

Below Josef Albers and Ricardo Legorreta at the Alberses' house in New Haven, Connecticut, February 1967, photo by Jon Naar, the Josef and Anni Albers Foundation

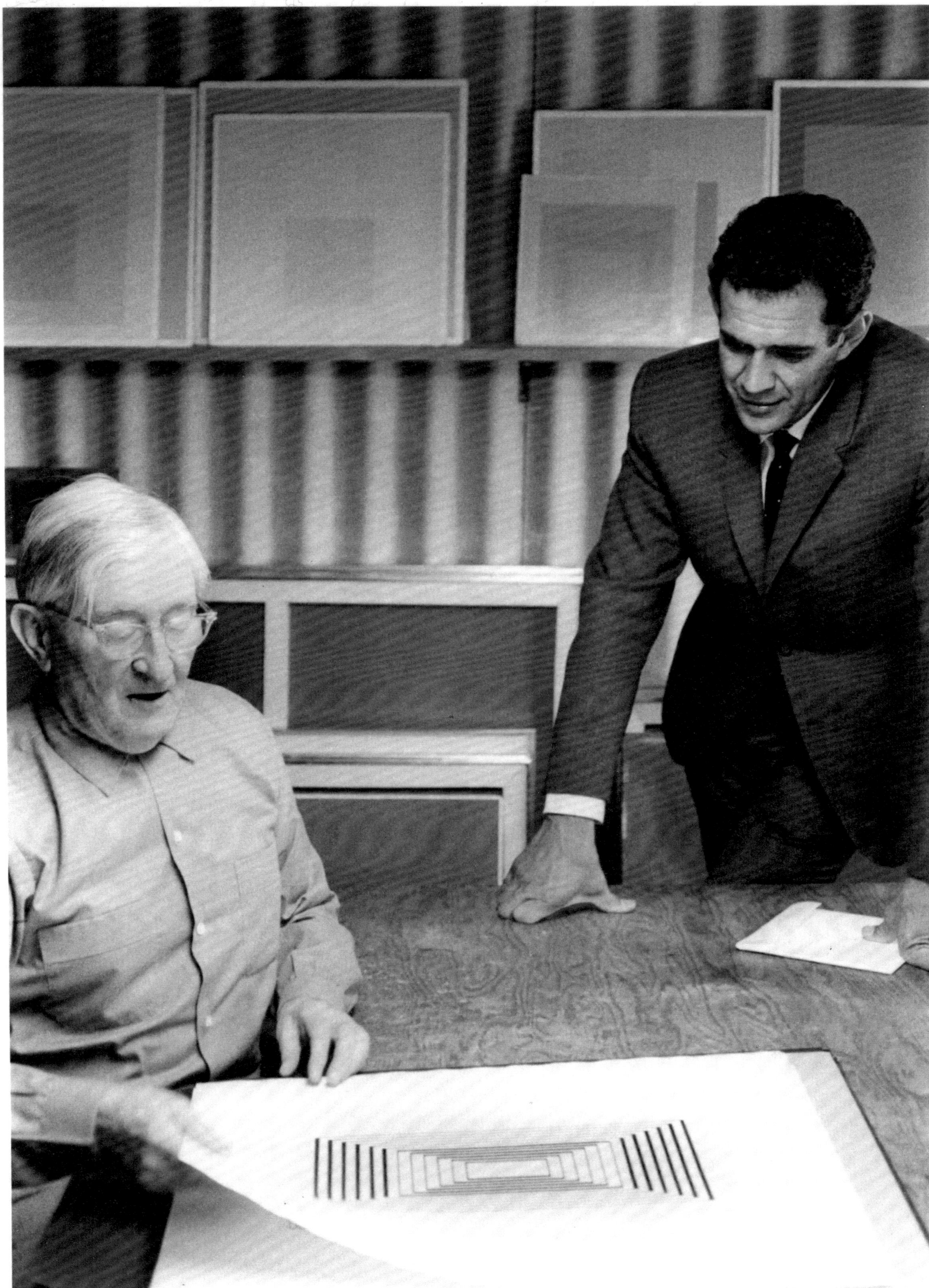

mass-market print on cloth, 'visitors [to Barragán's house] often thought it was an original painting by [Albers]'.[2]

This tension between reproduction and original—in this case, between a print of a painting on fabric and a painting on canvas—as well as that between mass culture and fine art was essential to the architects' vision for the space. They originally had approached Josef for the commission, following Barragán's intention, according to the photographer Jon Naar, to have one of his screenprints in every guestroom of the hotel. This is a gesture that would have democratised the expensive *Interaction of Color* portfolio and is consistent with the more general populism permeating post-revolutionary Mexico. The same nationalist ethos that was looking to indigenous crafts and agrarian traditions to solidify the country's new postcolonial nationalism likely saw an analogous project in the seriality of Josef's approach to painting.

The plan for Josef's screenprints never materialised; instead, the architects ended up commissioning Anni. One reason for this change of heart may have been her forthcoming book on miniature pre-Columbian artefacts, which was her main project at the time. Although the couple had frequently visited Mexico, travelling to archaeological sites and viewing collections of pre-Columbian artefacts, it was Anni who engaged with this history most deeply. While Josef was primarily interested in pre-Columbian culture for its optical qualities, taking hundreds of photographs and using certain motifs for his paintings and prints, Anni absorbed the culture's materials and technologies and particularly its weaving traditions. She studied objects in detail, paying attention to scale and size, and corresponded with the archaeologist Junius Bird, who had researched the earliest cotton specimens collected in the Americas. Her engagement was so sustained that she learned how to replicate ancient techniques and apply them to her own weaving practice.

This deeper engagement may have been the reason for choosing Anni over Josef, for the architects of the Hotel Camino Real also prioritised the integration of such ancient forms—some of those motifs are visible in the interior. The hotel was built as official accommodation for the 1968 Olympic Games and was intended to project a certain image of Mexican modernity abroad. As Luis M Castañeda argues in his book *Spectacular Mexico*, which examines the design of the 1968 Olympics, indigenous artefacts and motifs formulated a uniquely Mexican version of pan-American cosmopolitanism to be displayed for the international world. The year 1968 marked the first time a country within Central and South America had hosted the Games, and Mexico was the first Spanish-speaking country ever to do so; it was a unique opportunity for a historically marginalised part of the world to prove its membership in this international community. And it did so through an architectural and design program that combined the archaic, the colonial and the modern in ways that echo Anni Albers's approach.

Oaxaca's ancient Zapotec architecture, built around 1000 CE, was especially important here. Monte Albán, for example, the title of one of Albers's most important weavings of the 1930s, was an archaeological site important to both her and Legorreta, who also valued it for its geometric abstraction.[3] Such sites supplied Albers with certain formal motifs, for example those in *Red Meander* 1954, which also link to the uniforms of the hotel staff. These uniforms displayed a logo by the American designer Lance Wyman, who had also developed the graphic identity of the Olympic Games. Both Albers's maze-like line and Wyman's interlocking 'C' and 'R' of the embroidered logos were meant to evoke what Josef Albers called the 'meander' patterns characteristic of Zapotec architecture, which he also extensively photographed.

For the Alberses and Legorreta, it was this hybrid of modern and ancient, European and pre-Columbian, which defined postwar cosmopolitan Mexico, a formal language that—according to the manufacturer Knoll, which designed the hotel's furniture—'wonderfully bridges all of our worlds'.[4] The completed wall-hanging was installed

2 Sheila Hicks, 'A visit to his silent garden', in Yutaka Saito, *Luis Barragán*, Noriega Editores, Mexico, 1994, pp 238–39; cited in Brenda Danilowitz, 'Towards an ending', in Brenda Danilowitz and Heinz Liesbrock (eds), *Anni and Josef Albers: Latin American journeys*, Hatje Cantz, Ostfildern, 2007, p 202. According to Barragán's colleague, the architect Andrés Casillas, Barragán had bought these reproductions on a visit to the US and had them framed for his house in Mexico City (see Danilowitz and Liesbrock).

3 Ricardo Legorreta, interview with John V Mutlow, 28 May 1996, in John V Mutlow, *The architecture of Ricardo Legorreta*, Thames and Hudson, London, 1997, p 20.

4 Peter Andes on behalf of Knoll, quoted in Danilowitz and Smith, p 14.

Bottom

Paracas or Nazca people, south coast, Peru, Textile fragment (split-weave tapestry fragment of a border with step and spiral motifs) c 200 BCE–200 CE, wool and cotton, 16 × 42.8 cm

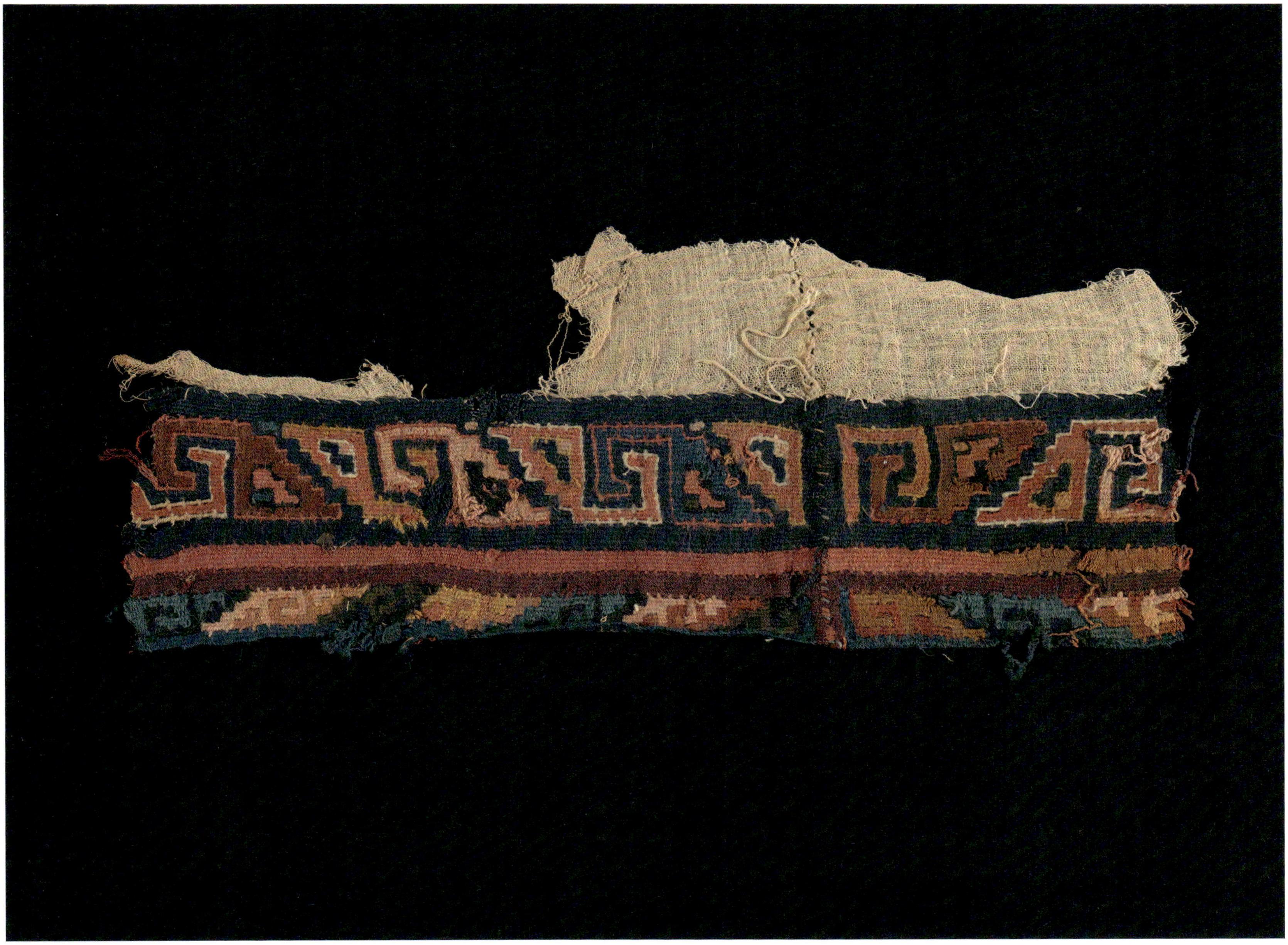

Below

Anni Albers, *Red Meander* 1954, linen and cotton, 52 × 37.5 cm, photo by Tim Nighswander / Imaging4Art, private collection

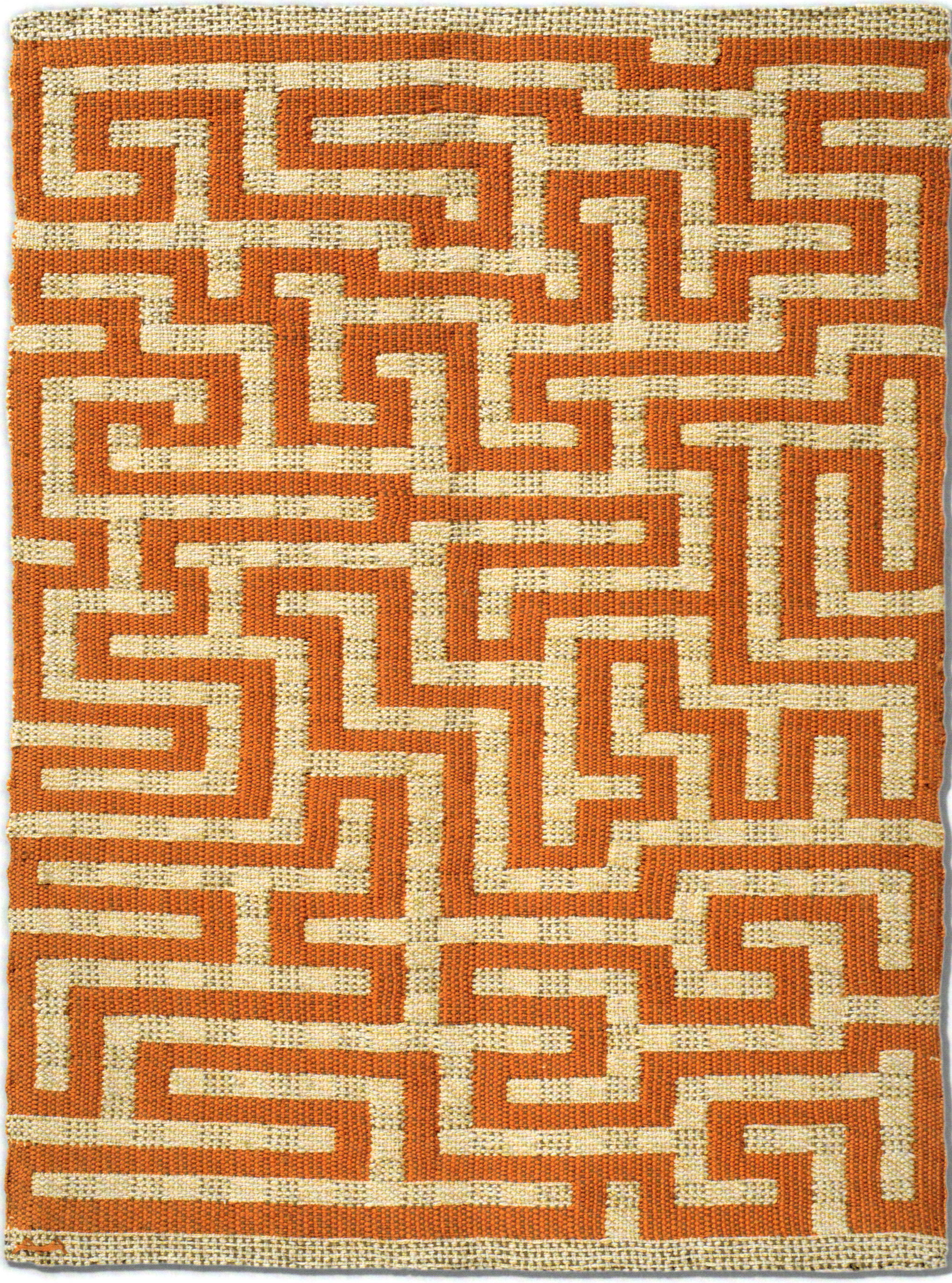

sometime in the summer of 1968, with Legorreta writing to Albers of how pleased he was with the work: 'Your wall-hanging is like everything you do: wonderful; it is perfect for the space.'[5] That space was the hotel's lobby bar, which also included a mix of furniture in ancient, colonial and modern styles. Albers had met with Knoll designers while she was in Mexico in 1967 and she must have been aware of the room's colour scheme as well as details of the furniture, such as the reflective round tables that now appear to distribute the colours of the textile into the interior space.

From the wall to the printing press

As Brenda Danilowitz suggests, the choice of materials and techniques for *Camino Real* was likely made in tacit dialogue with the art gallery Multiples, which had been established recently by Marian Goodman and Barbara Kulicke in New York and had invited Josef Albers to exhibit. The gallery institutionalised the notion of the 'multiple' in the United States, producing editions of artworks in a range of media, including felt appliquéd banners. It was essentially taking the concept of the print and expanding it from a two-dimensional surface to a three-dimensional object. A cancelled cheque in the Albers Foundation archive suggests that the same firm which had fabricated banners for Multiples had also fabricated Albers's wall-hanging, drawing a direct link between her work and that of a much younger generation. This would imply that although *Camino Real* was made by an artist whom we associate with the interwar avant-garde, the work is closer in its concerns to what print curator Richard Field described as 'the attitudes evidenced by many of the op, pop, minimal, and process artists of the 1960s'.[6] These were artists at least a generation younger than Albers—who turned 70 in 1969—and many of them, for instance Robert Rauschenberg, had been her students at Black Mountain College. What this suggests is a certain timeliness of *Camino Real*: its ability to respond to larger currents in contemporary art, primarily in its replicative affinity with reproductive media that inspired the overarching 'attitudes' of this younger generation of artists.

From 1968 to 1983, Albers devoted herself full-time to printmaking, creating increasingly complex prints—often in collaboration with a master printer. Although she had left the loom behind, its matrix persists in her continued use of the grid. We encounter another such permutation 15 year later, in a version of her textile *Red Meander* 1954. In *Red Meander II*, from the series *Meander* 1970–71, she submits the original motif to a series of alterations in which two colours are deployed to create the effect of four—an operation that is possible only in printmaking. This particular print went through the press four times. First, she laid down the background as a solid colour. And then, using the same colour, she ran the print through the press two more times, using a cut design screen that was half an inch smaller than the background, so that she could first align it with the top left corner, and then align it with the bottom right corner. And this second time, she also turned the screen upside down. This meant that the pattern would be inverted and off-register; wherever it overlapped, it created a slightly darker, ghost-like tone that was only minimally perceptible. The last step involved using the same screen, but a second, much more intense, colour. She flipped the screen back to its initial position and printed it centred on the page. This second colour was diluted to be translucent (which was in itself a tricky process, as only a few colours allow for this and still retain enough colouring power).[7]

As print scholar Marion Buzzard wrote: 'The idea, according to Anni Albers, was to start with a simple form and then make it more complicated in each succeeding print.'[8] Hence the many prints she made using the triangular unit that we first see in *Camino Real*. In *TR III* 1970, for instance, she reduces her palette to blind embossing, such that it is only the difference between a raised surface and an impressed surface—not the interaction of colour—that registers the pattern of triangles. Taking this one step further at Tyler Graphics in 1978, she joins triangles to create larger parallelograms. In further collaborations with printmakers, including Domberger, a

5 Ricardo Legorreta, quoted in Danilowitz and Liesbrock, p 202.

6 Richard Field, 'Anni Albers', in Nicholas Fox Weber et al (eds), *The woven and graphic art of Anni Albers*, Smithsonian, Washington, DC, 1985, p 106.

7 Marion L Buzzard, *Anni Albers: prints and drawings*, University Art Gallery, Riverside, California, 1980, p 9.

8 Buzzard, 1980, p 3.

Below Anni Albers, *Red Meander II* 1970–71, screenprint, image 50.7 × 40.7 cm, sheet 71.2 × 61.1 cm

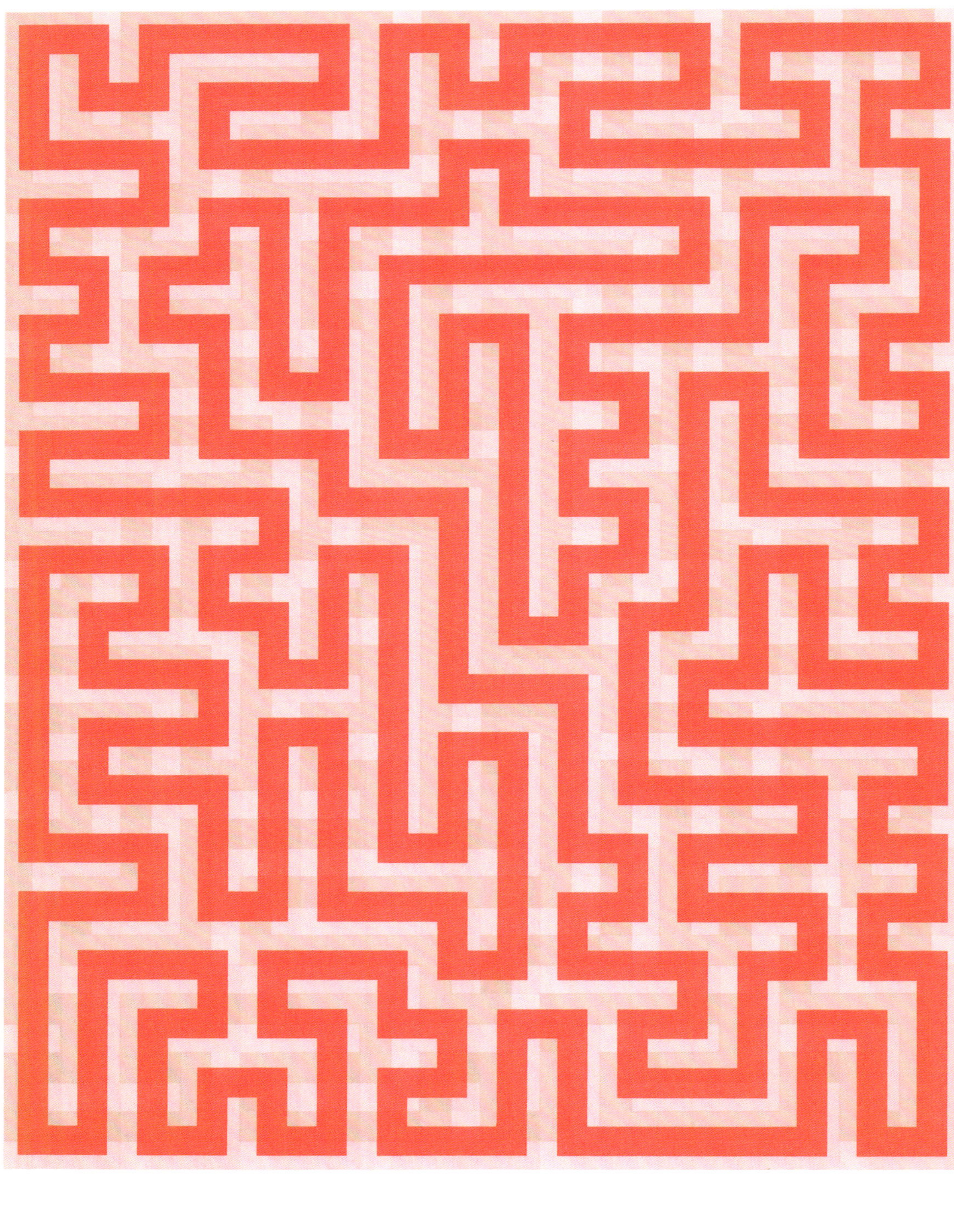

Below Anni Albers, *Mountainous IV* 1978, embossing, image 47.2 × 43.7 cm, sheet 56.6 × 52.7 cm

pioneering screenprinter in Stuttgart, she further developed these triangular patterns. Such prints speak to the complexity that Buzzard mentions, apparent even in those examples that may, at first glance, seem to be simply monotonous.

Anni Albers was able to do this only by working closely with master printers—another aspect of the so-called print revival in postwar America. Nicholas Fox Weber called this complexity Albers's 'uniquely "printerly" method', made possible through an extraordinary commitment to the medium's specific qualities.[9] At the same time, she was drawing on principles that she had learned from Paul Klee at the Bauhaus and with which she had long experimented in her textiles. We can see how she's deploying what Klee called displacement through repetition (which he termed '*Schiebung*'), for instance, where a unit is multiplied in a continuous direction. More specifically, through her use of the triangle, she deploys his concept of displacement with interruption (*Schiebung mit Unterbrechung*) and, in creating 'gaps' in the design, the concept of displacement through misalignment (*Schiebung durch Verschiebung*). In other examples, such as *GR I* 1970, a silkscreen of opaque red and blue triangles, she further complicates this through mirroring (*Spiegelung*) of individual units and their rotation (*Drehung*) at 90 and 180 degrees. This is further complicated by then applying these permutations not only to the units, to these chevron shapes, but to their colour as well, so swapping out the blue for red, or vice versa.

Camino Real, in other words, provided a formal language for many of Albers's prints to follow. Although differing in appearance and materials used, they share a common concern with what might be called a logic of permutations—of multiplication with slight differences. It may have even been that *Camino Real*, as a felt appliqué textile, unexpectedly solidified her fascination with printmaking—which she had first seriously engaged with in a 1962 residency at June Wayne's Tamarind Lithography Workshop. Albers may have exploited techniques specific to printmaking—the '"printerly" method', as Weber puts it—but then viewed such techniques as inherently intermedial. This was an attitude that Wayne shared, when she wrote to Albers about her turn to tapestry:

> Loved hearing from you. These days I have been making macquettes [*sic*] for tapestries I would like to have made. So you and I have traveled across intersecting affections in more ways than one. Meanwhile, although I have not yet seen one into reality, I hope my excursion will be as successful as yours into printmaking. After all, why not? An artist is an artist, and the medium is only a vehicle.[10]

Prof Jordan Troeller
Junior Professor of Contemporary Art History and Aesthetic Practices
Institute for Fine Arts, Music and Education (IKMV)
Leuphana University Lüneburg

9 Nicholas Fox Weber, 'Anni Albers and the printerly image', *Art in America*, July–August 1975, p 89.

10 June Wayne, letter to Anni Albers, 15 October 1969, the Josef and Anni Albers Foundation, Bethany, Connecticut.

Below Anni Albers's notes from Paul Klee's Bauhaus course, c 1930, photo by Irene Bayer, Bauhaus-Archiv, Berlin, 1995_17.105

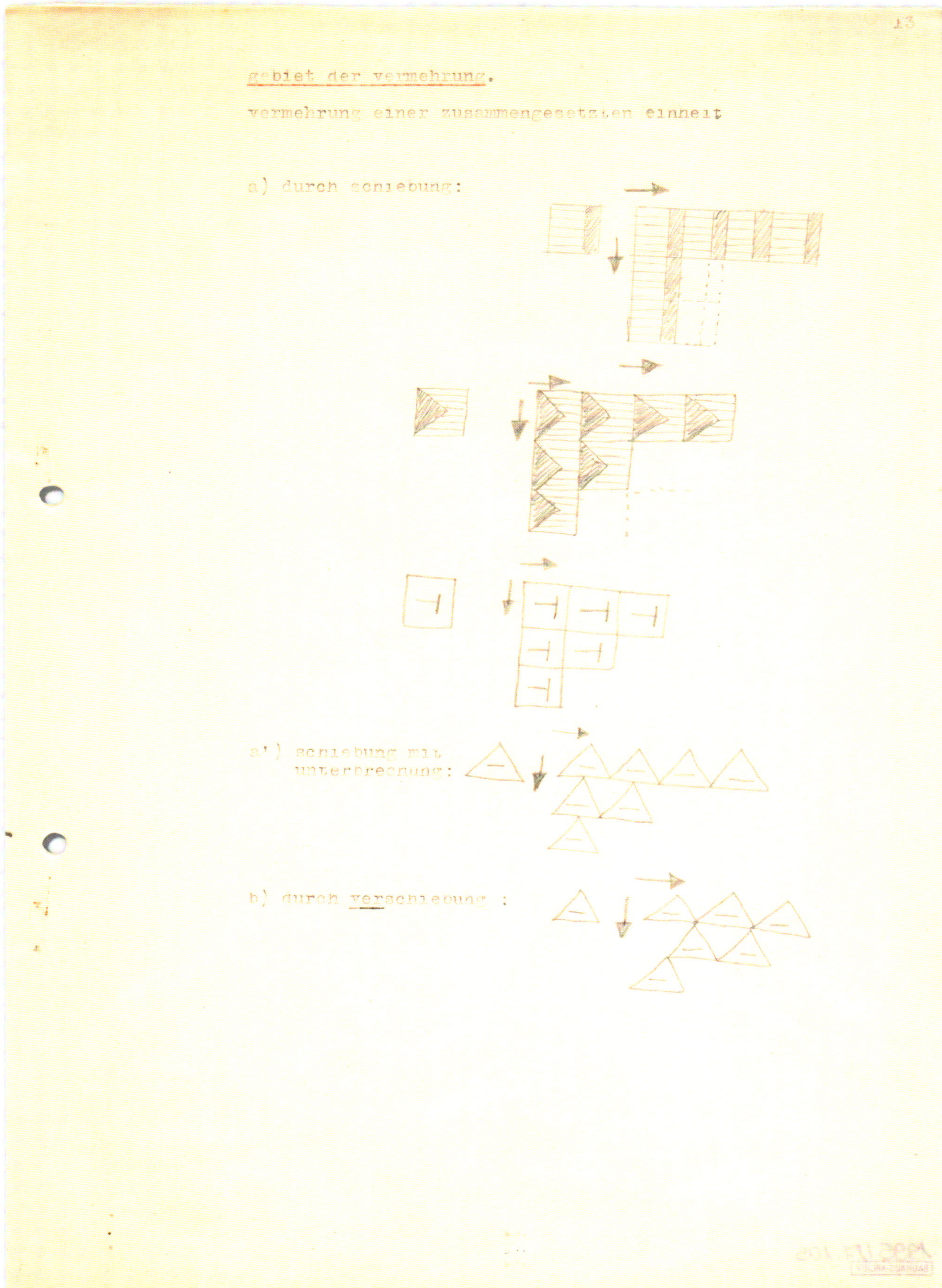
13

gebiet der vermehrung.

vermehrung einer zusammengesetzten einheit

a) durch schiebung:

a') schiebung mit unterbrechung:

b) durch verschiebung :

Below Anni Albers, *Blue Meander* 1970, screenprint, image 49.3 × 40.6 cm, sheet 70.7 × 60.7 cm

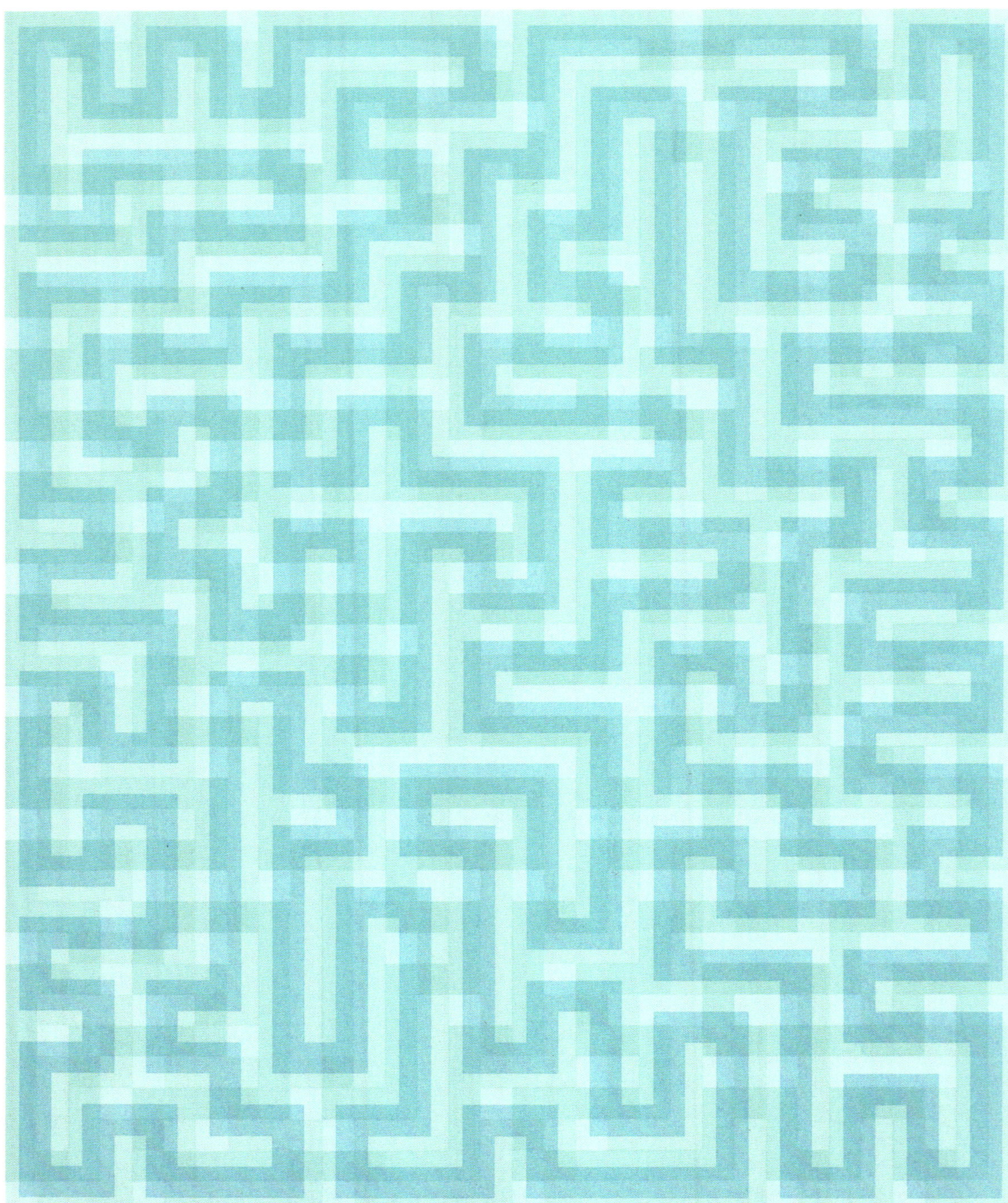

Below Anni Albers, *Red Meander I* 1969–70, screenprint, image 50.7 × 41.7 cm, sheet 71.2 × 62.2 cm

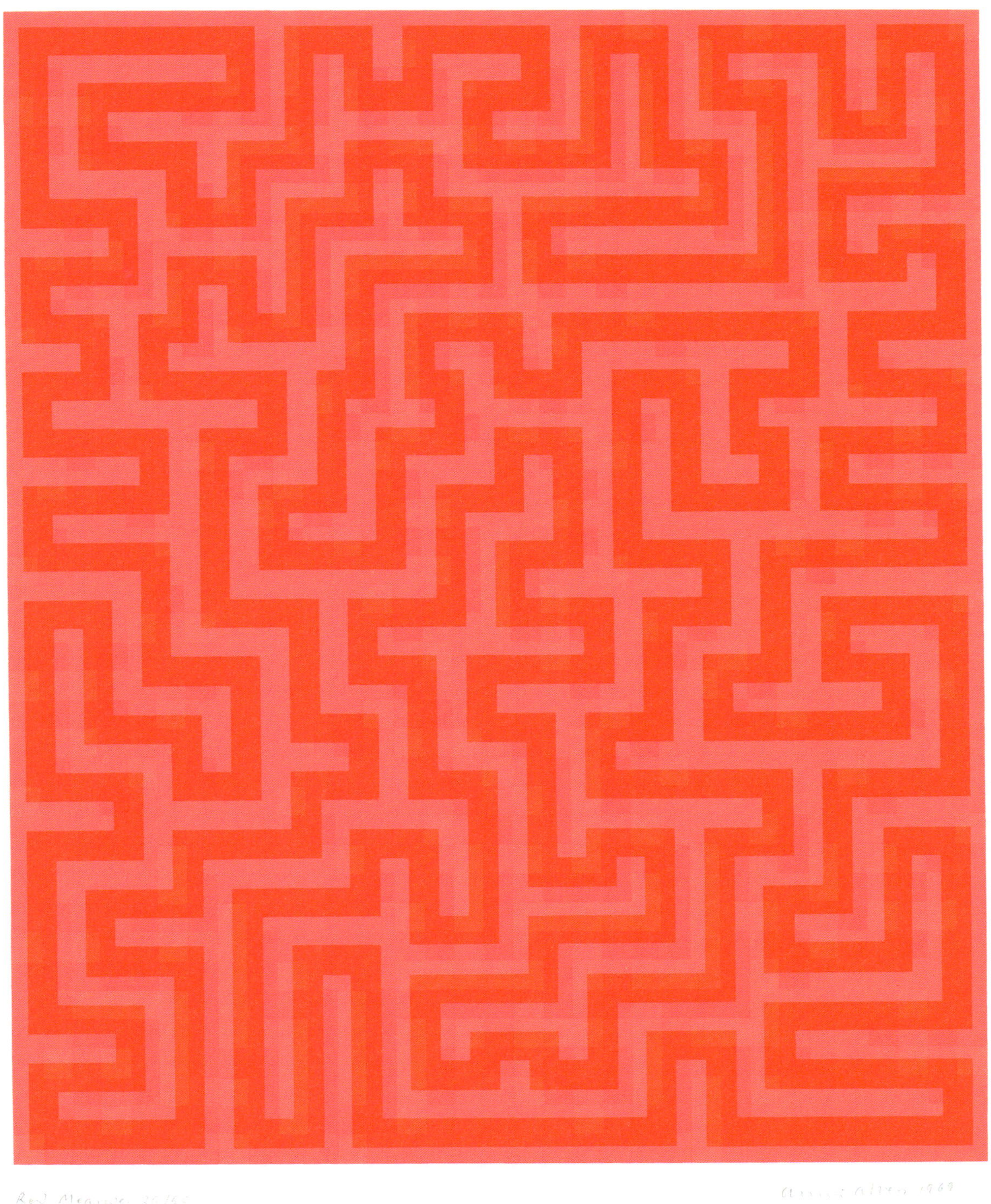

Below Anni Albers, *Mountainous III* 1978, embossing, image 47.2 × 43.7 cm, sheet 56.6 × 52.7 cm

Below Anni Albers, *Mountainous VI* 1978, embossing, image 47.2 × 43.7 cm, sheet 56.6 × 52.7 cm

Below Lotte Stam-Beese, *Group-portrait, weaving workshop at the Bauhaus, Dessau* 1928, gelatin silver photograph, image 8.4 (diam) cm

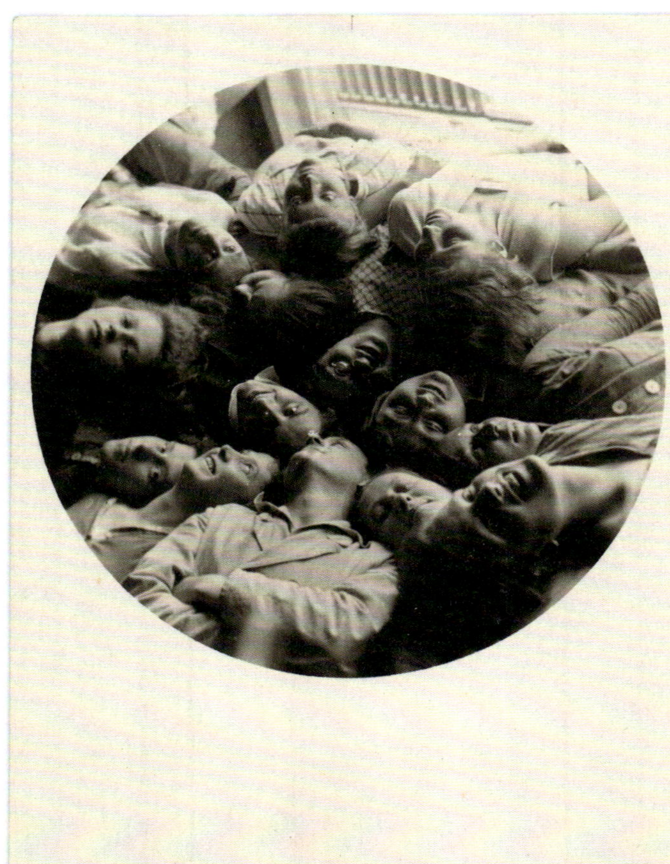

Below Wari (Huari) people, central, south and north Peru, Band 600–1000 CE, wool and cotton, 81.8 × 6.6 cm
Next Josef Albers, Study for *Oscillating* c 1945, oil on paper, image 30.5 × 22 cm, sheet 36.1 × 27.3 cm

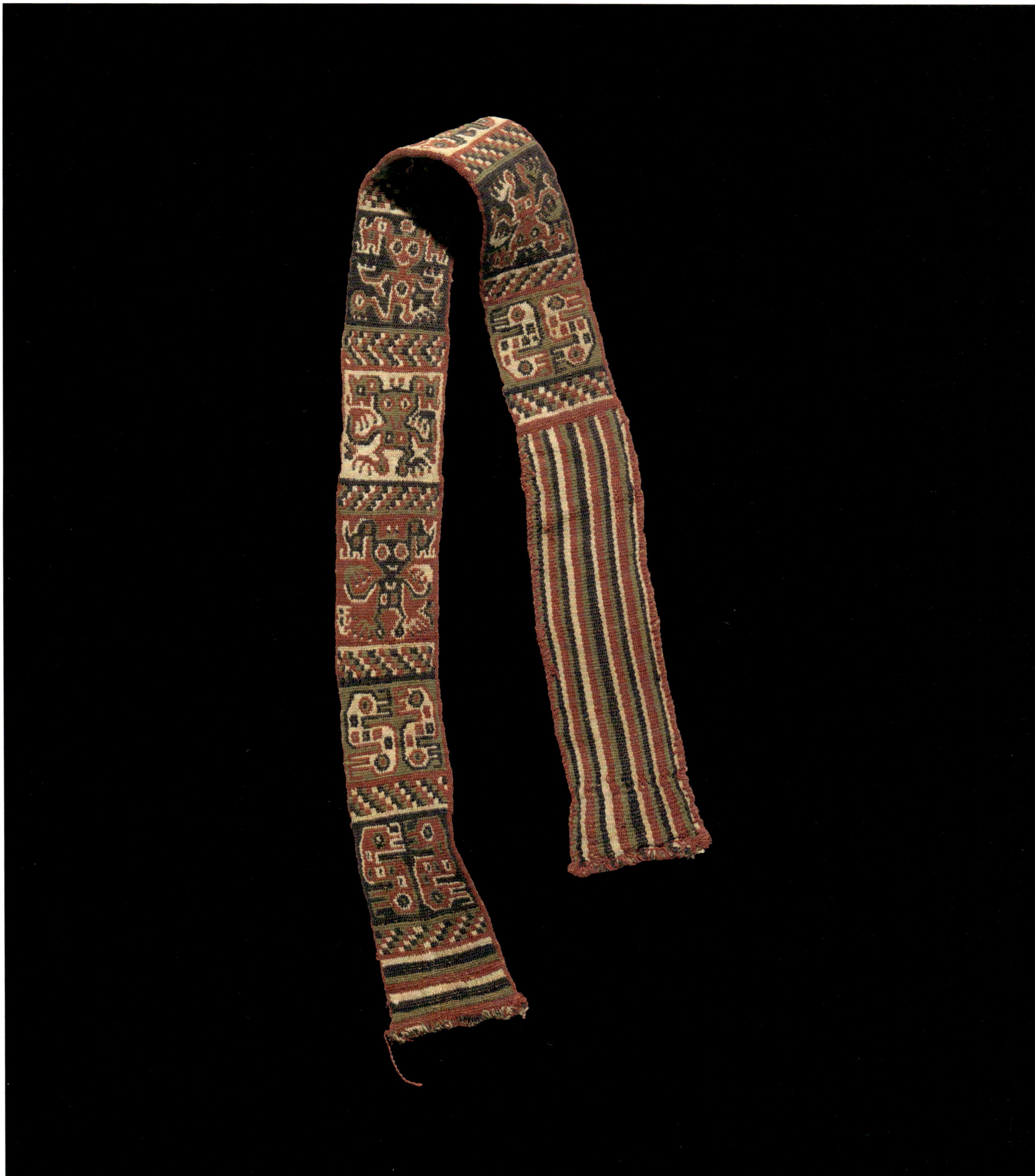

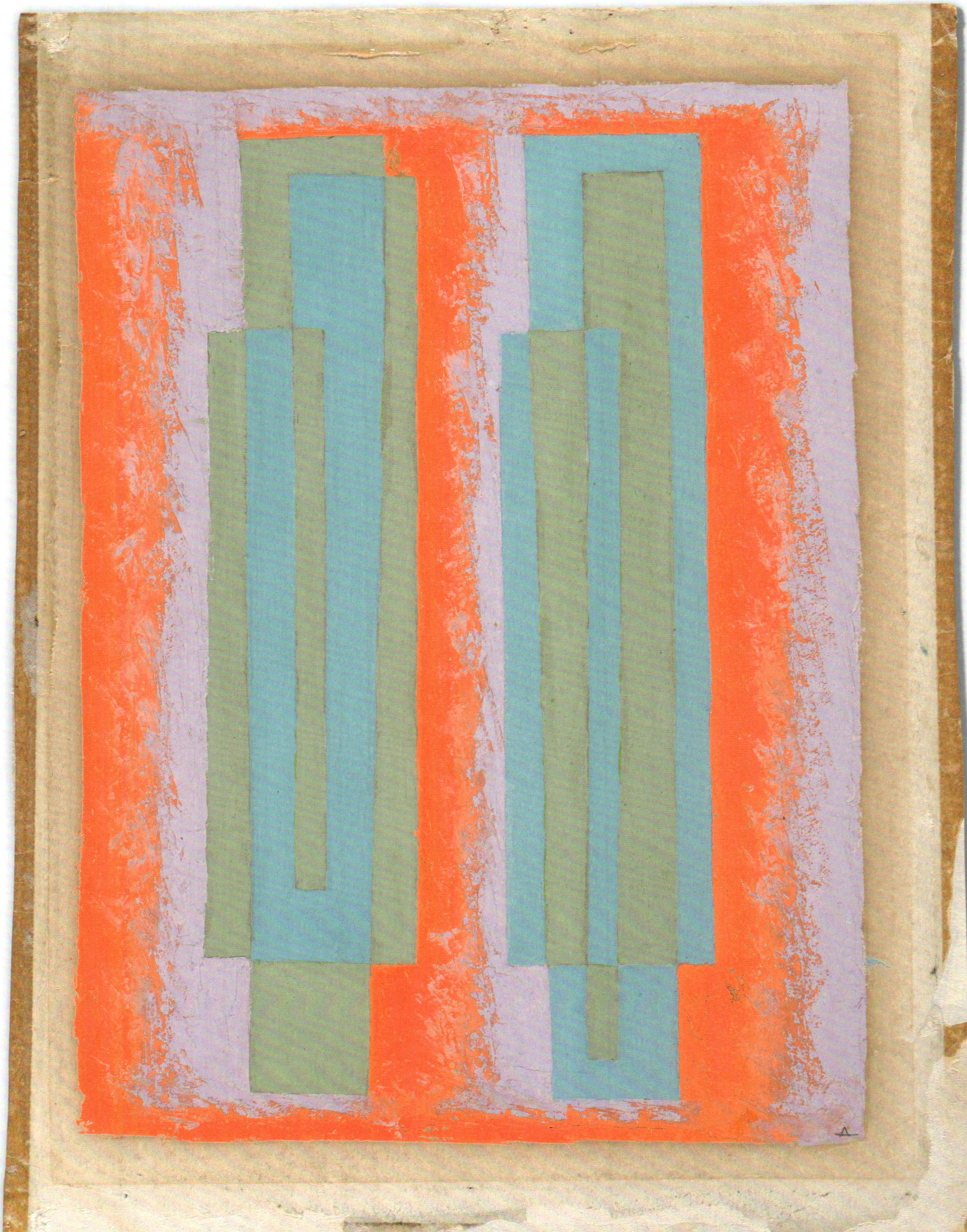

Below Josef Albers, Folio II, folder 12, from *Formulation : Articulation* 1972, screenprint, image 25.5 × 32.9 cm, sheet 38.2 × 50.8 cm

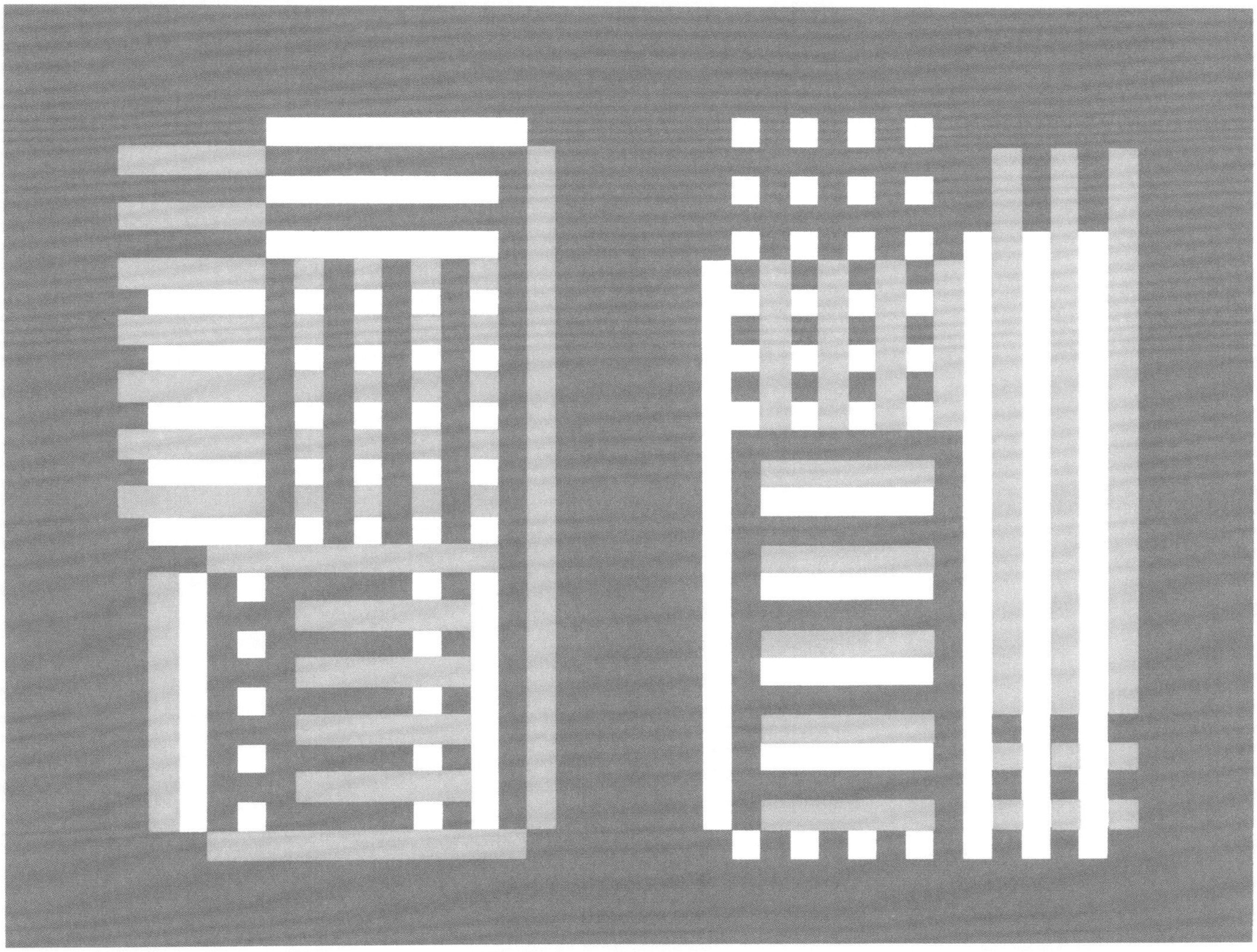

Below Josef Albers, Folio I, folder 24, from *Formulation : Articulation* 1972, screenprint, image (a) 28.7 × 29.6 cm, sheet 38.2 × 50.8 cm (folded)

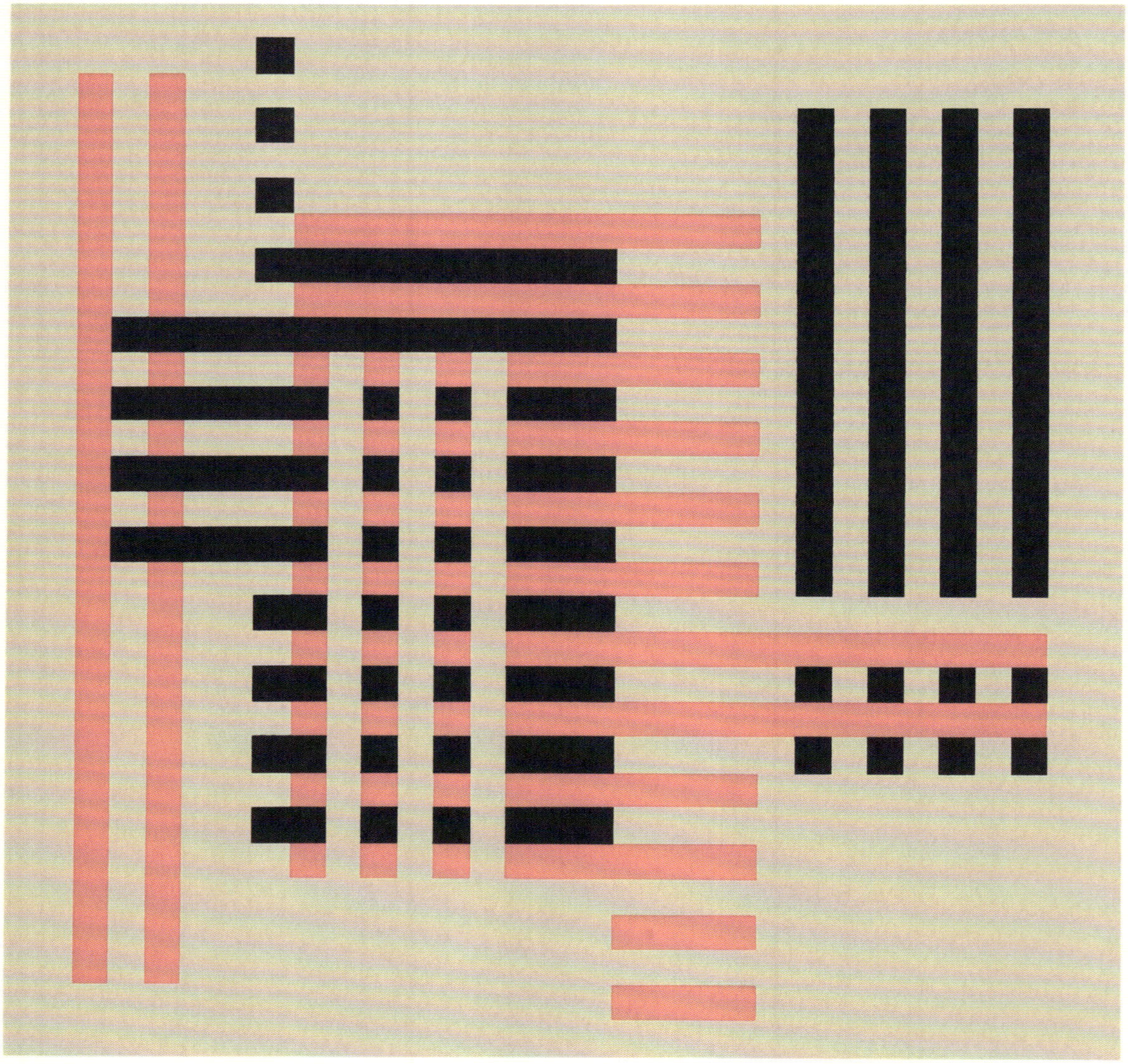

Albers

~~Hello, Ken, nice to hear you~~
Hello, Ken
Hello, Josef
Nice to hear you
Well, its good ~~t~~to hear from you, too, I, I'm sorry I took so long .
What, took long?
But the blue is beautiful. We're proofing it, we've been proofing it th;is week. One color on the outside keeps running to ~~the red side~~ dry a little ~~too much on the red side~~ much to the red side.
Oh.
So we're just re-proofing it again to see if we can improve that.
~~There is a distinct difference left and right of the white line~~
Although it has a distinct difference left and right of the white line.
Oh, it is beaufiful
It is broken.
It is very, very beautiful.
It ~~it~~ is not broken, the one you send?
No,
The very light gray one. It's very, very not so decisive.
Not so decisive
Yeah, and also the one I'm going to return is not so of great excitement. Although I wonder whether what that Roman number do you think for that one in the book now to be signed.
WEll that would follow B # X, if we did take them in order
They have signed already # 11. Number 11 is signed, as far as I remember.
Now, lets see, you have your first eight and then the gray one whichjust got back to us is # 9 . The yellow to ochre would be # 10.
Yah
Yes, is interruption one drawn
~~I~~I'll go see up my list and see whether that is right.
Yes, that would be the tenth one because what we are still printing is magenta and that is number 11.
That's what I mean, they have already in the making, numberll.
Oh, I'm sorry, Josef, that is correct, in the making is number 11.
Yeah, and number 10 we haven't done so far?
No, number 10 is what you have in the box at your house.
Is that so?
That's the yellow to the ochre.
Then let me write it down before I get confused again. Yellow to the ochre.
Yellow to ochre is number 10.
Yellow to ochre is number 10.
What you have there now.
And the one you sent me as trials interruption
Yes, is the light ~~green~~ gray
Is for the light gray one is a little bit also not so exciting . I wonder still, I'm studying still how we might still improve it. I didn't know.
Well, if ~~y~~you want to cut up any of those prints and move the colors around, change one frame, go ahead and do that if that helps any.
Well, I must see that, this cutting out makes always a shadow on this- horribly disturbing.
That's true, it's difficult.
For very simple selection is it absolutely impractical. I ~~have also a red in the making~~.
Well, how ~~we will~~ will we proof it any way you want me to.
I have also a red in the making.
That excites me
It is similar to the blue, it promises very much, but knows, you know.
That's very exciting, it would go very well with the second series.
Did you ~~ge~~ get my letter?
Yes, I have your letter.
Then send me some brochures.
There in the mail to you Josef, you should have them today or tomorrow.
You promised me also the five frames for me on my bill.

Well, those were shipped to you.Those had been shipped to you for over a week. Let me write this down, I will check ~~ag~~ this again with the shipper.

Now, let's see the contemporaries, and ..

Both have been written to, Josef. The multiples we wrote to ~~ove~~r about a month ago.

Did you give them a promising margin?

Well, yes, we told them that we would have to wait until we decided what we would increase the price to for them, you see, so we can give them a regu~~ll~~/lar dealers discount.

Yes, that's what I mean.

So we've taken care of that.

Probably that's the price now and the brochure is a pre=publishing price.

That's right and October 1 we will bring the price up to a standard retail so ~~w~~we can offer the galleries a discount.

What does that mean, how high is it going?

We're going to bring it up to 200 so we can give the galleries 50 % off.

That means each print is 200 dollars?

Yes, remaining prints. We have ~~ato~~ to have at least that mark up in order to do business.

Yeah, good.

~~Do~~ So that we will still be able to make what we have to make to get our cost back and

Annie is calling, how many orders ~~do~~ you have?

Well, we, let's see, the yellow is almost sold out in the singles.

That means number 1 is sold out?

Almost sold out in the singles. You see what we did, we put aside so many sets, we will not sell those as singles, only as sets.

How many complete sets are fixed?

Well, I don't have the records in front of me but I would imagine somewhere in the neigh~~bor~~borhood of 30 %.

of 30% you ~~ma~~ are making portfolios.

No, I would say about 30% is sold. Is sold. Of the total series. Now we issued number 75 to no. 100 as singles. Now we are already into the 90's on the yellow, we're almost in the 90's on the orange, the blue-green and the red to brown is doing ~~good~~ very well

So then you get orders for ma~~il~~inly single sheets.

No, no we have sold a great deal of singles and sets. WE are selling mostly the sets to the collectors who want all of them, you see. To the professional students and the teachers who don't have a lot of money, they're buying the singles.

Ah, they're buying the singles.

Like one or t~~ow~~wo, some of them have bought two of the colors, two of the gray, but they can't afford the whole set .

But also lots of customers among the students and not so abled people.

That's correct , and this is where we did a very good thing by pre=publishing at a very reasonable price. See many of the architectual students could only afford a 100 dollars And many of the university art students, and the artists, too-- many artists have bought your prints-- which is about the highest compliment I can tell ~~you~~ you about the single prints,

Does that mean that you are selling them now for 100?

Yes, until ~~Oo~~ October 1

For one print~~s~~ 100, and after October 1 equals 200.

That's correct.

Oh, boy.

After October 1 the galleries will be handling them. And the European distributuion will probably be taking care of out of ~~London/and/Germany/~~ London and Germany. ~~We/will/probably/take/care/o/~~

What was that?

We will probably take care of the distribution in Europe. In the fall, very actively. That way we will be able to cover the continent. Because then we will be able to sell to dealers there, too.

So you are satisfied with the form.

Oh, yes.

That's good.

Well, it was very thin this summer s, Josef, because many people were on vacation.
Summer is thin.
VERy thin.
All correspondents and all mail men thats very thin. Me too, I have very little, very less.
And then of course with the museum show, opening October 25, this will create a great deal of activity, too, we're very sure the catalogue will excite people .
Now you said the first one is probably sold out. Let me tell it to Annie. You said you have how much sold of the first one?
The yellow is now- the singles- we're about ready to stop selling them. WE're sold into the 90's. Which means we'll probably have to stop selling them as singles very soon.
Yeah
The same way with the orange one.
Now are you in a hurry to have the prints back, signed, I am just terribly tied up.
Yes, I know that Josef, when you can get to it, that's fine.
Your not that in a hurry.
No, no. I would be more in a hurry to have another one to proof.
Well, just a moment. Annie wants me to remind you that we on September 20 we will go on vacation for a while.
That's one of the reasons I'm calling you. I'll be in New York
Everything piles up now on me. Particular my book for that trial is very hard to finish now., right away.
Let's see, you are going on September 20?
Yeah
Now, I will be in New York right after Labor Day, which would be around the 6th of September. I would like to show you the catalogue at that time. All the texts, and go through the proofs which the museum wants to put into the show with yours to make sure we have your approval. And then, also to see, I'd probably like to bring some proofs back, too. So if we could proof the red one by that time, and the gray one, then I can have them with me at that time.
On the 5th or 6th of September.
Yes, it will be in that week.
And is also, Hopkins coming?
I don't know whether he can make it at that time. But I will probably be in New York on business for about a week.
What makes telephone calls so expensive? Annie said ago I talk too long.
No, no thats alright, we have lots of things to say. Now the prints documentation for the first eight that we have - the print documentation - that tells you exactly how many prints were pulled and when they were pulled, and everything will be sent to you shortly, and you sign one copy and we keep the other copy on file.
OK.
Because we will start sending that to museums who have bought the prints.
Although the first part of this is one through eight.
That is correct.
And then you have now how many more?
Well now we have the nineth gray one., which you signed and is returned to us, we have the yellow to ochre which is at your studio now, to be signed, we are almost finished printing the magenta, then we have proofed the light gray one which you have over there to look at, and we are proofing the blue one, which you will receive in a couple of days, as soon as it is dry, and well, you are working on a red one, and I have that one very beautiful red to yellow which we decided we would not work on about three months ago.
What we call peach.
No, the peach is yours. That is your edition.
So another one you have.
It was a red to yellow.
Let me see it because I brought home some other things in red and orange, also.
Alright, you should have some proofs of that there, Josef, You have the proofs of the red to yellow ones I am discussing.
to

I mailed those to you about three months ago. When I mailed you the three prints together and you asked that we not do anything with it for a while, you were not too happy with the second color, and you didn't know which way you might want to move it. I'll see if I have one copy here and I'll send it to you and you can tell me what way you want me to change it.

I must know which one is still in your drawer, you know, I don't remember and I can't continue unless I see the duplicate.

There are two of them actually, theres one that was a yellow ochre one which is

I cannot see them clearly now.

Okay, I will find a proof of it somewhere and send it to you. I will put that in the mail today.

Then you come on the 6th.

Yes, any day in that week which is good for you, then we can get together, and I will see if Henry will come with me

VEry good

I'll be very interested in your response to the catalogue also. Now we have chose to reproduce in the catalogue in full color. We will start out with the blue one because it has a different kind of quality than the other prints. Then we will do the umber black to the gray, the blue to the green, the red to the brown.

That sounds very good.

And the red to the orange.

That sounds very good.

Now that gives all the white lines in their three different positions

Oh, that's good, too.

We will give color separations of the blue to the green becasue the second color on the blue to the green is unbelieveable, when you print it by itslef. And we have made new inks of that so we have a closer color match to what the original is like. Then we will also have one page of black and white break down showing how many plates are used for every print and the three series of white lines.

Right. You said you have no over lappings this time.

Theres no overlappings.

All fitting.

And I want to show that in all black squares, so everyone understands that.

Very good.

So that will make a catalogue of about 40 pages.

Oh boy.

It will be quite handsome.

And how much does this coast?

It's going to cost us about $1.70 a catalogue. The museum can't afford it so we're printing it for them.

Oh, good.

But, I promised you a catalogue and its going to be in three languages; German, French, and ENglish.

VEry good.

And I will have theGerman translation to you in about a weeks time, since that is your native tongue, I think that you should edit it. To make sure it says everything you want it to. And we have an expert in French who will do a beautiful job of tranlating.

Sounds all good.

One thing Henry Hopkins asked me about, is that you said you were writing some more things on the white line squares

No,he has all my writing.

He has all that. We thought perhaps you might be doing a poem or something.

I have no time, I have no time.

Okay, alright, I'm just checking. Because if you did

I would like to but I can't.

How long will you be gone on vacation?

Well, maybe four weeks.
Four weeks, now will you be going to Mexico?
Yeah, probably.
Do you believe there might be a ~~change~~ chance that you could be here for the opening?
No, No, I hate openings. I do not like to shake hands with everybody.
Oh, you'd be so close it would be a shame not to see you.
Oh, its still quite a detour, you know, so for us its a little resting in other landscapes.
But you worked very hard this year. You need a rest.
I can say that, yes. Oh, Ken, let's not ~~ma~~ the telephone bill make too high.
Alright, ~~Josef,~~ fine, Josef.
Thank you very much.
Alright. ~~B~~ Bye, now. ~~Josef~~
Bye, Ken.

Below Josef Albers, Folio I, folder 24, from *Formulation : Articulation* 1972, screenprint, image (b) 28.7 × 36.5 cm, sheet 38.2 × 50.8 cm (folded)

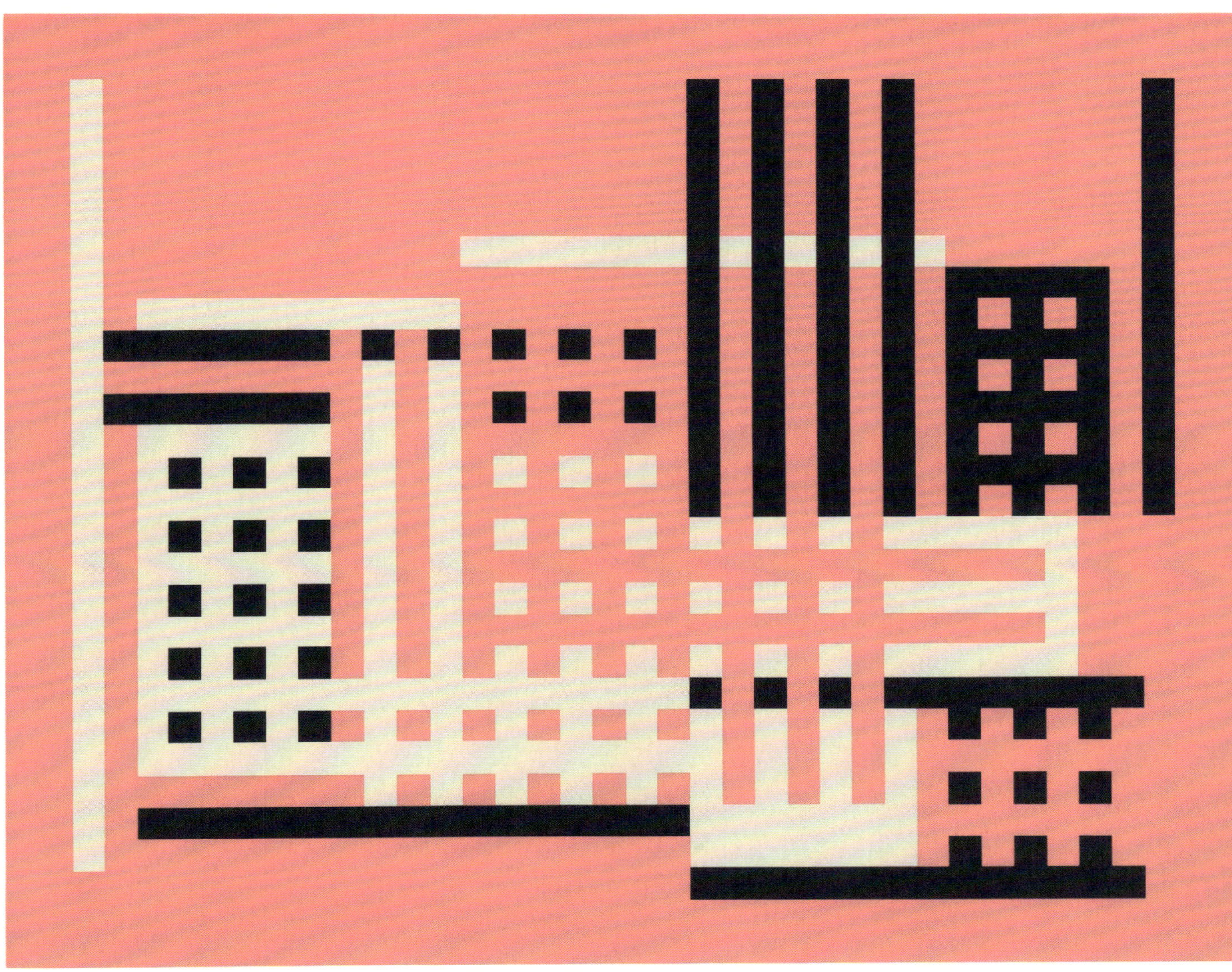

Below Josef Albers, Study for *Vice Versa* c1943, oil on paper, 22.5 × 44.6 cm

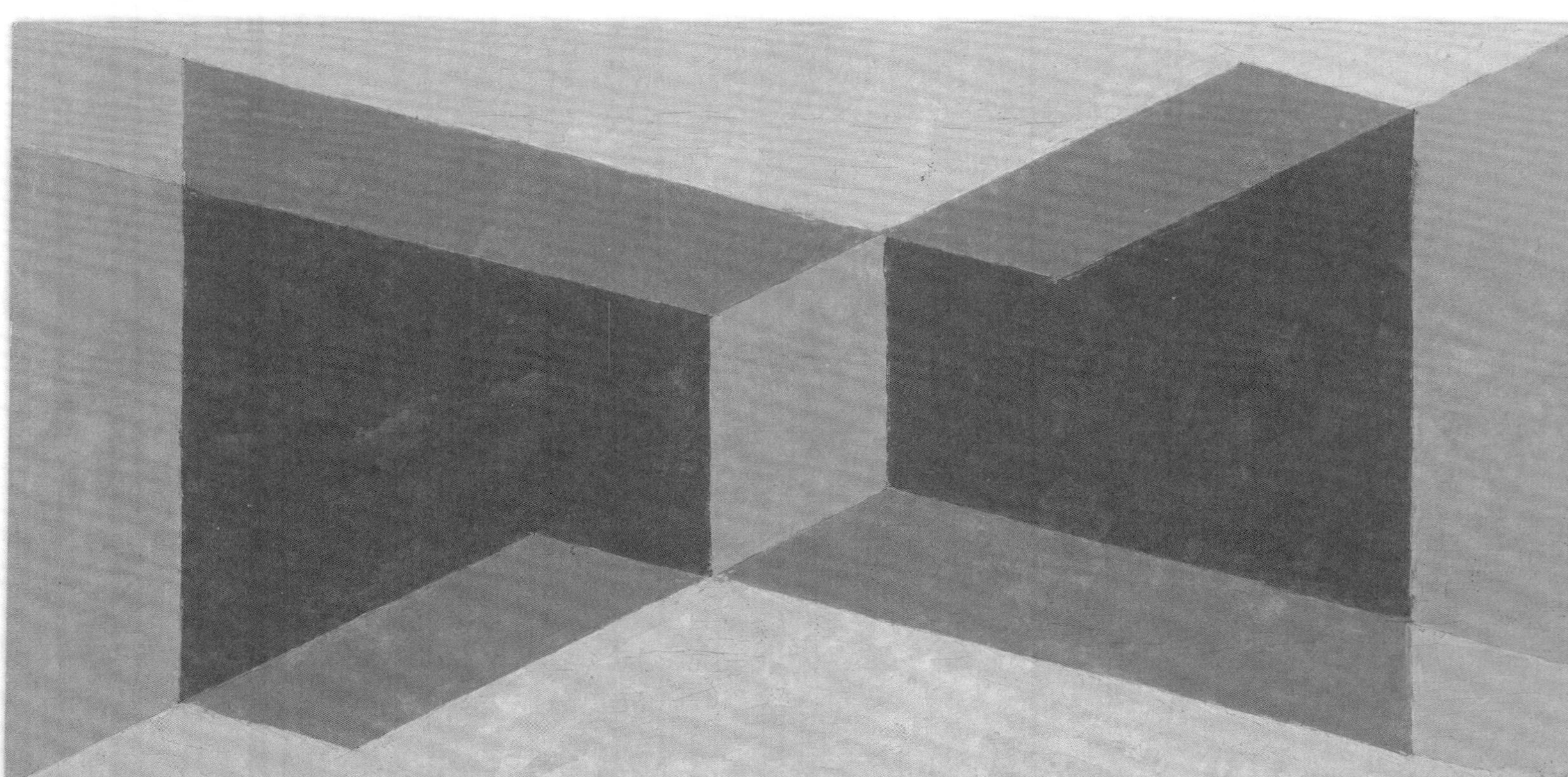

Below Josef Albers, Study for *Biconjugate* c 1943, oil on paper, 25.4 × 42 cm

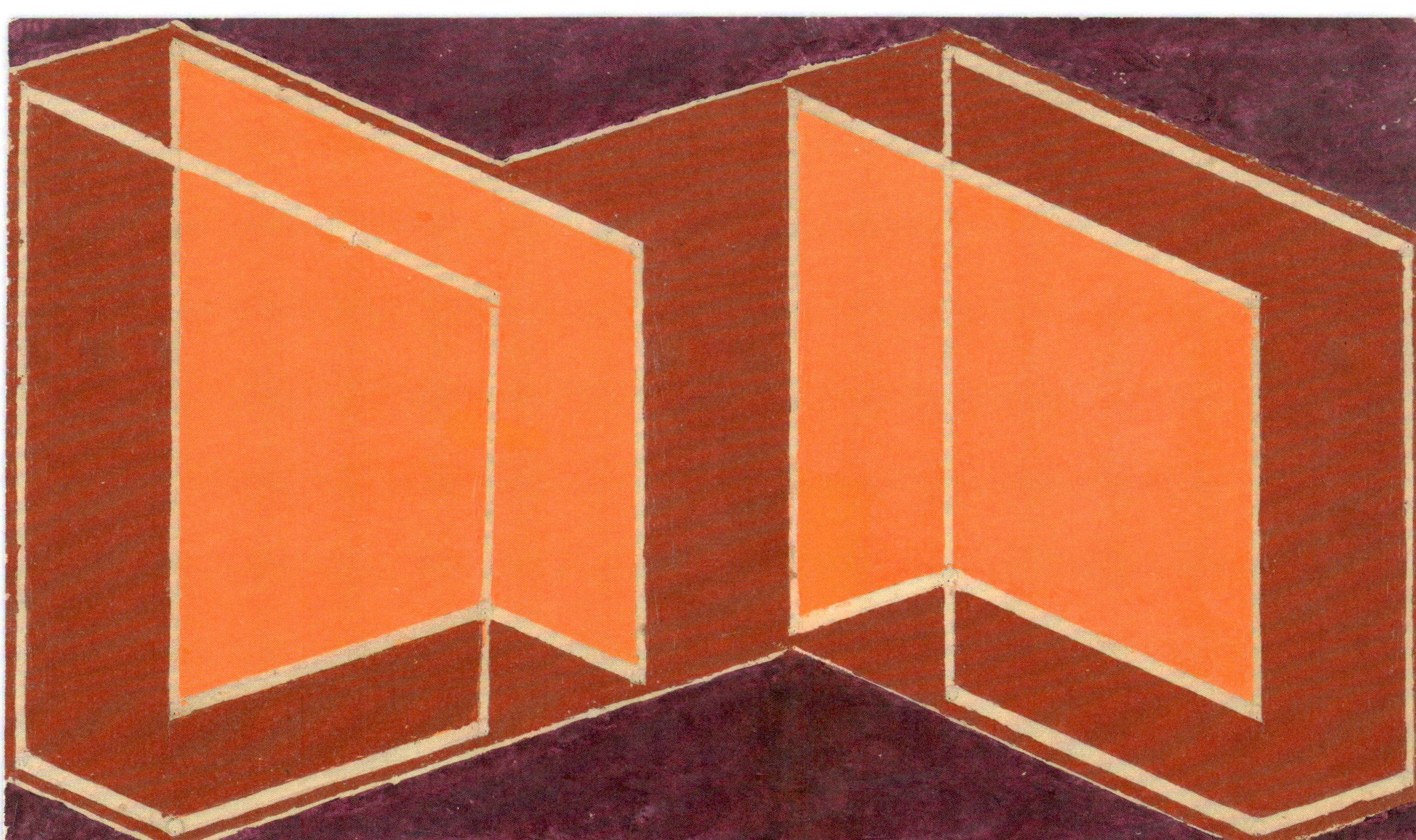

Below Harry Seidler & Associates, MLC Centre forecourt (today's 25 Martin Place), Sydney, 1972–78, with Josef Albers's *Structural Constellation: Wrestling* 1976, photo by Max Dupain, Mitchell Library, State Library of NSW, PXB 237

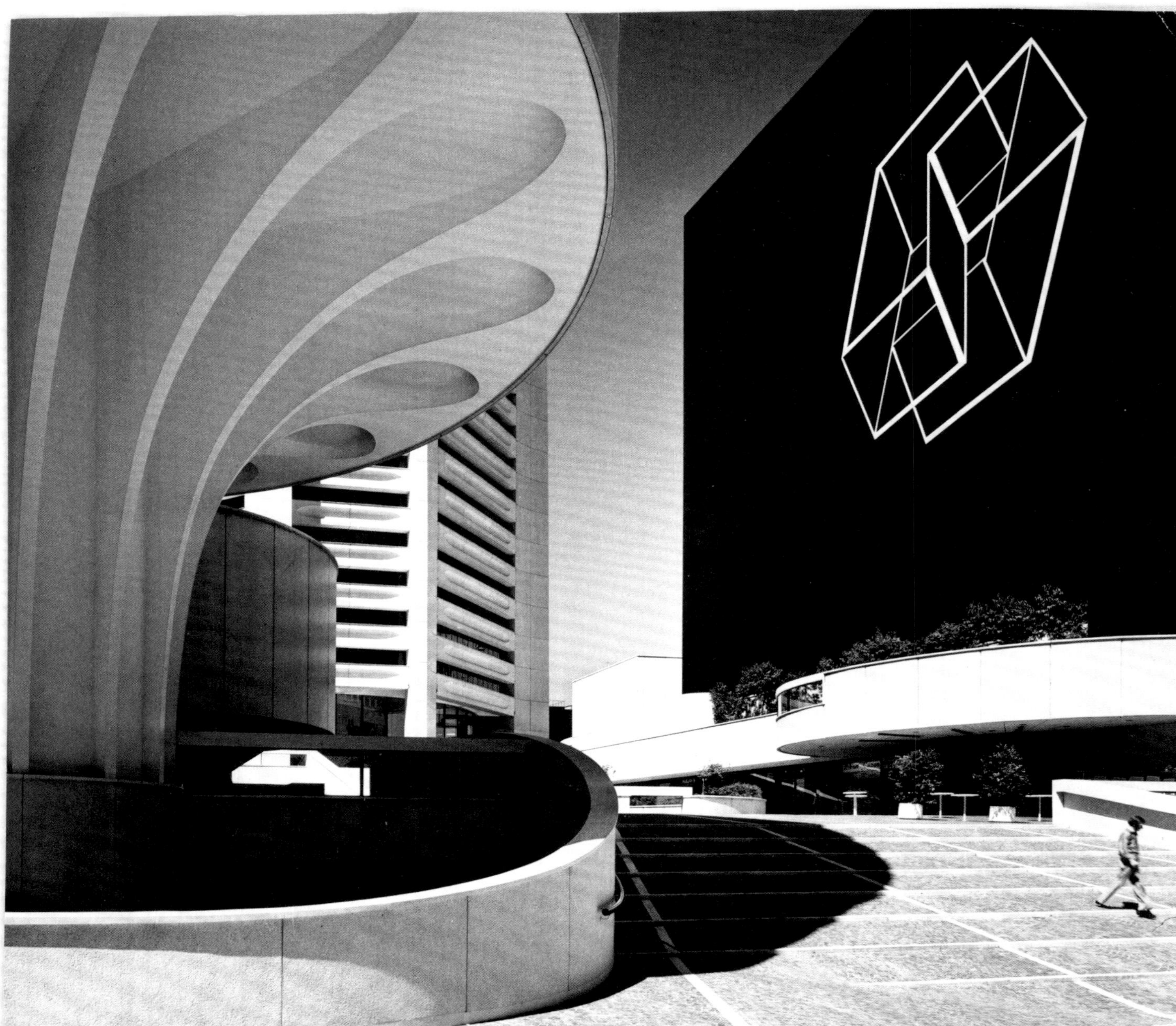

In conversation with Penelope Seidler

Philip Goad

Philip Goad: Your husband Harry Seidler counted Josef Albers as one of the greatest influences on his architectural ideas. How did Harry first come into contact with Albers?

Penelope Seidler: Harry had been in the Master of Architecture course at Harvard University under the tutorship of Walter Gropius. As he was concluding this, he asked Gropius, 'I wish I could understand more about the visual appreciation of things. Why do some things look better than others? What is it about visual experience that one can learn?' And Gropius said, 'If you are interested in these things, I think you should go to Black Mountain College where Josef Albers is teaching.' Josef was his colleague at the Bauhaus in Germany. So Harry applied and got to go there for a summer course, and he was very happy about that.

PG: I get the sense too, that Harry enjoyed his time there.

PS: Oh, he certainly did. He enjoyed his time there very much, mixing with very creative people and living with fellow students, and they travelled around.

PG: And he took the two courses, one on colour and the other on design. These were fantastic courses that Albers offered, and Harry recorded his experience in a series of notebooks.

PS: Oh, yes. We had them at home on our bookshelf for a long time. And we'd look through them. But later he was in contact with people at the Museum of Modern Art in New York, particularly [architecture curator] Barry Bergdoll, and Barry persuaded me that the museum would be the appropriate place to house these notes. Apparently, they've been very well received and they're available to everybody now.

PG: In the notebooks Harry quotes from Albers. He also makes sketches and drawings. Do you think Harry made use of them through his architectural career?

PS: Oh, yes. I don't think he had to refer to them so much, because they were embedded in his brain. I think it was part of his focus. He just knew it.

PG: That experience at Black Mountain in summer 1946 must have been quite extraordinary, but also very affecting in terms of becoming wedded to Josef Albers's ideas. He also began to collect work by Albers in New York in the years afterward.

PS: Yes. After he finished at Black Mountain he was working in New York with Marcel Breuer. There was an exhibition of Albers's work at the Sidney Janis Gallery and Harry bought three lithographs. He had them in his room at 222 Riverside Drive. And he brought them to Australia, of course, when he came here.

PG: That must have been an extraordinary thing to do--to actually buy them then. I noticed that they may have been somewhere around $12 at the time, which seems, well, unbelievable.

PS: Yes, they weren't very expensive. And when he met Albers some years later and he told him that he'd bought these, Albers apparently said, 'I always wondered who bought them as they were the only ones sold.'

PG: So they travelled with Harry to Australia, and then they ended up on the wall of his apartment in Point Piper. Do you remember them?

PS: Of course, because I lived there the first year of my married life in 1959. And they were on the wall then.

PG: And were there other artworks on the walls?

PS: Yes, there were reproductions. I think there was a Klee. And then of course there were Max Dupain photographs of Harry's early work.

PG: Right, so in some respects, Harry was placing Albers alongside his own work.

PS: Yes, very much so.

PG: Both Harry and you would've admired these works in their own right. But do you think they also acted as mementos or reminders of the Black Mountain experience?

PS: Well, I'm sure they did. Like any collector, one buys things as a memento as well as admiring them in themselves. When you look at artworks you admire them, but they also bring back the association of how you came by them.

PG: They would've been extraordinary mementos of his experience at Black Mountain, as well as being fundamental lessons in contrast and spatial depth--and the complexity of the projections themselves were such clever visual exercises in geometry.

PS: Indeed, yes. He was always rather disappointed as he didn't think his enthusiasm was shared particularly by people here in Sydney.

Below

Page from Harry Seidler's Black Mountain College notebook, showing notes from Josef Albers's Colour Lectures, 1946, pen, pencil and coloured pencil on notepaper, 27.9 × 21.6 cm, photo by Museum of Modern Art, New York / Scala, Florence, gift of Penelope Seidler, Museum of Modern Art, New York, SC87.2009.1

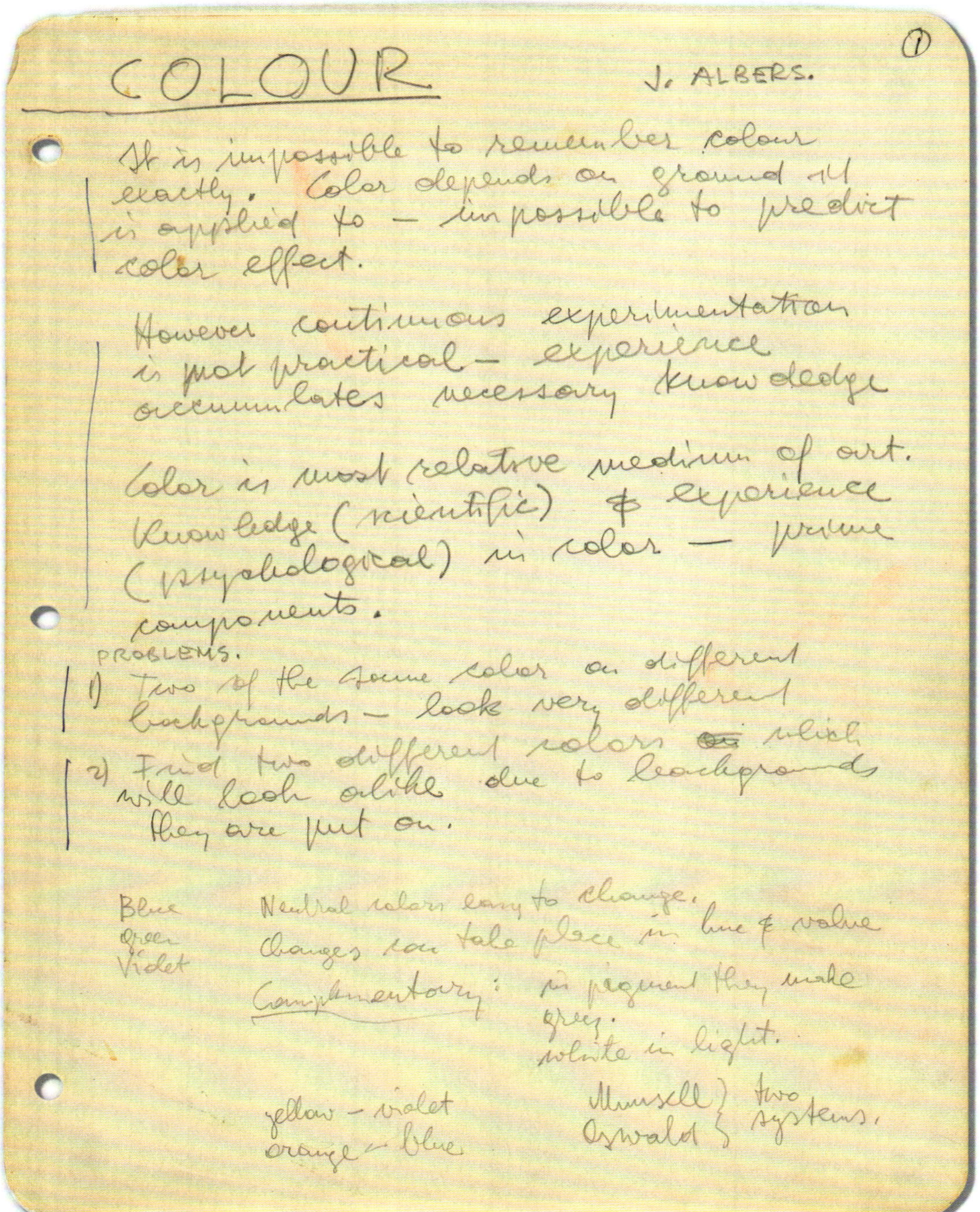

Top — Josef Albers, *Wings* 1934, woodcut, image 18.7 × 31.5 cm, sheet 20.6 × 33.6 cm
Bottom — Josef Albers, *i* 1934, linocut, image 20.6 × 28.8 cm, sheet 32.3 × 40.1 cm

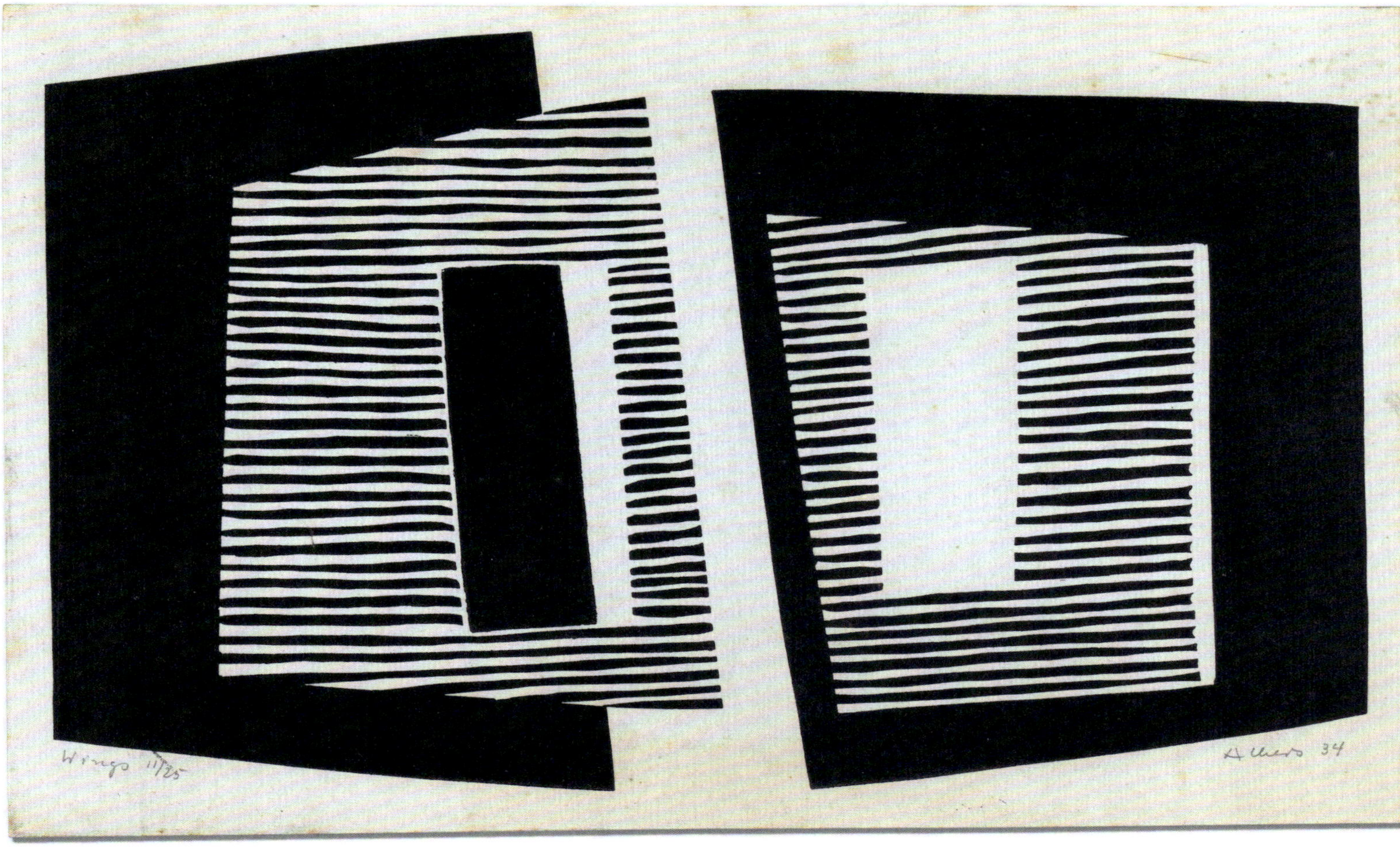

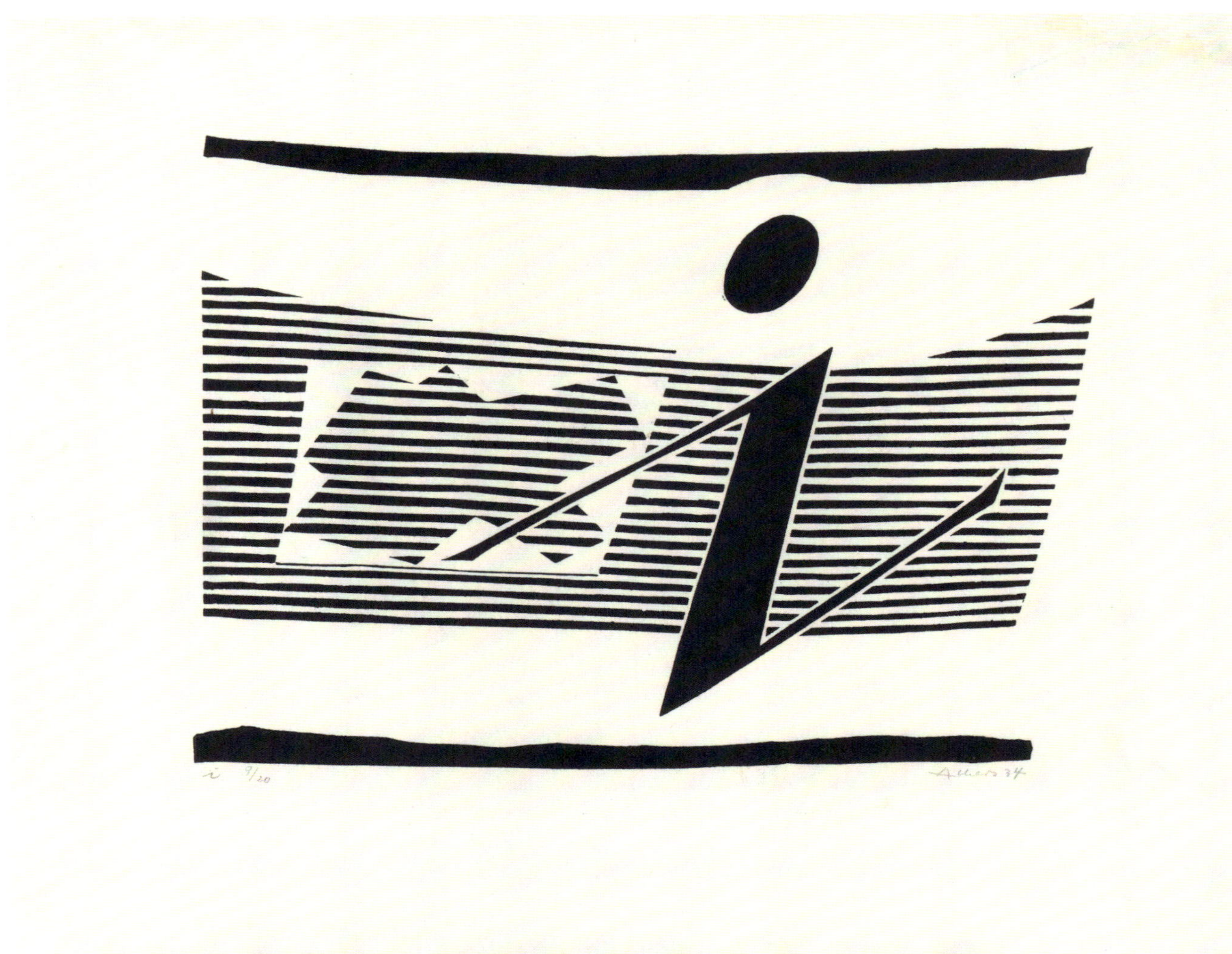

Top	Josef Albers and Harry Seidler at Anni and Josef Albers's house, Orange, Connecticut, July 1966, photo by Penelope Seidler, digitised by Eric Sierins
Bottom	Josef Albers and Penelope Seidler at Anni and Josef Albers's house, Orange, Connecticut, July 1966, photo by Harry Seidler, digitised by Eric Sierins
Opposite	Harry Seidler architecture, Blues Point Tower apartments, McMahons Point, Sydney, April 1962, gelatin silver photograph, cardboard, 59.1 × 49.2 cm, photo by Max Dupain, National Gallery of Australia, gift of Harry Seidler 2001, 2001.236
Next	Josef Albers, Folio I, folder 8, from *Formulation : Articulation* 1972, screenprint, image 15.8 × 44 cm, sheet 38.2 × 50.7 cm

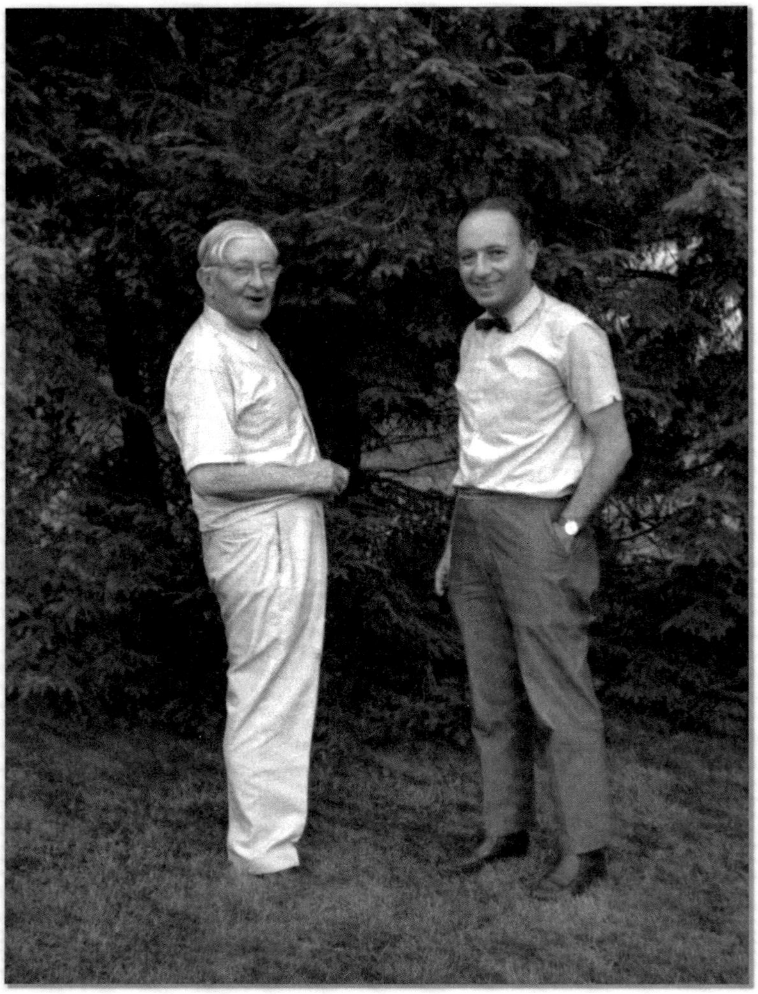

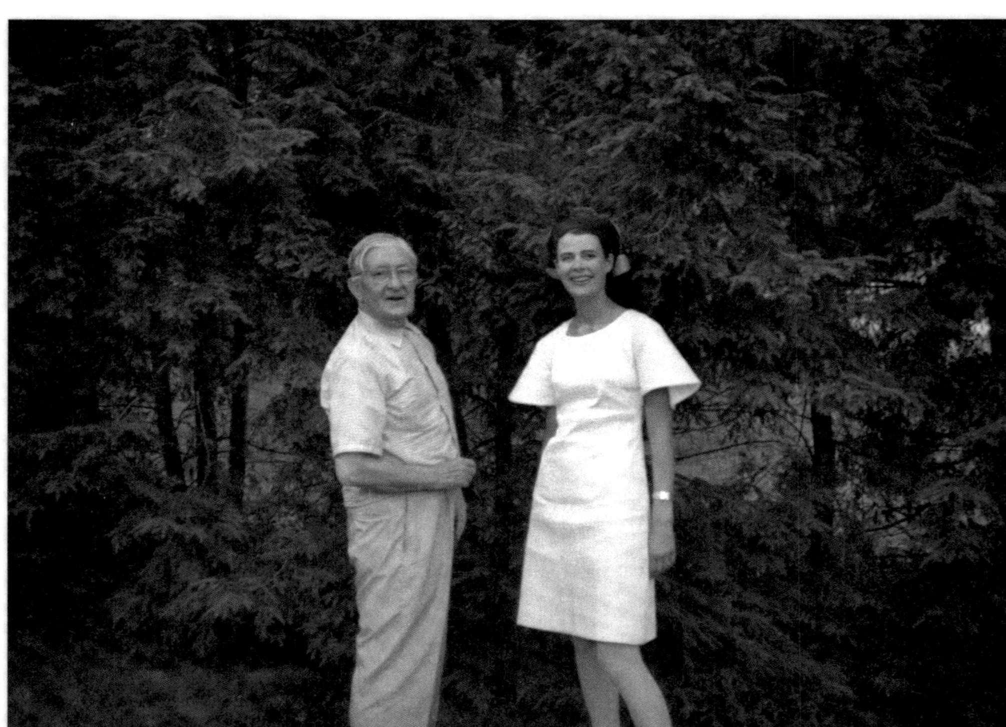

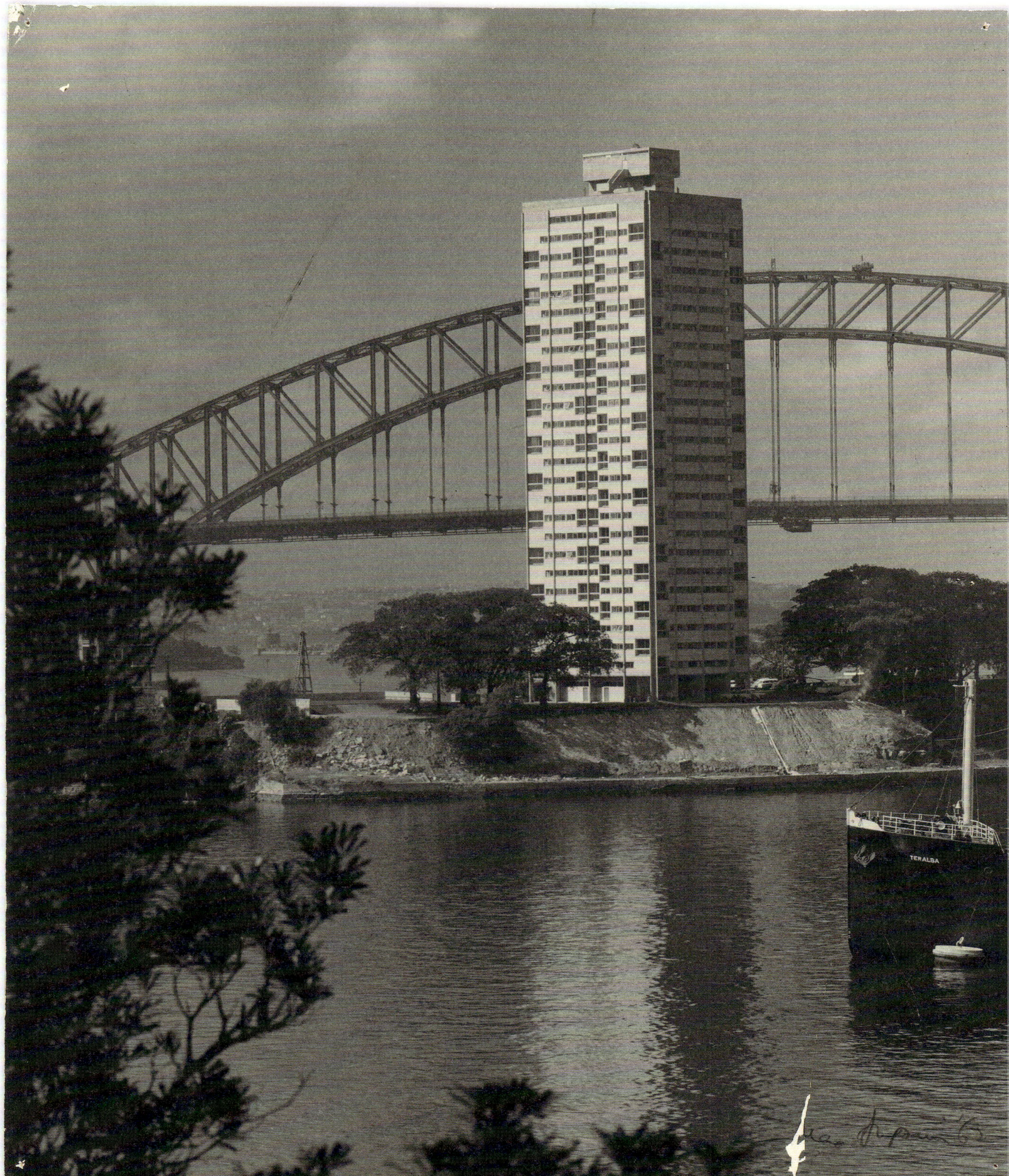
TERALBA

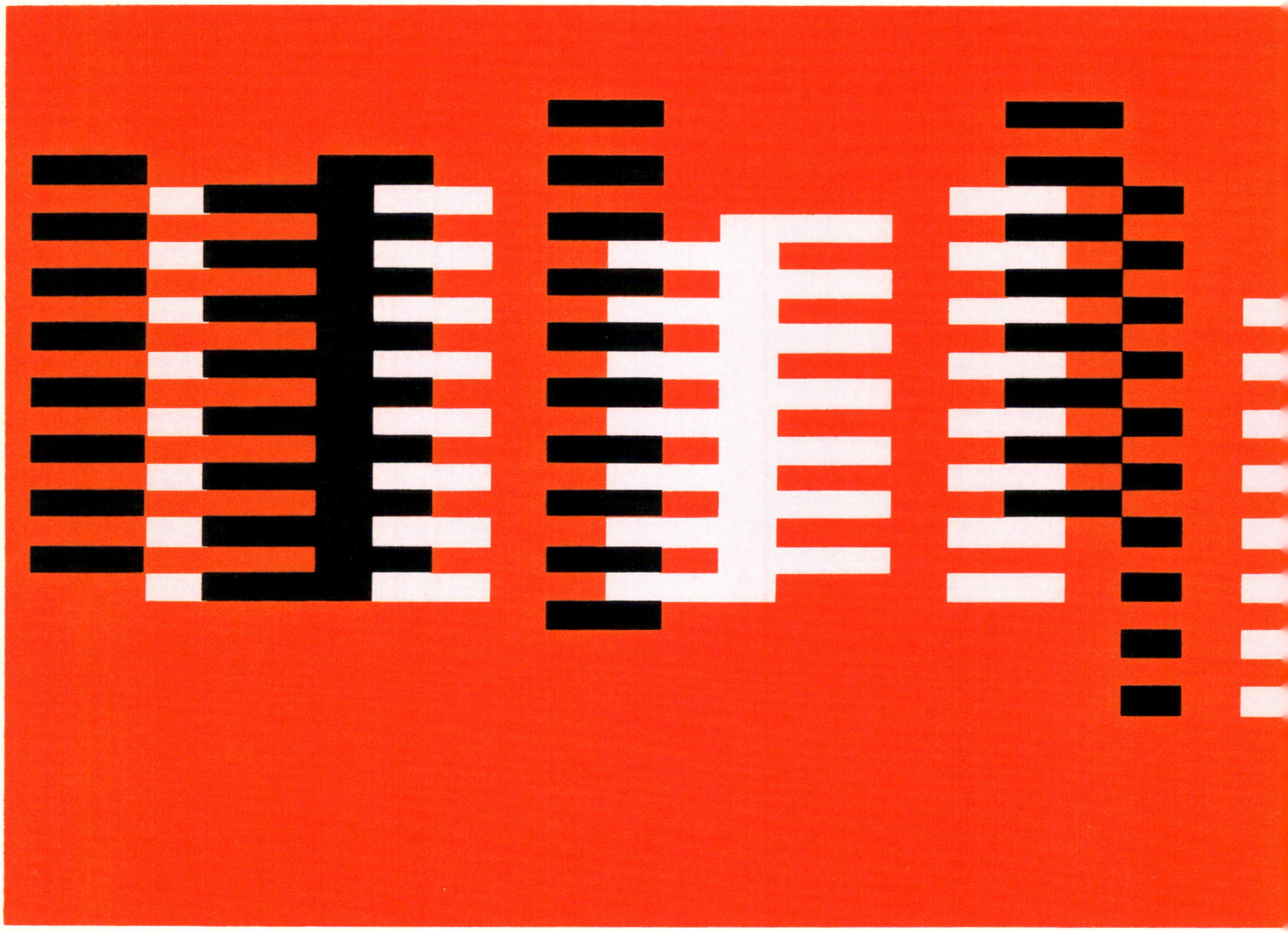

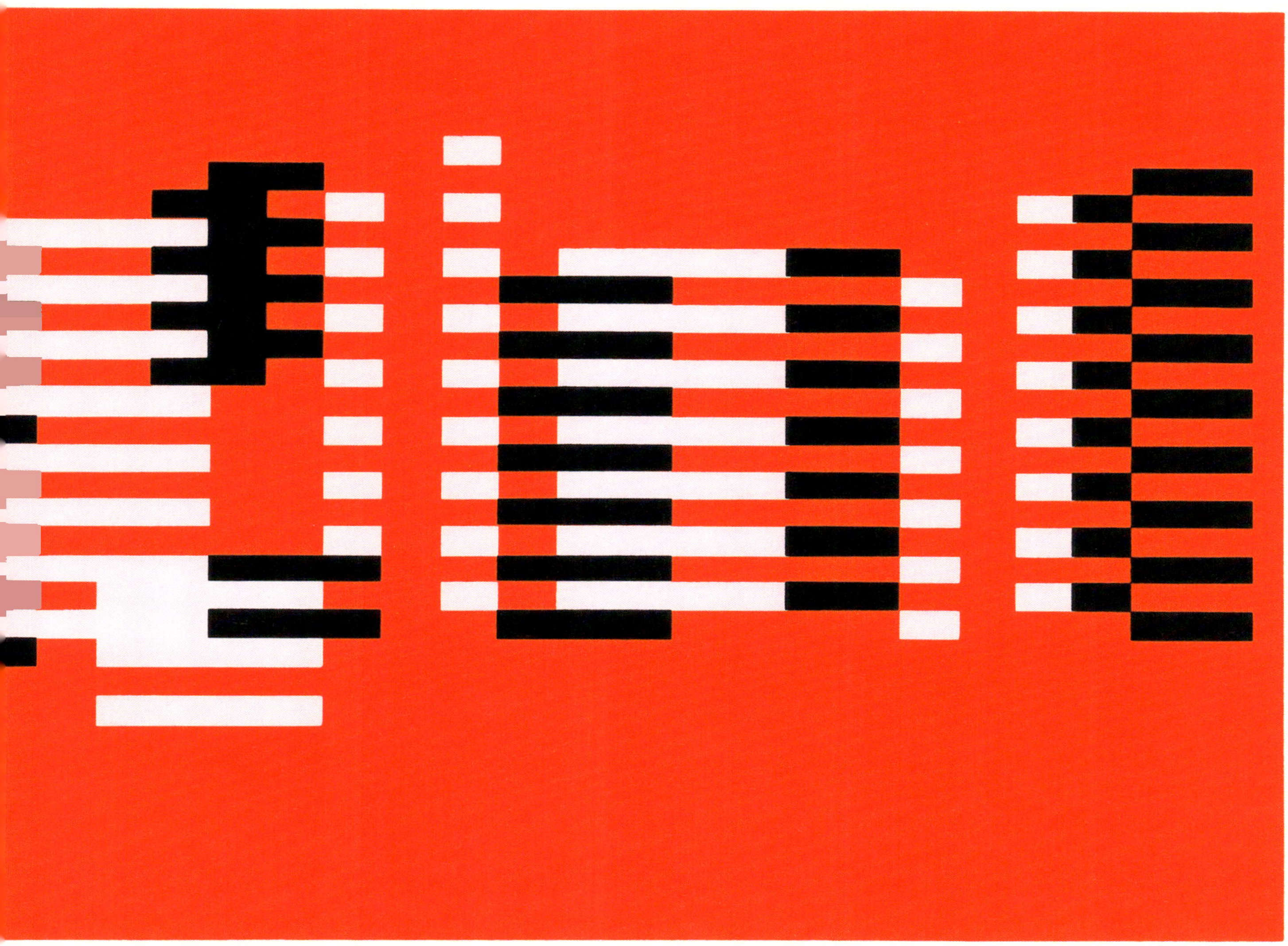

PG: Right.

PS: At first.

PG: Harry also used these lithographs in his own writing. There's a famous article he wrote in the journal *Architecture* in 1949 called 'Painting toward architecture', and in the 1954 book *Houses, interiors and projects* he uses an Albers. Do you think he felt Albers's work helped to explain his own approaches at the time to design?

PS: I think so. I think he saw parallels in his designs and Albers's methodology. From one creative process to another.

PG: Yes, because in both cases he used examples of the work of Jean Arp and Piet Mondrian, and Albers as well.

PS: Yes.

PG: And in some respects, I get the feeling that the introductory essay in *Houses, interiors and projects* was a way of also educating his architectural readership here in Australia.

PS: Oh, indeed, yes.

PG: I wondered whether it was also a tactic to challenge people here in Australia to become familiar with modernist art more generally.

PS: Well, that was part of it. When he arrived in Australia, Harry quickly became associated with several artists and joined the Contemporary Art Society. And I think he was a little bit of a snob, you know, artistically, because he felt that they weren't aware of the amazing developments or aesthetic activities happening internationally, particularly in New York. In those days there were magazines which took several months to arrive in Australia, and there were very few colour pictures available. So, people might have seen a small copy of a Picasso painting. Maybe not even in colour. But it was very hard to get firsthand knowledge of artistic episodes in other countries. Today you just click your fingers and you've got everything, any artist anywhere in the world, their whole oeuvre.

In those days, he used to say, it was like a faint echo of what was going on in other places. He used to give lectures and show slides of developments in painting as much as architecture. And people were very interested when they heard these lectures because there was little exposure. He arrived in Australia in 1948, only three years after the war ended. He'd learnt from the great masters, and he felt absolutely full of all these developments and wanted to get them out to the world and tell people. He was a sort of evangelist for modernism. You know that energy; he couldn't get it out fast enough. And he felt that he was sometimes disappointed with the reaction.

PG: Now, when you and Harry married a few years later, you had a Christmas card printed for friends and clients and there was an Albers lithograph on it.

PS: Oh yes. We used to send a lot of Christmas cards, as we all used to do. I don't much do that anymore, but every year we would get a card printed.

PG: The Albers card was one of the *Structural Constellations*. As compositions, I think Harry seemed to be particularly preoccupied by the *Structural Constellations* because of their geometry. But also there's a really strong sense of implied spatial depth, even three-dimensionality, even though they're two-dimensional images.

PS: Yes. When you look at them in various ways, your eyes are a bit dazzled because they do tricks.

PG: Exactly. The facade of Blues Point Tower at McMahons Point has sometimes been compared to the abstract compositions of Albers. Famously, Peter Blake compared it to Albers's glass painting *City* 1928. Do you think Harry was conscious in thinking about that at a large scale?

PS: Well yes. It was a big influence. Rather than have every floor the same, he juggled them around a bit and moved the balconies from one side to the other. It was a very rational plan, but he was able to articulate the facades to make it more interesting, more dynamic.

PG: More dynamic, yes. It seems that that is a preoccupation which Harry and the office pursued throughout his career--these sort of syncopated rhythms across facades.

PS: Yes, that was deliberate, of course.

PG: And later it became obvious with balconies that curved out and projected. Never formal compositions, but always over a large canvas of a facade or a skyscraper. These were huge artistic compositions. Am I stretching it too far?

Top Portrait of Josef Albers in his studio, New Haven, Connecticut, 1969, digital file from black-and-white photo print, photo by Malcolm Lubliner, Kenneth E Tyler Collection archive, National Gallery of Australia

Bottom Harry Seidler and Josef Albers at Anni and Josef Albers's house, Orange, Connecticut, July 1966, photo by Penelope Seidler, digitised by Eric Sierins

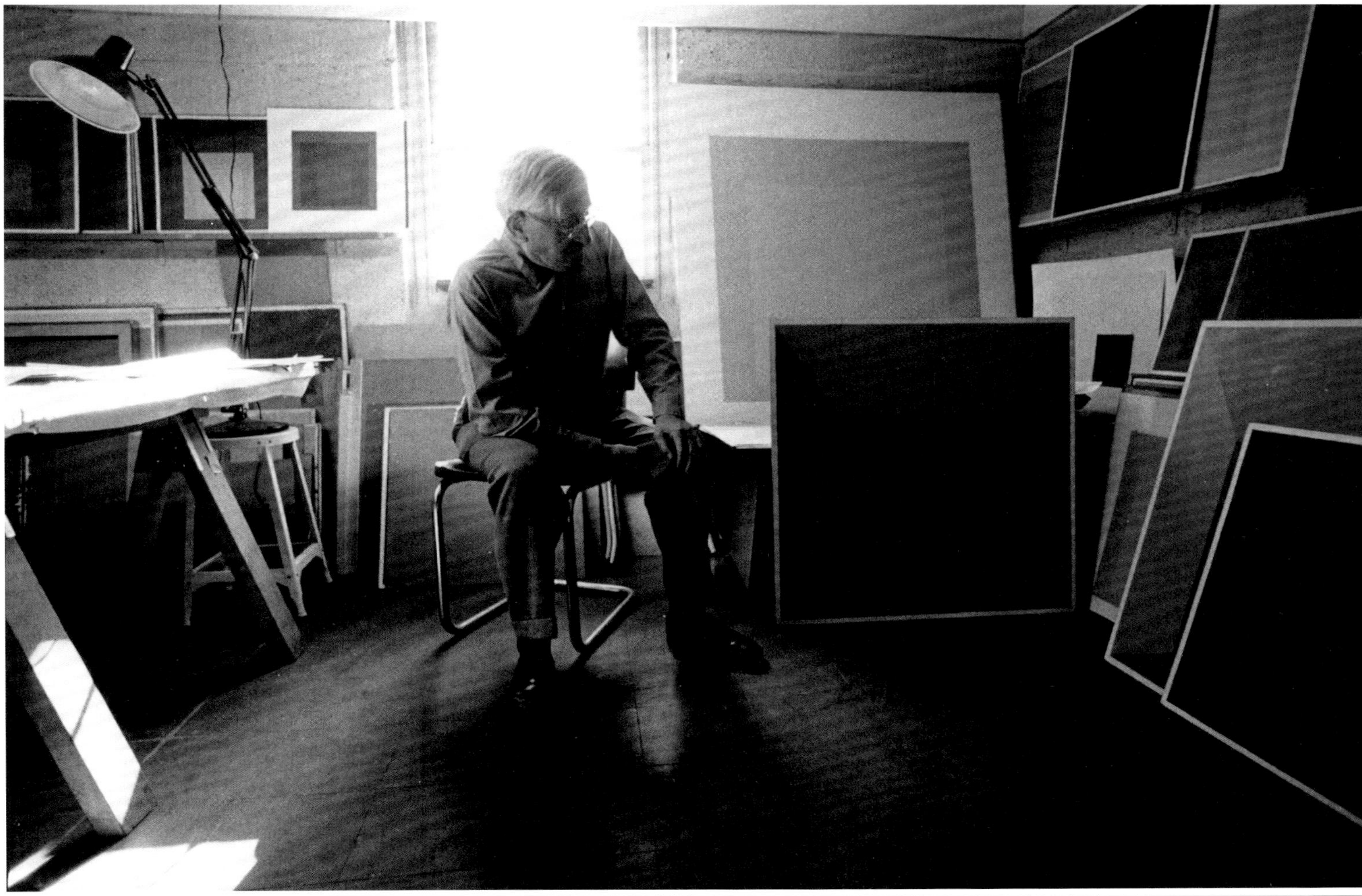

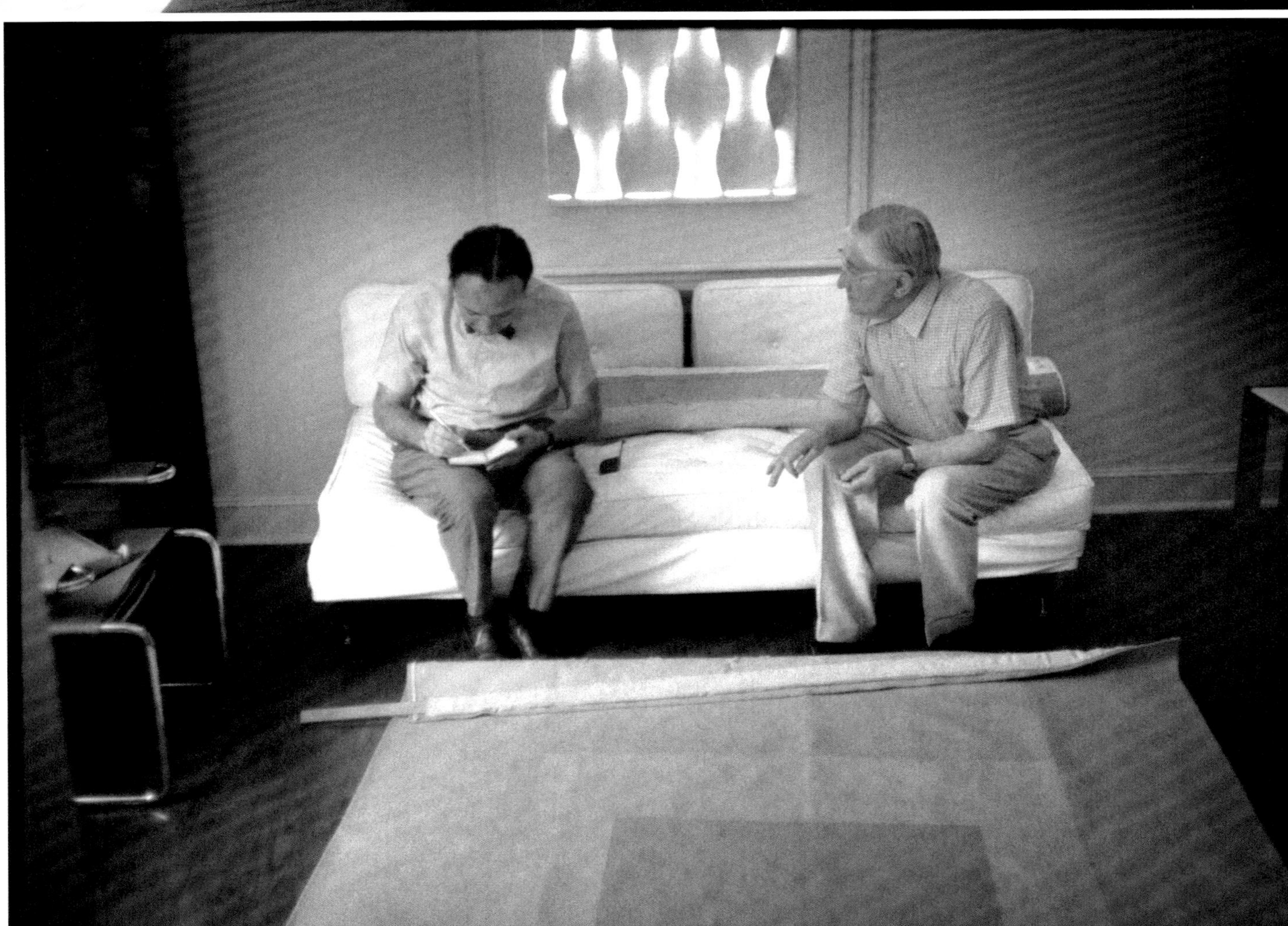

Top Josef Albers with Kenneth Tyler in the workshop studio, discussing his Stanford University wall maquette made by Tyler Graphics Ltd, Bedford Village, New York, 1976, digital file from black-and-white photo print, photo by Betty Fiske, Kenneth E Tyler Collection archive, National Gallery of Australia

Bottom Josef Albers, Ink drawing for *Embossed Linear Construction IV, 2-D* 1964, black ink on paper, image 22.4 × 52.6 cm, mount 47.3 × 68.7 cm, National Gallery of Australia, 2002.1.1323

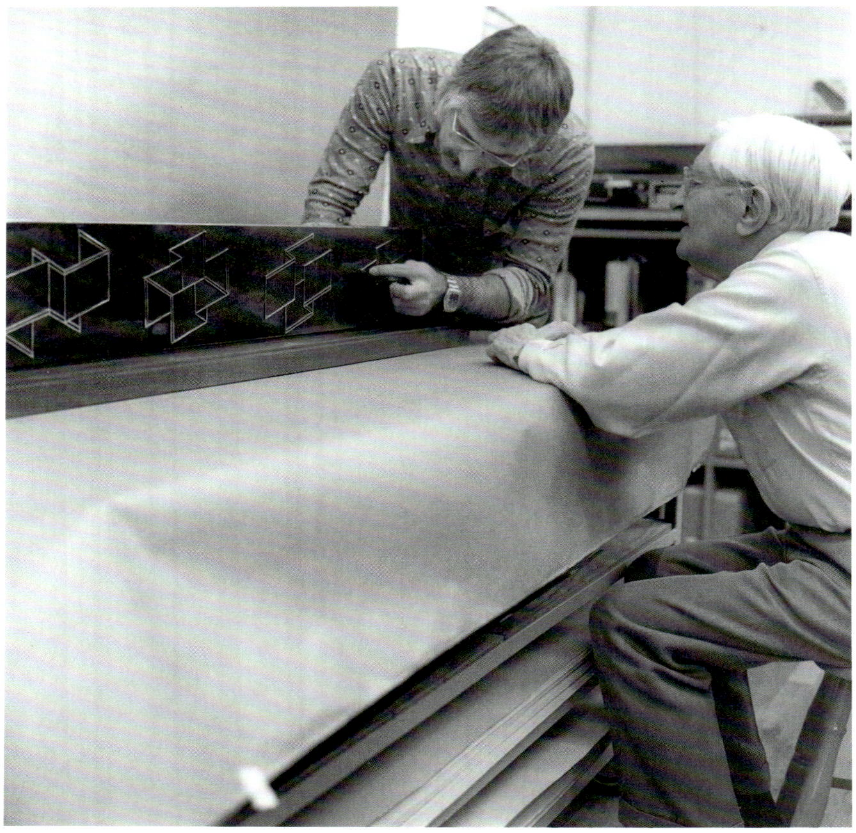

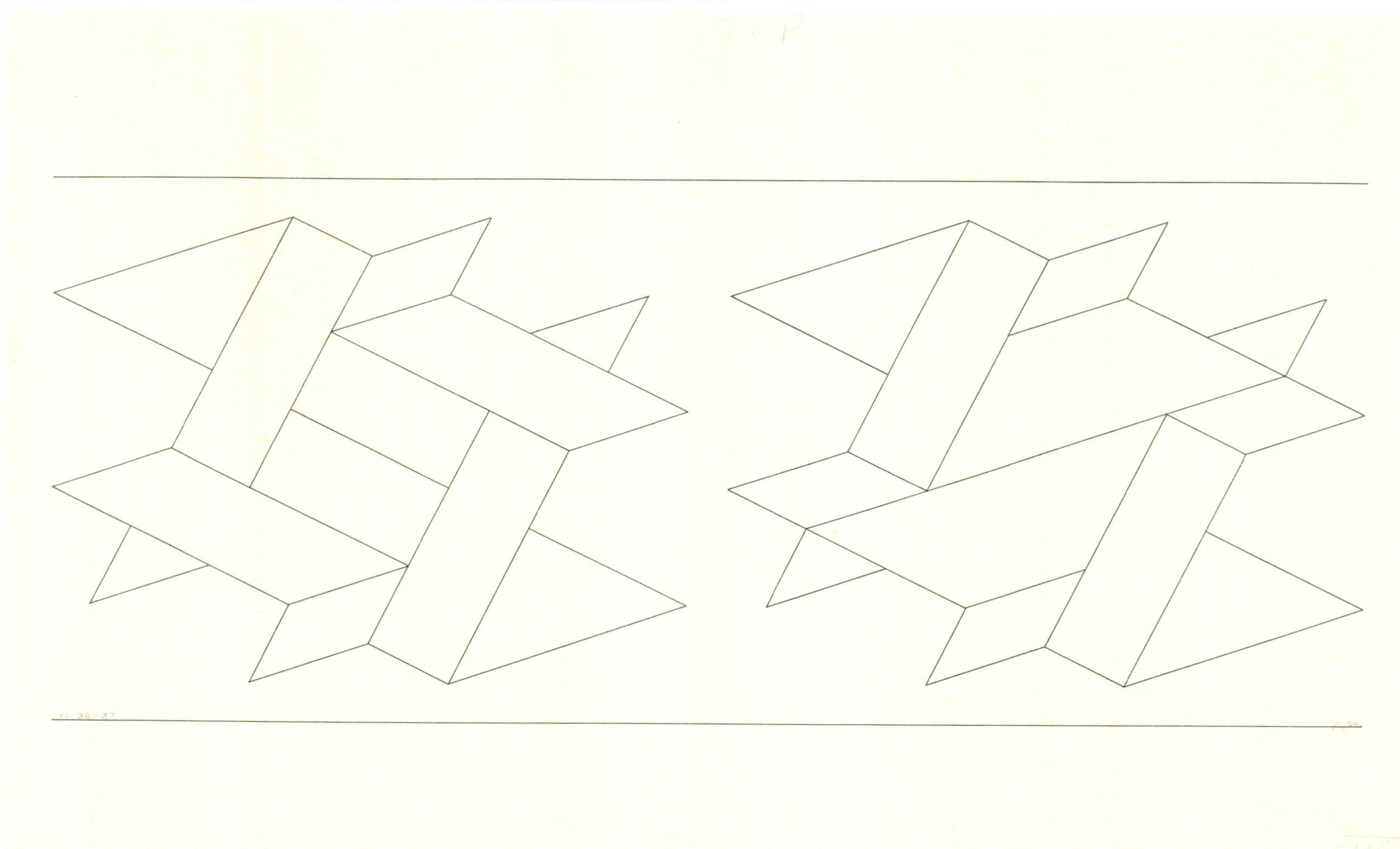

PS: No, you're not. But there's an interesting development in 1963 when he lived in Rome working with Pier Luigi Nervi. It was then that he discovered Baroque architecture. He would go around and visit all the churches and other buildings by Borromini. And his buildings from that period onward started to develop curves, which he really hadn't done before. Our house doesn't have a curve in it. But subsequent to that, he became extremely influenced by Baroque architecture and its possibilities structurally. And that became a predominant influence, integrating it with what he absorbed from Albers.

PG: Yes, because curves--I might be wrong--are notably absent from Albers generally.

PS: Yes, the famous works, of course. I remember when we visited Albers in 1965 and he said to us, and I can remember his words exactly, 'I'm going to devote the rest of my life to the square.' And I thought at the time, How far can you go with the square? But that's what he did. He devoted the rest of his life to the square. He took us into his studio where he painted, and he had all these colours, you know, little tubes of colours. He said, 'I have every colour of yellow here and I make it so that I get the perfect colour to match with the other colours.' And he was very sweet the way he described the whole thing. But he was very determined--'I'm going to devote the rest of my life to the square.'

PG: So where did you first meet Albers?

PS: In his house in Orange, Connecticut.

PG: And that was in 1960?

PS: Probably, yes. We went there several times.

PG: Right. And can you describe his home and studio?

PS: Well, he lived in a very ordinary, wooden house of no pretension. In a very nice area called Orange, which seemed appropriate for him when you think of all his ideas around colour. It was very modest and frugally furnished. It wasn't what you'd call a Bauhaus house, but it was very simple and logical. He thought it was a typical American house.

PG: Did you met Anni Albers too?

PS: Oh, yes. We met Anni and spoke to her, and she was very charming. But, you know, in those days people--and I think my husband was one of these, not in a derogatory way--they regarded weaving and artworks composed of materials as women's work. It was not celebrated the way it is today. Anni Albers's fame has been particularly notable in the last 20 years or so, but it was always Josef.

PG: Which is interesting because you and Harry commissioned tapestries from Albers, which are woven. It's like the men's weaving is okay if it's woven by others.

PS: Yes, that's right. We talked about this when Harry built Australia Square. There was the round, circular core, and the idea was to get a permanent artwork which would hang on the core. Obviously, a regular painting would not take the curve. So, the first artworks were two tapestries. The [Victor] Vasarely tapestry was at the back and at the front was the Le Corbusier tapestry, which was from an edition of two or three. One of these was in the UNESCO building in Paris. And that was because the tapestries took up the curve, and that's basically why most of the tapestries were commissioned. Another factor was to get a tapestry made quite large, bigger than Albers could paint himself.

PG: Right, yes.

PS: But he selected the threads of course.

PG: So in 1965, and I think also in July of 1966, you and Harry visited the Alberses again in New Haven. Why did you go again?

PS: In 1965, it would've been in connection with Australia Square. In 1966, it was just friendly in a way, to keep the lines of communication open.

PG: There was a visitors' book at the Alberses' house, and it is remarkable to see all those names. You and Harry would've been two of a long line of eminent visitors coming to visit Albers.

PS: Yes. He didn't go out much. He didn't go to New York much, he liked to stay at home, so the visitors would come to him. I must tell you: he was very fond of me.

PG: Right.

PS: He gave me a dear little piece on Formica, one of these beautiful drawings, and etched into it is 'For Penelope'.

PG: Oh, lovely.

PS: It's a beautiful thing, very special.

PG: Yes. And you also had works made for the house in Killara. It must have been important to you and Harry to continue to be patrons of Josef's work. At home you had Marcel Breuer chairs, you had maquettes by other artists in the house as well as at the Seidler office. Do you think Harry felt his office-study in Killara was like a sort of studio?

PS: Oh yes, of course.

PG: So he's not just designing in the city office. Did he also design buildings at home?

PS: Oh, of course, absolutely.

PG: So the study at home was almost like his studio--and artists often do this--where they have work by other artists around them in addition to their own work. Did Harry work like that?

PS: Yes, absolutely.

PG: And many of the drawings that Harry did, do you think he would develop designs in the way that Albers had taught him? Was he working across disciplines in terms of making a form for the entire building, or thinking about a particular unit of the building?

PS: He used to say he thought of all those things all at once in his head. The structure, the planning requirements and the site. The site was very important of course, the orientation. He thought in three dimensions.

PG: Right, he's always thinking like an artist would. The structure, the form and the ideas of contrast are all being thought about at the same time as he is getting everything correct, everything functionally in place.

PS: Yes, all together. We could be in a restaurant, and he'd start drawing on a napkin. It's a shame one didn't keep all these things, he used to throw them away. He'd only regard the final, elegantly drawn plans as the product--or only the building, actually.

PG: And for the office at Milsons Point, you also acquired some works by Albers?

PS: We have a tapestry and there are a few smaller pieces.

PG: Can you explain how you commissioned or bought a tapestry? You don't go to an Albers exhibition and buy a tapestry. How did you do it?

PS: Harry was instrumental in commissioning several. And I think Albers quite liked that, because he could do works which were much larger. He could see a way that you could make quite a large piece if the colours were right. Albers's gallerist in Paris, Denise René, she was very helpful in this regard. We met her several times, and she made the introductions to the weavers.

PG: The Albers is there in a major public part of the Seidler office. Do you think that among the employees working in the Seidler office, among these works of art, there was some osmosis of influence?

PS: Definitely. They were all influenced. If anybody took up the discussion, Harry was very pleased to be able to talk about that. And I think everybody in the office had an appreciation of the aesthetics of Josef Albers.

PG: Now, you and Harry often commissioned pupils of Albers for public artwork. Artists like Norman Carlberg and Charles O Perry. How did you come to choose these artists?

PS: Albers himself told us about Norman Carlberg, and showed us one of his *Positive Negative* sculptures. Harry sought him out and liked the work. And then, I think in the late 1960s, we had a party at Killara for a visiting British professor [Charles Mitchell] associated with the Power Institute and he came in and saw the Carlberg. He said, 'This is very interesting, I think you'd like the work of Charles Perry.' We did not know about Charles Perry, so Harry visited him in Rome. He became enamoured with Perry's work too, who was also an ex-student of Albers from when he taught at Yale.

PG: And I think it's a fantastic shift with you and Harry commissioning these artists, because they're not largely painters or lithographers like Albers, they're sculptors.

PS: Yes, three-dimensional.

PG: And the number of projects where these students of Albers have done work for you is quite extraordinary. At what used to be called the Trade Group Offices [now Edmund Barton Building] in Canberra, there were two very large Carlberg sculptures. There was the precast one, *Twist column* 1970–72. And the fantastic one, *Black widow* 1974. These students of Albers--Carlberg and Perry--how do you think their work complemented the Seidler buildings?

Top Study at Harry and Penelope Seidler House in May 2023, architecture by Harry Seidler and Penelope Seidler. On wall: Josef Albers, *Homage to the Square: Impartial* 1966

Bottom Josef Albers's tapestry *Homage to the Square* 1976 (woven by Ateliers Pinton, Aubusson) at the MLC Centre (today's 25 Martin Place), architecture by Harry Seidler & Associates, Sydney, August 1978, photo by Max Dupain, digitised by Eric Sierins. *Homage to the Square* since relocated to the Josef and Anni Albers Foundation.

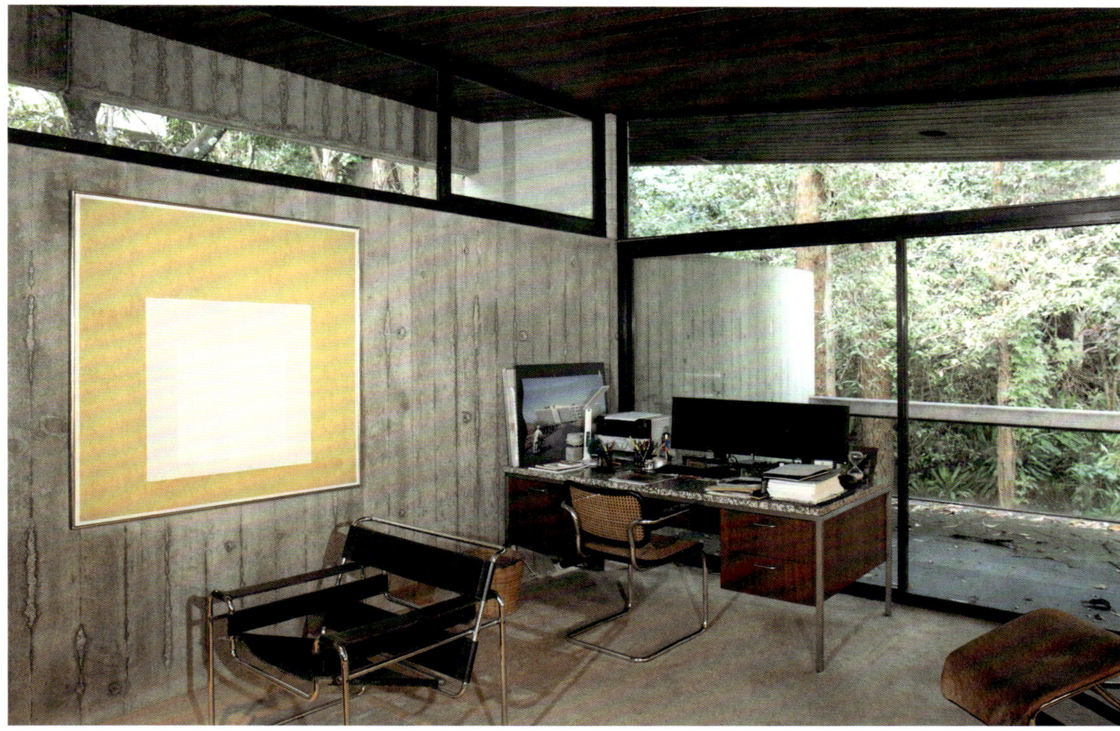

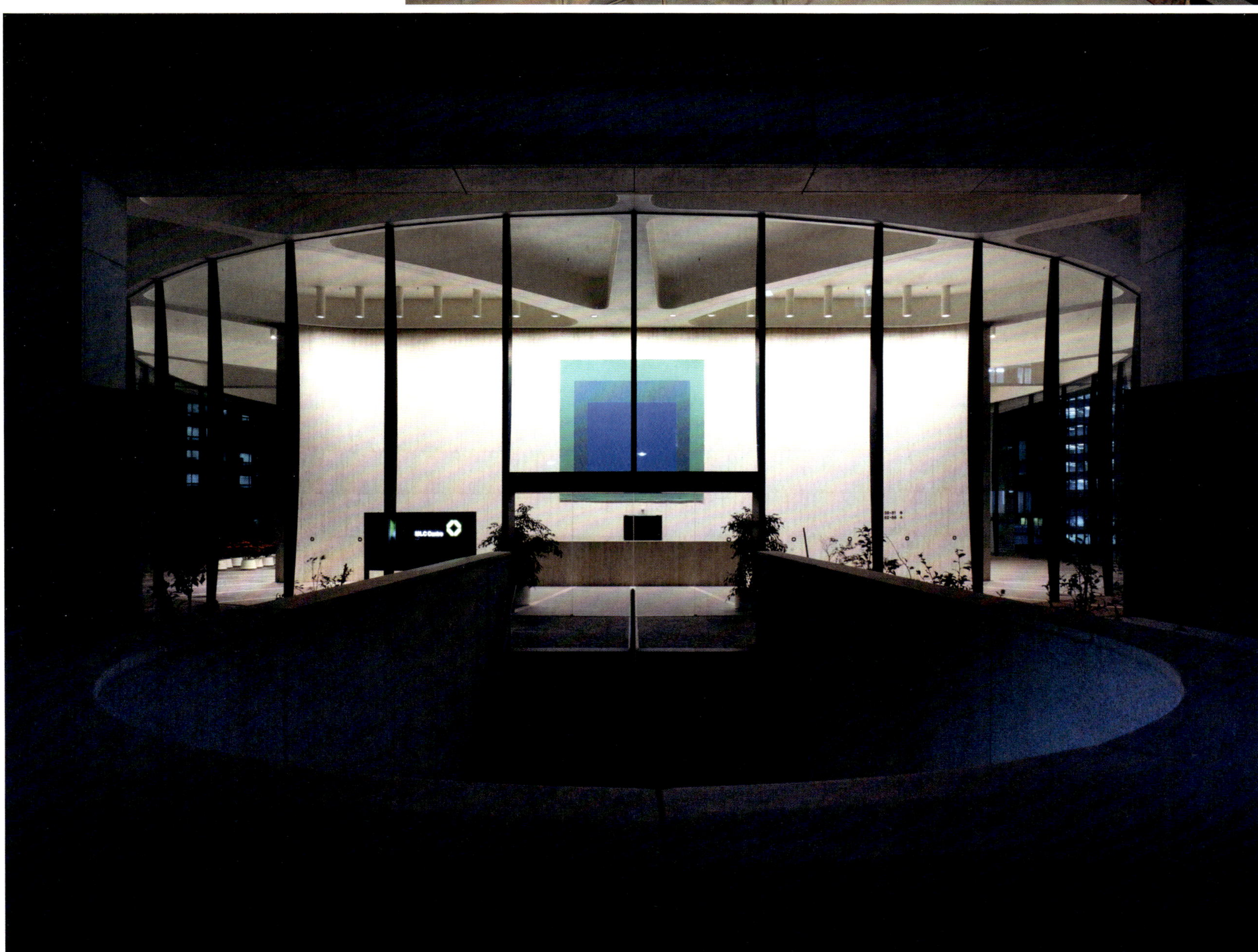

PS: Well, they were built in a so-called modular way. They had very interesting aesthetics, they kept you puzzling. When you looked at them, you wondered what was going on.

PG: To me, they remind me of Albers's drawings, but in three dimensions. Albers's work prompts the same compulsion--you want to study it; the mind is asked to think. Looking at these remarkably simple forms, Perry and Carlberg ask you to do the same with their sculptures.

PS: That's right. We felt a particular affinity to their work.

PG: And it seems that in much of the Seidler work in that period, the buildings themselves are often made up of repetitive elements. Then these complex sculptures work well together in dialogue.

PS: Yes, complementary.

PG: Which brings us to the MLC Centre, 1972–78 [today's 25 Martin Place]. Inside, there was the huge tapestry *Homage to the Square* 1976 commissioned to hang on the wall. Was this Harry suggesting the artwork to the client?

PS: Oh, yes. Harry would have suggested it and convinced the client; he was very convincing.

PG: Outside in the forecourt you've got the Perry sculpture *S* 1977, bright yellow. And *Structural Constellation* by his master Albers is on the black wall.

PS: Yes.

PG: I just think it's an incredible conversation between master and pupil. And Harry's architecture is in some respects the pupil too.

PS: It is, yes.

PG: Can you tell us about *Structural Constellation: Wrestling* 1976? How did it all come about?

PS: There was a building with a huge blank wall facing the public plaza of the MLC project. It was crying out for something to be on it rather than some sort of advertising, and Harry thought it'd be a perfect place for an artwork. It was his idea to commission Albers to do that. We have the correspondence, and I have the original drawing. It was quite specific how it would be implemented, and how wide the lines would be.

PG: Right, and in the final design you have public space, the Charles Perry--the brilliant canary-yellow *S* sculpture--and the Albers to your right as you're heading up to the entrance. It must be, in Australia, one of the most complete spatial experiences concerned with big-scale public art.

PS: Well of course, I think so. I think it's monumental. It's on a monumental scale, which one never really gets in a city like Sydney because Sydney is very dense. The roads are not too wide, mostly, but you have this huge public space around the MLC Centre, which needs big-scale art.

PG: Now, I've often thought that a number of Seidler buildings, like the Seidler offices at Milsons Point, or even earlier, the Printers Union offices in Sydney [now demolished] with the giant-size *brises soleil*, resemble the paper studies that Albers might have encouraged at the Bauhaus or at Black Mountain. Is this an unreasonable supposition?

PS: No. That's not unreasonable. But he was very influenced in Brazil by the *brises soleil* of architect Oscar Niemeyer that he saw. And Le Corbusier's love of them too.

PG: Yes, Harry seemed to be more--and I'm going to go out on a limb here--more artistic in terms of their placement, particularly as he moves into the curves as well. Harry's aim, I think generally, is that they become huge compositions in much the same way as a painting.

PS: Oh, absolutely.

PG: Albers's paintings, in particular his Homages, invoke the power of colour, contrast and visual perception. In the work of the Seidler office, colour doesn't seem to have been intrinsic. Am I wrong?

PS: Not so much. Harry always thought of materials as having contrast in their natural colour, you know--granites and wood and whatever it was, the colour was extremely important. But apart from the very early buildings, he didn't use much colour at all. Just superficial colour. They were more accents. Colour in the art or in parts of the furniture, but not in the actual building.

PG: I think you're right. It's more about the inherent nature of the materials. In October 2002, Harry gave a talk at the National Gallery in Canberra on Josef Albers and visual perception. In it, he spoke about a scientific approach to colour, a way of moving away from history, about the essence of what we see. Did he talk about these ideas in the office with clients or with staff? And did he have books by Albers in the office?

Below Gustav Hassenpflug, Paper sculpture made in Josef Albers's class, 1927, photo by Irene Bayer, Bauhaus-Archiv, Berlin, 6460

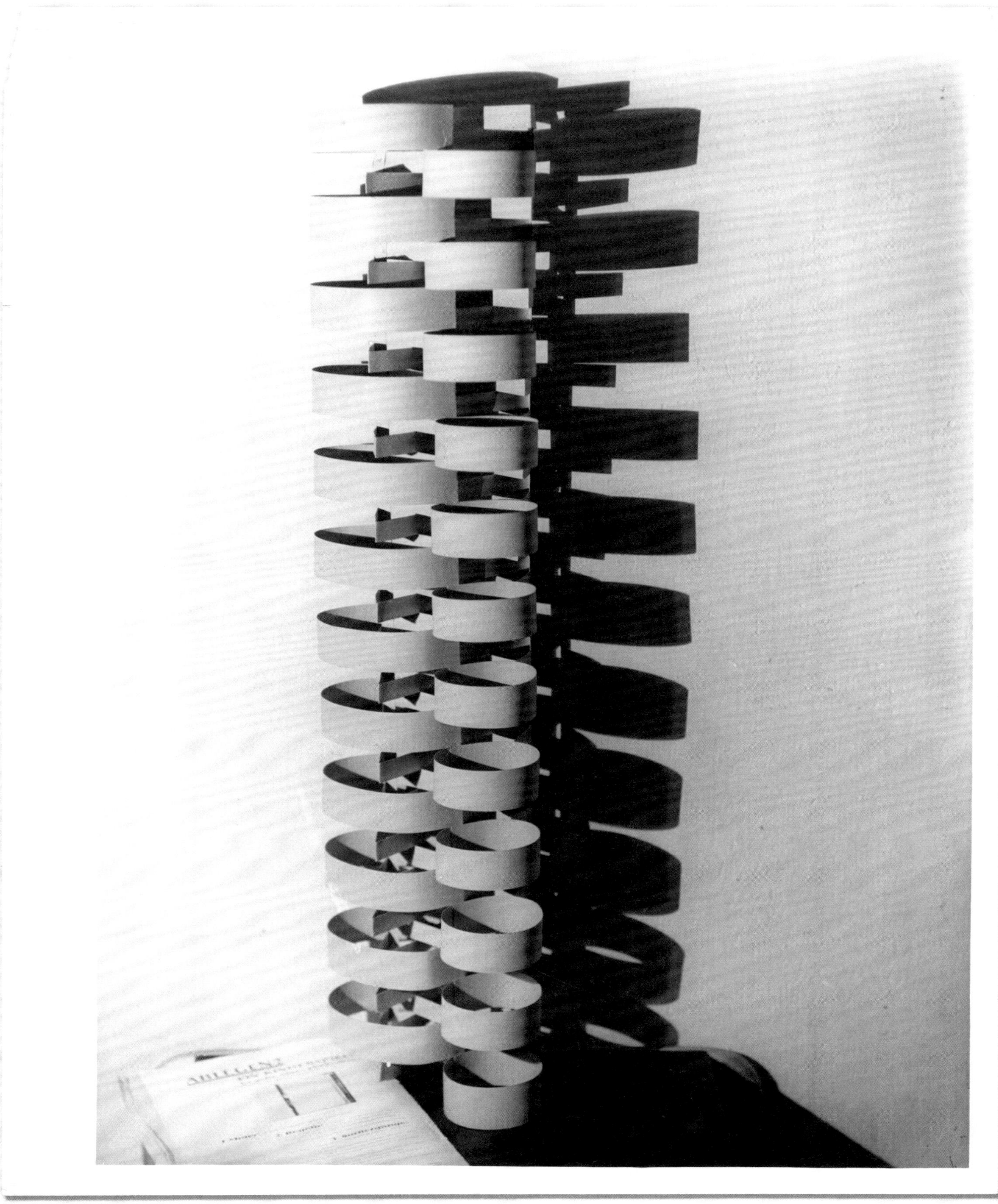

PS: Yes, but that was a sort of 'high art' talk, the one in Canberra. He wouldn't have lectured his clients in such a didactic way.

PG: No, it seems to me that Harry would have just led by example.

PS: He was very loyal to his teachers, you know? They were the gods. And he was the follower. And he always used their teaching wherever he was. He was aware of it.

PG: I think Harry was consistent throughout his career in keeping to those early principles that he'd gained at Harvard under Gropius, under Albers at Black Mountain, through Breuer in New York. And then his experience with Oscar Niemeyer. I mean, it's remarkably consistent. And at the same time, there is a developing career, but the artistic principles seem to have been held dear and been consistently applied.

PS: Yes, he held them dear. He regarded himself as an artist, most of all.

PG: Right.

PS: Architect, yes. But an architect–artist or an artist–architect. Art was the goal. Art.

PG: And at the same time, he's a brilliant structural technician.

PS: Well, he was absolutely concerned about structure, that it had to be pure, that it had to be rational and integrated into the design, rather than doing a design and then getting an engineer to work out how to build it. I mean, he was very much concerned with the whole integrity of the building. He thought that a building couldn't be a good building if it wasn't structurally pure as well as everything else.

PG: Yes. But it seems to me that also Harry understood the art of structure in much the same way that Albers in those cut-paper studies at the Bauhaus was instructing students in the fundamentals of formal experimentation in three dimensions. For Harry, these studies were about holding something up--towers or the like--and showed him that structure could be art.

PS: Yes, that's why he was so excited to work with Pier Luigi Nervi, whom he admired. Although they didn't really speak a common language, on the drawing board they understood each other very well. The structure and the art. It all goes together. Every great building you could say that about, whomever it was by, it all goes together.

And, you know, Albers's art has survived. His art has been more and more appreciated. Many artists are famcus and then their work goes out of fashion. Some of them come back in fashion, but the reception of Albers has been pretty consistent. His fame and reputation are increasing, I would say, on a global level.

PG: And do you think that's because colour is such an essential, emotional trigger for us?

PS: Yes, the colour--and the compositions too, they're so pure. Look at when he said, 'I'm devoting the rest of my life to the square.' I didn't say anything but that's sort of strange, because you don't think of the square being an artwork really, do you?

PG: No.

PS: But it's the square within the square within the square, and the relationship of one to the other, and the colours and the way they float together, or the proportion. It's very dramatic.

PG: Yes, and the way colour can come forward and recede.

PS: Yes, it's all there.

PG: It's all there. Makes you feel terrific, or it doesn't. It is remarkable.

Prof Philip Goad
Chair of Architecture, Redmond Barry Distinguished Professor and Co-Director of the Australian Centre for Architectural History, Urban and Cultural Heritage (ACAHUCH)
The University of Melbourne

Penelope Seidler AM
Director
Harry Seidler & Associates

Below Harry Seidler architecture, Blues Point Tower apartments, McMahons Point, Sydney 1962, gelatin silver photograph, cardboard, 58.2 × 48.6 cm, photo by Max Dupain

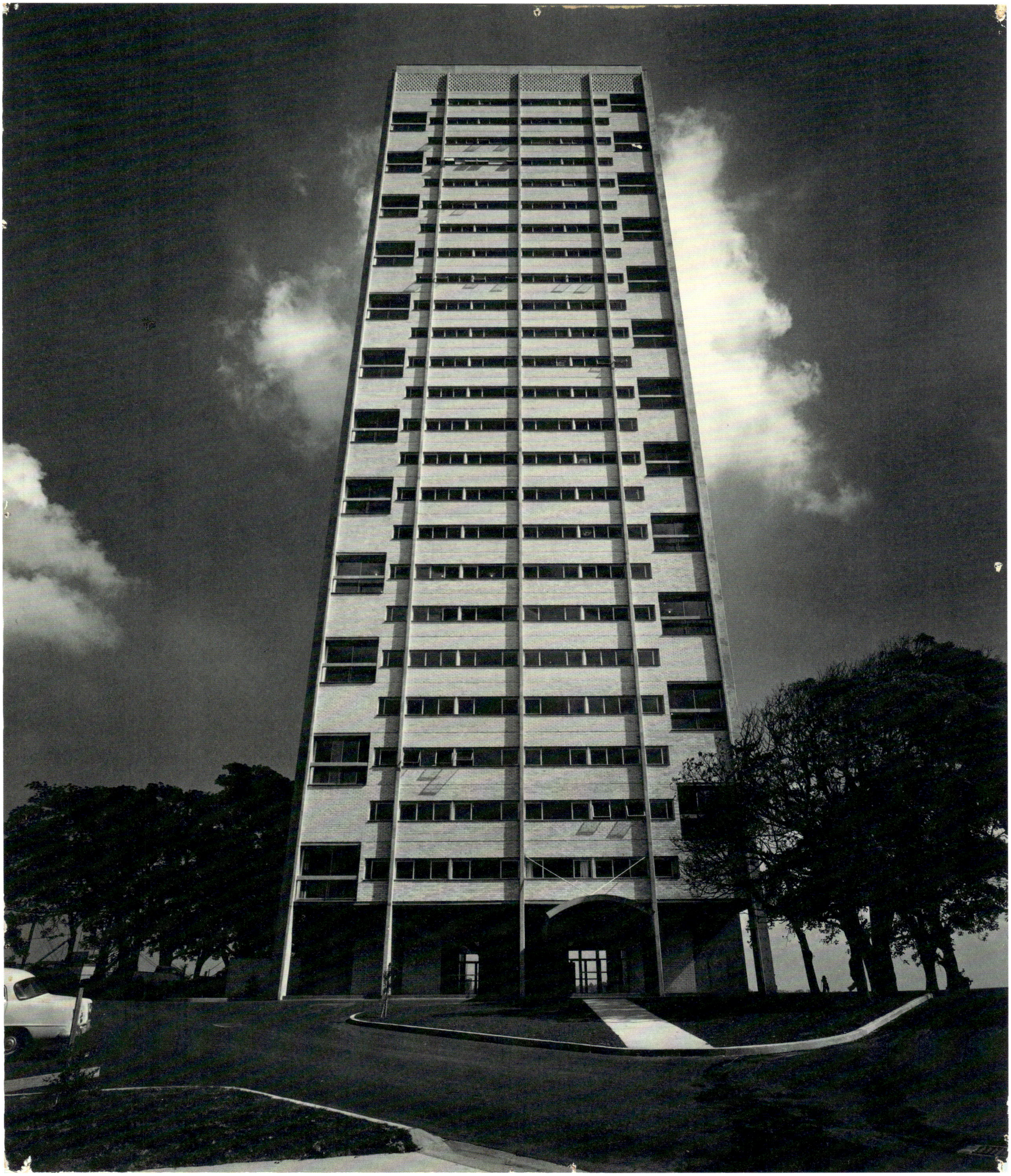

Below Harry Seidler architecture, Printers Union, Sydney, exterior (since demolished) January 1959, gelatin silver photograph, cardboard, 47.5 × 59.7 cm, photo by Max Dupain

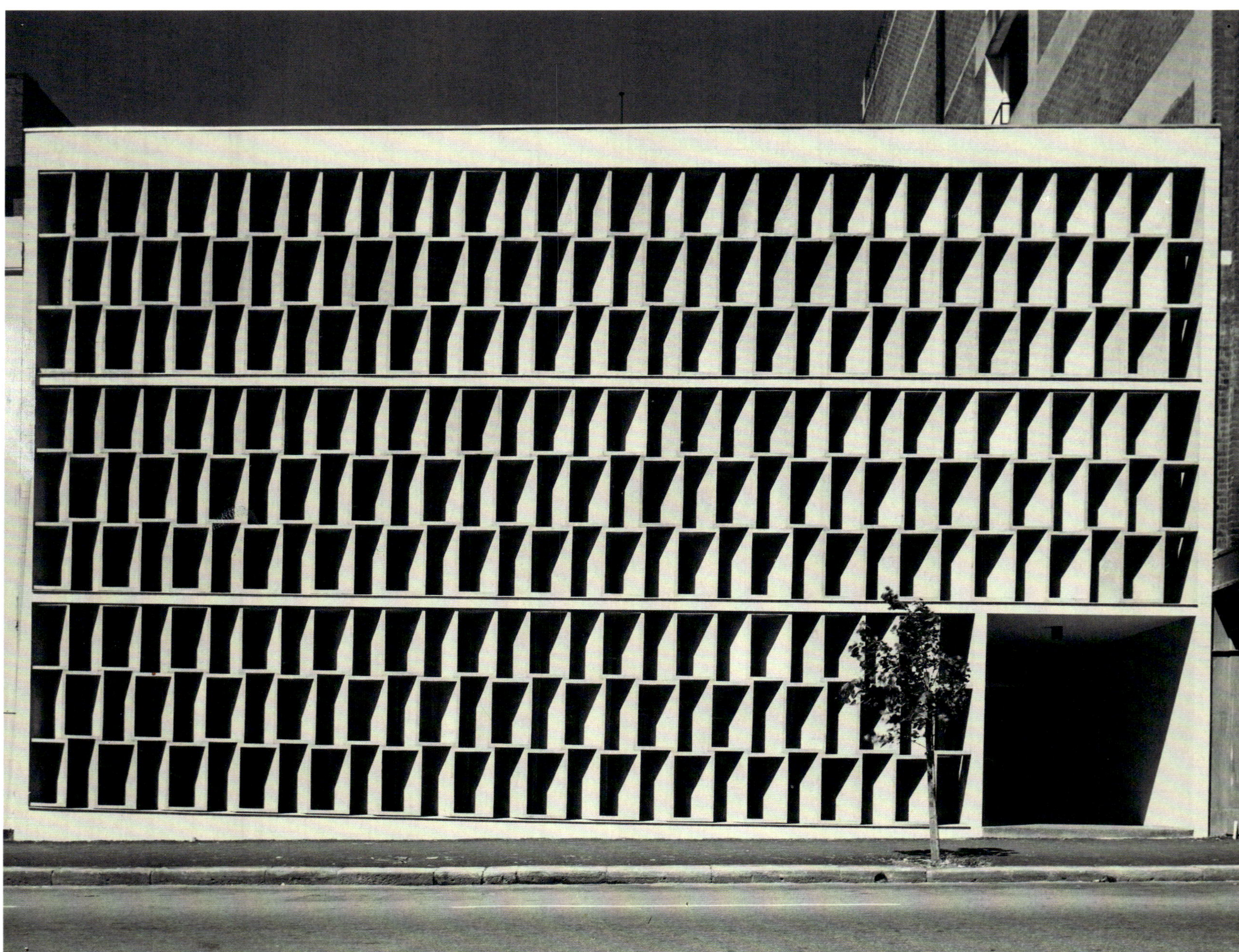

Below Harry Seidler architecture, Horwitz House, Sussex Street, Haymarket, Sydney, exterior November 1955, gelatin silver photograph, cardboard, 59.1 × 47.8 cm, photo by Max Dupain

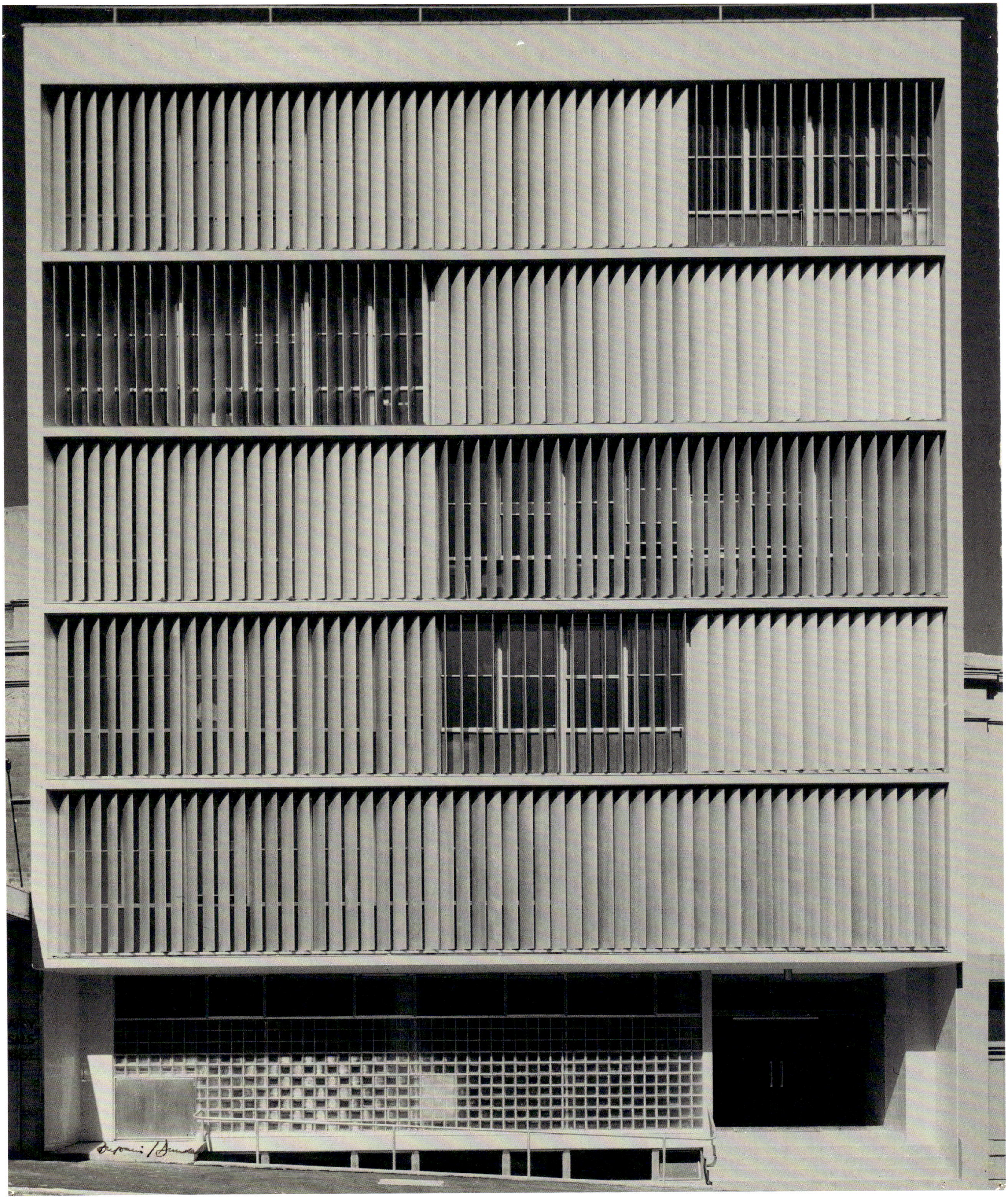

Below Harry Seidler architecture, Harry Seidler's Thurlow House, Blakehurst, NSW June 1954, gelatin silver photograph, cardboard, 58.1 × 47.5 cm, photo by Max Dupain

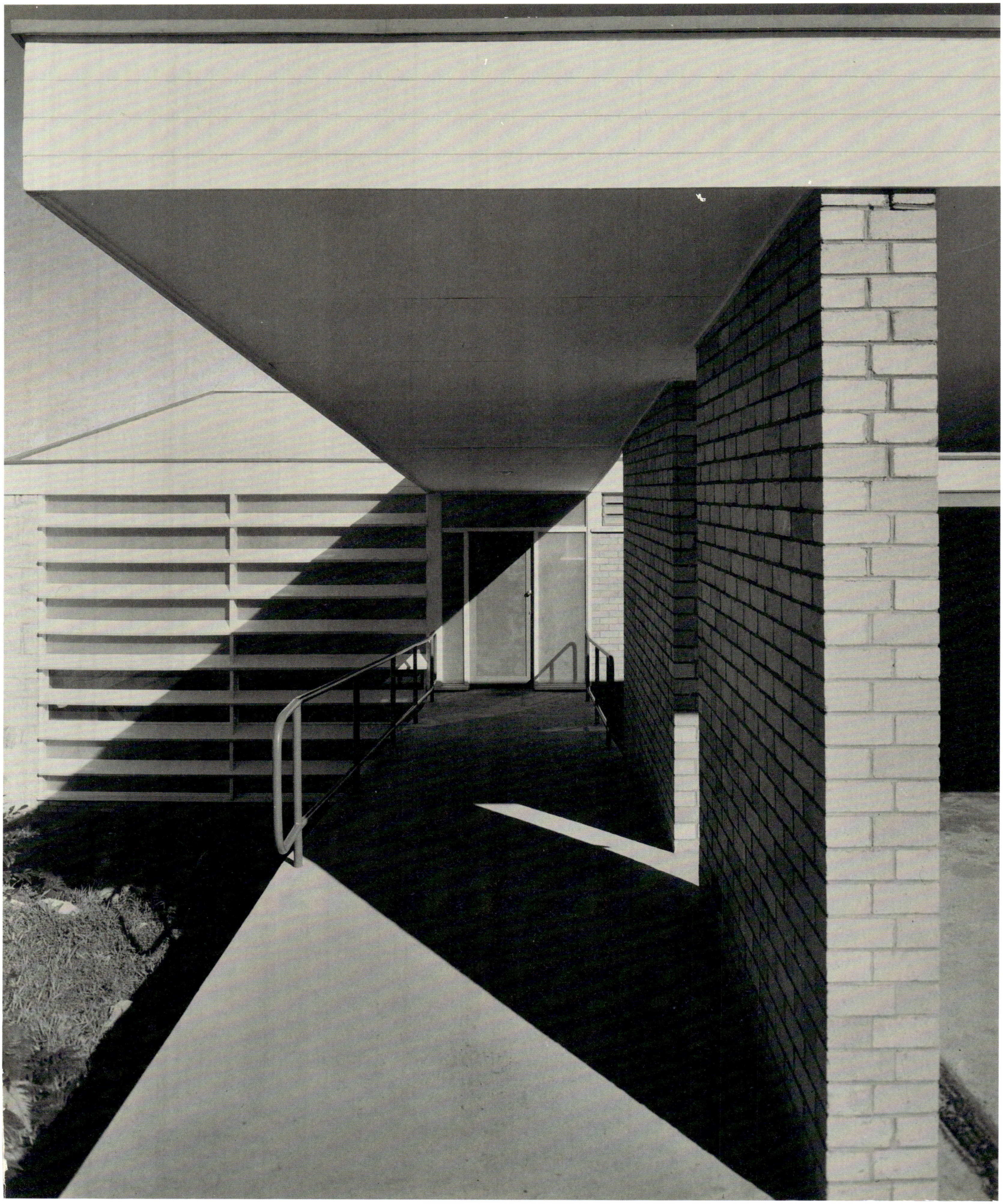

a gray one and it looks beautiful.

Wonderful, andnow will you send me the sizes that you want your frames made?

No, no, no, I am not ready for that now. Thank you awfully much, that's very good of you to remember.....there signing your things. Good, I'll call him quickly. Hold on. Ken Tyler is on the phone. How are you, are you feeling alright?

Very good, Annie, thank you.

All repaired?

All repaired.

That's good. Thats very wonderful.

It's hard to keep me down.

Very good, he is coming.

And how's the weather hhere? Has it rained up some?

We don't have time for it!

Well, when things go well the weather looks nice, and if its pouring. Just a moment.

Ken.

Good evening, Josef.

How are you?

Fine, how are you.

Ok, I'm signing now.

Wonderful . That's good.

~~Doggie would like to hear that now. He is standing in front of Annie's bed~~ Annie would like to hear that now.
Here stands in front of Annie's bed that frame you have sent her.

Good.

I have put in one of the grays, it looks just wonderful.

Yes, I'm glad you like it. Well, we're going to make up a set for you.

You probably called on Monday as you said in the letter/

Yes.

We were in New York so you missed us.

That's ok,

Did you get the new ones I sent?

Yes, the new samples are beautiful. We have already started work on one.

You brought in today this one, orange and deep orange here. Well, anyway, two things I feceived ;yesterday, and I send them tomorrow morning. That greenone and that deep orange one. Both are fine, particularly with the extra outer frame. Still better.

:You like that better? It's deeper.

The outer orange is a little bit lighter and therefore in that mixed color a little bit deeper.

Do you like the one with the lighter orange?

Yes.

Fine, and the green one worked okay when we increased the second frame.

I have to sign now, the 125 of number one.

Yes, the yellow.

Your yellow one.

Are you signing that Josef Albers?

With my initials A-66.

A-66.

Reduce it.

Reduce your surname. But Josef, will you sign the Gemini copies and the copy with your full name?

Yeah, I do not know where to put it. Behind the......now, on the left side now.

Is thenumber.

No, let me think of something....WLS-1. And then comes a little space and then comes 1/125, but I discover now you have 15 artists. Is that a little bit much?

No, they varyanywhere from 5 to 20, Josef, in this. We have to pull 50 extra prints to make sure that we have 125 good ones.

You see, I have discovered already in one of them, is a little spot in the lower edge of the yellow. I do not control the machine. That is your job. But, I put them so nice over each other that I can find them without doubling....make double numbers or leaving some numbers out.

Will the numbers of this print help you?

There wonderful, they are very helpful.

Ok.

Now you want to have a large number of artists pull?

No, not a large number, Josef, but we would like to have at least 15, and these would be the prints that we mail around to people.

so if they get damaged, we can then throw them away.

Gemini...Roman I and Roman II.

Those are perminent and they go to the museums for shows.

Where should I put that?

Anywhere that you want.

WLS is the title of that print, then comes number I. And there I say Gemini I and Gemini II and I put also there, trial proof and artist proof. And then I say ....you have an English word for it.

We use the English word right to pull.

Does that come after the trial proof instead of the number?

Yes, the only thing you put is "right to pull" and your name.

And the name's always on the right corner.

Your name is usually on the right corner.

This is my singature. A-66. Always on the right corner. And all these titles, Gemini

Is usually on the left side.

Like artist proof and trial proof. All on the left side right next to the title?

Yes,

Where the numbers are, the pull numbers.

That's correct. It is permissableto either sign the title first or the state proof first, whether it be artist proof or right to pull or what have you. It works either way......interruption

I start always with what?

WLS.

Is that one number Roman I? and then comes number of the pull number. IV, artists proof IV, trial proof IV, Gemini Roman I and Roman II, and then also .....

Well, the numbered impressions. The edition numbers.

A few on top, I put them on top, when YOu come I will ask ...a few have no red ink indications of what to put on them.

Oh, well those are probably extras, Josef, in case something happened when you were signing. But when I come to see you we can go over those. I am concerned aba out.... can you manage to repack those?

The man, when I came back today from Richport, I was there in the early afternoon, there was an auto and one of your boxes. and I said to him, you must be the boss, because the big ....in your hands. He said he would after an agrreement with you, do the packing. Well, I should call him and get the calling cards? I put the boxes in and just ask him to put the rubbers around? and inside and then

use the same boxes, I guess.

Wonderful. That would be very nice. If you could ask can ask that gentleman, give my address, I will write him a letter authorizing him to re-pack and to bill us and thlen we will also make arrangements for insurance with him.

He asked me, shouldn't he do the re-packing, and I said that I had an agreement with you. He said yes.

That's fine, we could not find any information regarding the packing from over here so if you have the gentleman's card I would you appreciate you telling him to just write me.

He is not in New Haven, but in a little town. But he is working with the packing.

Anyway, I will show him the boxes and I will call him to tell him.

Wonderful

It seems that is going very smooth now.

Yes, its picking up, Josef, we---- the gray is very, very, difficult to print, very slow, because we had to be very careful because the color was very transparent. But we are all through with that and we are starting on the brown one that you sent me. And now, the color ones will go faster.

The brown one, I think we put more to the middle.

To the second frame? Or to the center?

No, I mean in numbering them, the Roman numbers WLS number I is the first yellow one, and then comes one of the gray ones,

It wouldn't make any difference which one you chose first.

I would like to ask that somebddy shows the whole collection, that there is a rhythm in it that the black ones I fit all of them on one spot. Then we have a yellow, and then gray, and then orange, and then black-brown, something like that.

Well, if you want them Josef, this might be better, why don't you just sign WLS and your name, and then when we finished all of them, you will decide which order to put them, in, and then we will just put the Roman numerals in ourselves.

I think that makes another pencil, though. That makes looks funny.

Well, couldn't I use the same pencil you use?

No, your handwriting may be different, I shall do it here. I have three boxes from you. I have the full set of number Roman I, and then from the gray I have only half of it but you said in your letter that two boxes are on the way.

We made sure that they were very dry before we sent them to you. They were drying very, very slowly, and I didn't want to send them to you if they were a little bit wet for fear that they might scratch.

Have more of those frames?

Yes, I have made a whole set for ;you.

That means ten.

Yes, so we will keep sending you the plastic frames as we finish the prints.

Let's also watch that the arrangement of the white lines, that is either within the center, or it is in the double , or the outerone. I have the feeling that we have more of the ....type and very few of the outer range.

Yes, right now we have the yellow one which is in the center, we have two grays which where it is in the second frame, we have one gray where it is in the center, we have the brown and red one where it is on the outside, we have the green.

A little bit evenly distributed.

Yes, and you have the green and the blue which is on the outside. Now you sent me two more with tehe lines on the outside.

I like the outside especially because they are the most difficult ones for me to make.

They are the most difficult for us, too. That is very difficult to get the interaction when we have the big frame. It has to do with the amount of color, but it is helping each time I talk with you you give me more clues.

How many prints do you have now to be done?

Right now I have nine.

You have nine. Isn't there a duplication of that that you sent me today with the green one, the orange one, the deep orange one. Didn't I send you one that's almost the same?

No, yours is brown on the outside, Josef. You start with brown ....

Yellow.....

And then you have one you sent me that's yellow that goes to red in the center.

Don't we have duplications of the reds in the center?

No.

That's godd. Because that wouldn't be so nice. I wouldn't like that. Well, anyway, it seems...I have sent you enought color samples that you can just continue to finish this year. But this exclusive one, yeah.

Yes, we have been talking with the Los Angeles County Museum of Art. Mr. Hopkins. We hope to visit you the first week in June.

The first week in June you want to come.

I was going to come sooner and help you sign, but evidentally, we're doing okay by themail.

No, you don't need to come for that.

Okay, fine. Mr. Hopkins will be in New YOrk that first week, and we wanted to talk to you about the Museum show, of the prints, and to arrange for an international showing. Along with the catalogue.

Why is that man from..........

Becasue he did not have the time and I felt Mr. Hopkins was more simpathetic

to you. He understands you very well, he has watched you all of his life, and he is a great admiéer of yours. I feel he will get a better job. Beside that, it is a bigger museum and they will be able to do a better job on the show. /I/ I'm very ///// much in favor of having a very beautiful catalogue and a very nice show to travel.

You are happy with the material I send you?

Excellent, Josef.

YOU think its promising?

Oh, I think its ver, very, promising, /////the white lines

The white lines have been a new inventioN????

Yes, and this is why I think we should put a beautiful catalogue in a show together because of it.

The gray one is dark on the outside.

Thats a beautiful ////

So you are pleased with the whole affair?

Very, happy, Josef.

That is good. Now, then I think I should stick now to the signing of the things I have and then you send me as soon as you can these new proofs and gray on that and it seems that I have to paint one more.

Yes, we would also......

Explain in a note which one is needing and edition. Let's say the small white , or it goes in the middle or it goes in the outside, you know. Which one is in the minority. I cannot/ You will count that, I cannot......

Okay, I will count that and get a letter to you in the next day.

I am not in that hurry. But Annie just said... I had no blue one. It was my plan to bring something blue into it.

The only ones that have any red to them are the green..yellow outside, that goes to a red center, and the brown one that you approved that goes to a red center. The one we're working on now. But they are two different reds. And they will not read as red.

How do the boys like that stuff?

They love it. It's a real challenge, Josef, I think we have done a great deal for lithography. The fitting is working beaufifully.

The fitting is so excellent.

I think we have made a break through, and we congratulate you. I believe the white line and the tight fitting has produced a very remarkable print.

It is remarkable....at first things were sometime s lost, you know. It's now so convincing.

Its because of you. I would like very, very much, if we possibley could, to eventually come up with about 15 to make this show.

In different prints?

Yes,

No, these prints ten, or the nine so far, have taken derrific time of my life. Really, it so a delicate affair to develpp these things, I put themiddle the yellow, I use all of my expectations, it just doesn't do what I hoped it would do.

Yes.

With this color you are fooled all yur life, it, never you can prddict how much it truly means.

I would like to be able to produce more than ten.

In oneportfolio?

Not necessariyly, one portfolio Josef, we were thnking more in terms of having more for the museum show. And I would like to go over the many proofs that I gave you that one time. To see if we can't pull some more from there.

No, I don't think there is much possibilites with the white lines. Otherwise if we would produce gray.... with the white lines, this is a devil not easy to get under command. It's vrry, very, difficult/ really, it makes my neck all...... Well, but I think it came out.

I think its worth it.

Very good, worth it.

Well, wonderful, and we will continue this and I will get you the new samples as quickly as I can. And then I'll correspond with you.

I'll send you tomorrow the green .

And the blue.

The green-blue one and the other deep orange one.

Right, now do you have any studies for a blue print.

I have one began, but it has for me, most other grays, and I don't like to ingringe the grays in that series.

If I sent you some of the paper which we printed in blue, when we first started in February, and you cut the paper up, would that help ;you? Let me send those to you, Josef, there are some interesting views perhaps you can make something from them. And it might give us another color for the series.

Annie is right, blue is absolutely missing .

I agree, I think blue would be very beautiful. It would give a nice balance.

Yea.

I will send you those, then. Wonderful. Then we will get a hold of the man who will do the re-crating. And then we will instruct him as to the amount of insurance. Wonderful, Josef. Then I will correspond with you by letter soon. Wondefful.

Nice talking with you.

good night

Bye now.

Below Ludwig Hirschfeld-Mack, *Optischer Farbmischer* (*Optical colour mixer*) 1950s, wood; drawing in fibre-tipped colour pen on paper, 10 × 6.8 (diam) cm (each)

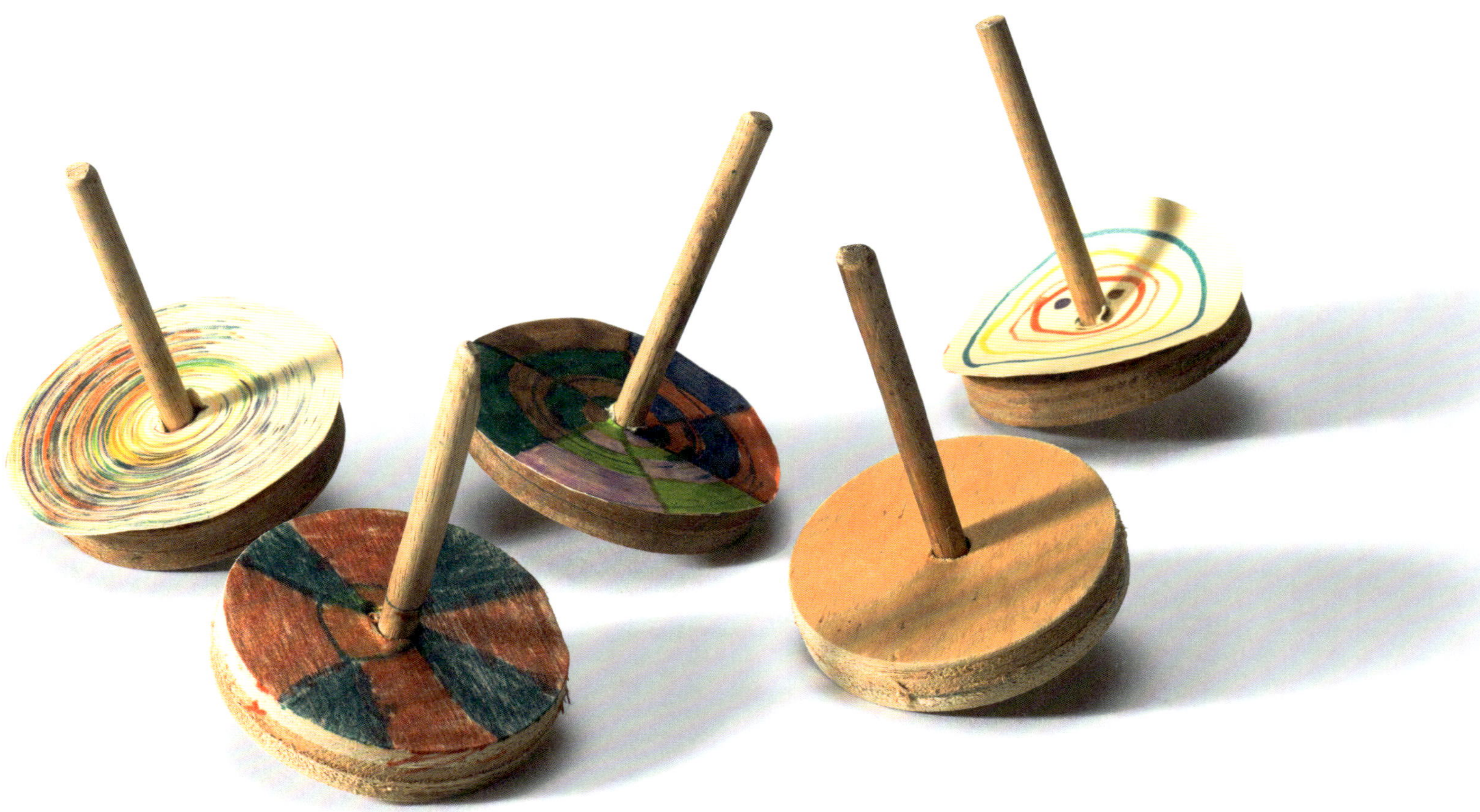

Top Ludwig Hirschfeld-Mack, Stringed instrument (12 strings) 1950s, wood, wire, 8 × 25.5 × 37.5 cm
Bottom Ludwig Hirschfeld-Mack, Piano accordion, c 1933–36, wood, vinyl, pearl shell, leather, metal, paper, paint, 16.9 × 30 × 35.7 cm

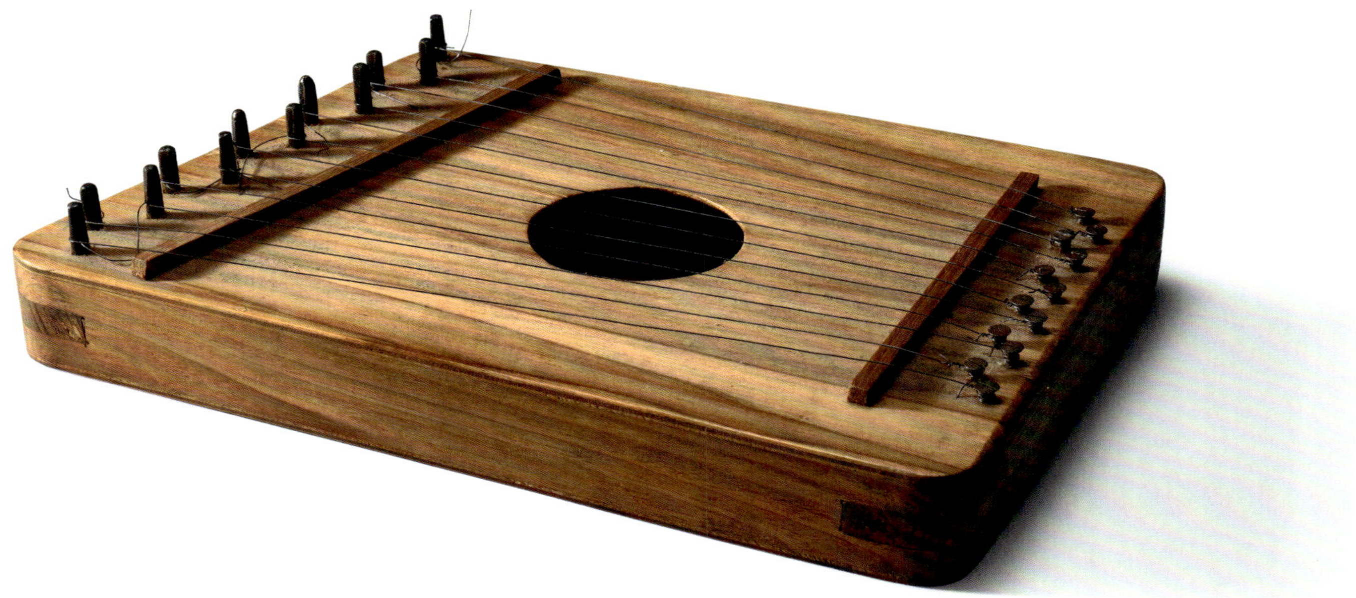

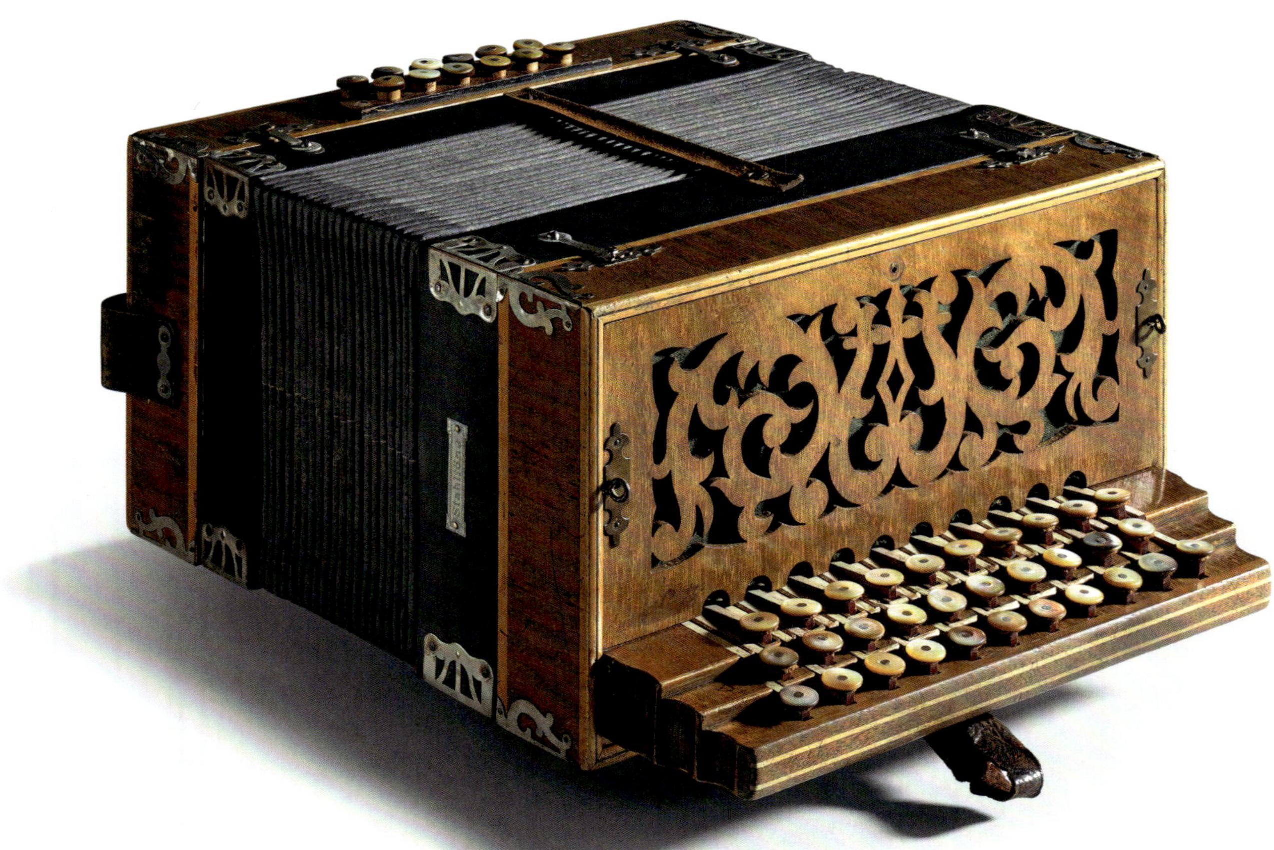

Below Ludwig Hirschfeld-Mack, *Colour chord (Queen Mary)* c 1936–39, wood, wire, 11.7 × 97.5 × 12.1 cm

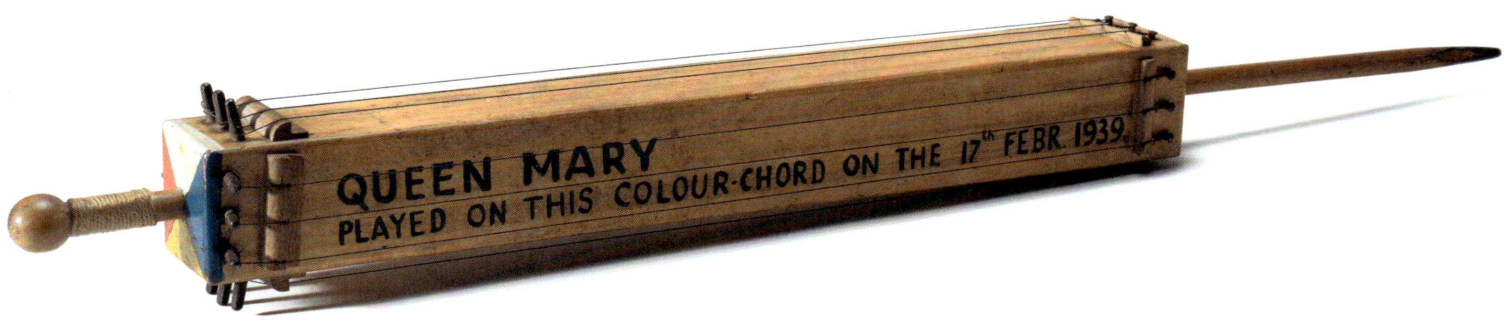

 Below Ludwig Hirschfeld-Mack, *Not titled* 1921–22, oil on canvas, 77 × 53.5 cm

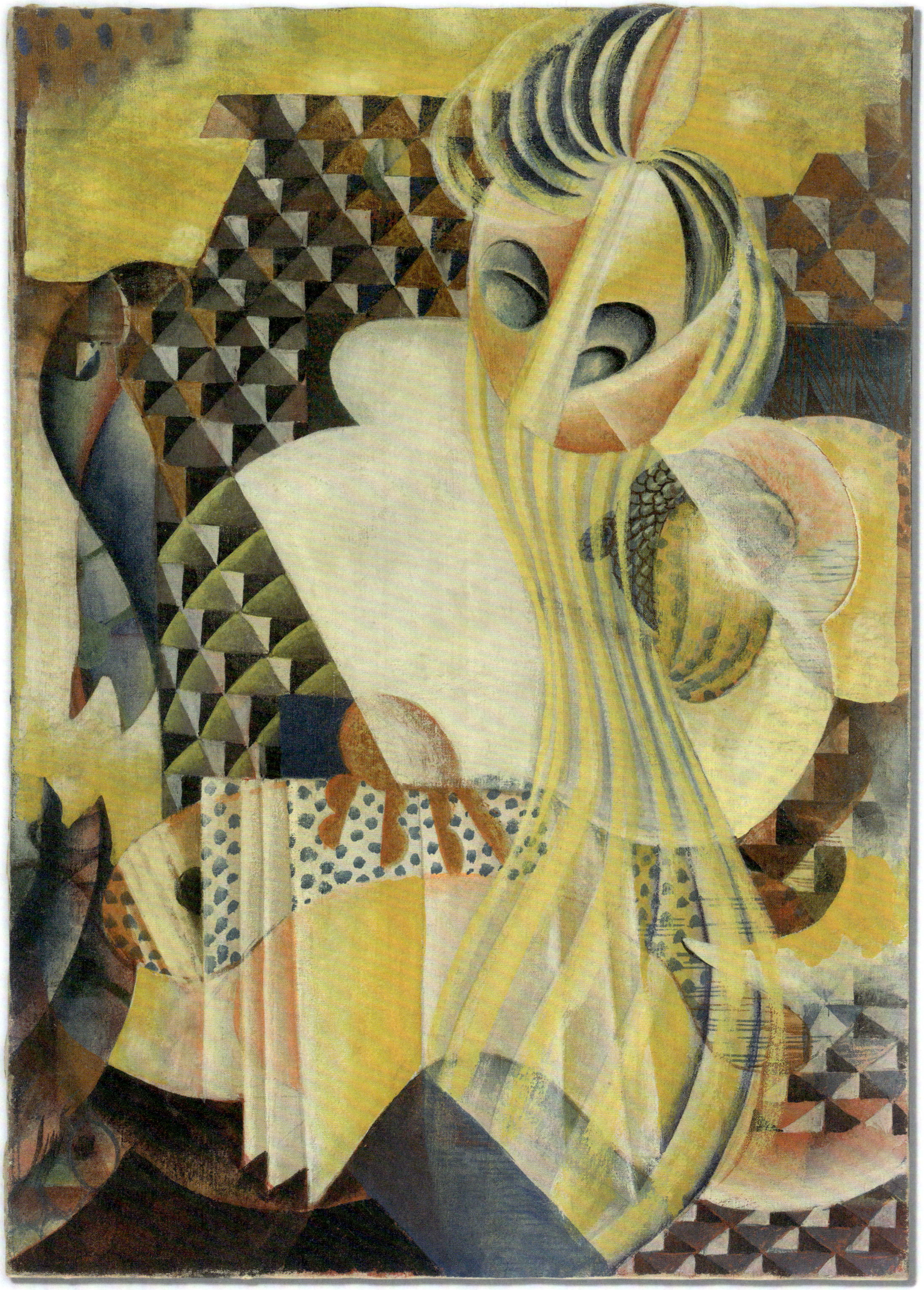

The Alberses and Hirschfeld-Mack: a Bauhaus friendship

Ann Stephen

The friendship between Josef and Anni Albers and Ludwig Hirschfeld-Mack developed during the short life of the Weimar Bauhaus. Though subsequently separated by cities, then continents and, in the case of Hirschfeld-Mack, extreme circumstances, they built a long-distance relationship that would span more than four decades based on a shared passion and belief in Bauhaus ideas. The following account begins when they were Bauhaus students and then draws on personal correspondence from the mid 1930s and a later exchange between 1958 and 1965.[1]

Bauhaus days

When the architect Walter Gropius launched the State Bauhaus in Weimar with a manifesto in 1919, Hirschfeld-Mack was among the first to enrol in October that year, for the winter semester. He was mature beyond his 26 years, having studied art in Munich and then later Stuttgart, in between serving five years in the German army. Albers arrived the following year in the autumn of 1920. At 32 he was the most senior Bauhaus student, and had worked as an art teacher during the First World War after training in Berlin, Essen and Munich. His future life-partner, Annelise Fleischmann (later Anni Albers), enrolled in 1923 aged 23. Most Bauhäuslers, as Hirschfeld-Mack recalled, were 'in their early twenties; two thirds of them were men, half of whom had served in the army during the war'.[2] They took the preliminary course (*Vorkurs*) on material studies conceived by the artist and teacher Johannes Itten. Classes began with breathing exercises, after which the students engaged in collaborative work alongside nature studies, compositional analyses of 'old master' reproductions, and workshops on the principles of colour, design and form. Itten applied the theories of colour and abstract forms taught by Adolf Hölzel, with whom Hirschfeld-Mack had also studied at the Kunstakademie Stuttgart in 1918–19.[3]

One of Hirschfeld-Mack's student paintings, made in 1921–22 at the Bauhaus, recently acquired by the National Gallery of Australia, reveals his fascination with colour and music. In the composition, curving lines of transparent yellow paint cascade from a Brancusi-like head with enlarged almond eyes, through hands and across an accordion. The popular folk instrument had a special significance for Hirschfeld-Mack as he played one in the early days of the Bauhaus band, joined by fellow students on xylophones and some homemade percussion instruments. Years later he mentions to the Alberses that 'my old *Ziehharmonika* [accordion] which I used in Weimar is still alive & I still play old tunes. If you have a tape recorder, I'll make a tape recording of them for you.'[4] In the painting its abstracted button keys and bellows generate a series of horizontal bands in muted primary colours, across an optical grid of coloured triangles that sweep around a figure to indicate waves of sound. The golden light that flows from the musician's forehead conveys Hirschfeld-Mack's belief that 'creativeness is given to every human being. It springs from a quiet point of concentration, a divine centre or inner light within every person.'[5] As an apprentice, then journeyman, in the Bauhaus print workshop, his vision of a synthesis of art and music found its finest expression at the time in a colour lithograph, *Sterntänzer* (*Star dancer* or *Reaching for the stars*) 1922. A cubist dancer, made of chord shards and shafts of light, straddles the earth while playing the moon like an instrument.

In contrast, Josef Albers approached coloured light as a materialist, shedding any symbolism associated with colour. As a student, he scavenged discarded coloured glass bottles, cutting and assembling them into grids that he mounted in square

1 There are 22 letters in all: 11 Albers letters are held in the University of Melbourne Archive (hereafter UMA) and an equal number by Hirschfeld-Mack are held in the Josef and Anni Albers Foundation, Bethany, Connecticut (hereafter JAAF). The UMA also holds considerable correspondence between Hirschfeld-Mack and Bauhaus director Walter Gropius. All translations from the German are by Raoul Middleman, unless otherwise identified.

2 Ludwig Hirschfeld-Mack, *The Bauhaus: an introductory survey*, Longmans, Croydon, Victoria, 1963, pp 4, 5.

3 Éva Forgács, *The Bauhaus idea and Bauhaus politics*, trans John Bákti, Central European University Press, Budapest, 1995, ch 6.

4 Ludwig Hirschfeld-Mack, letter to Josef Albers, 27 June 1961, Papers of Josef and Anni Albers, JA 4–50_1958–1965_Lud series 1, box 4, folder 50, JAAF.

5 Ludwig Hirschfeld-Mack, art education lecture, UNESCO, 1954, quoted in Resi Schwarzbauer with Chris Bell, *Ludwig Hirschfeld-Mack: more than a Bauhaus artist*, HistorySmiths, Thornbury, Victoria, 2021, p 244.

frames like secular stained-glass windows. These 'translucent compositions' have been described by art historian Jean Clay as introducing 'an unpredictable, changing element into painting' with 'the light ... a convenient medium to demonstrate (thanks to its transparency) the kinetic instability rather than a symbolical idea.'[6] By 1922 Albers had advanced rapidly in the Bauhaus, becoming master of the glass workshop. At that time, Hirschfeld-Mack was struck by the possibilities of projecting coloured light when he observed the accidental effects produced by a Bauhaus shadow play. He presented his experiments *Farbenlichtspiele* (*Colour light plays*) on a specially created apparatus accompanied by his own musical score at the 1923 Bauhaus Week. The performance caused a sensation and was described by art historian Éva Forgács as one of 'continuous motion', in which 'the series of colour- and form-compositions were constantly changing and the picture not only moved, but moved out into space', and 'light endowed [the] works with a cosmic character'.[7]

At this time, however, the mounting economic crisis of the Weimar Republic confronted Gropius with an existential dilemma, forcing him to reorient Bauhaus teaching towards industrial production so that the school could survive. The shift to utilitarian concerns caused irresolvable differences with Itten and his mystical Mazdaznan teachings.[8] Itten resigned, and Gropius appointed Albers in his place to teach the preliminary course. In the interregnum, during the winter of 1922–23, Hirschfeld-Mack made charts to demonstrate principles of colour theory for a series of seminars he delivered on colour.[9] Albers, in line with the new direction, wrote that his aim was 'to bring the art training hitherto isolated from practical life into harmony with the actual demands of contemporary life' for a special issue of *Junge Menschen* (*Young People*) in 1924, devoted to the Bauhaus.[10] In the same issue, the precocious young Annelise Fleischmann published her first essay on Bauhaus weaving, arguing for a future of mass textile production and experimentation. The art historian T'ai Smith has observed that she had astutely 'crafted a flexible text that addressed, all at once, weaving's past, present and future'.[11] This turn to industry, as Hirschfeld-Mack noted, acknowledged that 'nearly all the students were poor and had to earn their living at the Bauhaus by producing saleable goods in the workshops'.[12] Josef Albers designed domestic ware, while Anni Albers and her fellow weavers created fabric to be sold by the metre.[13] Hirschfeld-Mack's coloured spinning top, which he described as an optical colour mixer (*Optischer Farbmischer*) was licensed as a toy in 1924 and was among the Bauhaus's most successful products. However, by 1925, when Gropius was forced by a combination of economic and political forces to relocate the school to Dessau, Hirschfeld-Mack parted ways with the Bauhaus and directed his energies to *Farbenlichtspiele* performances, alongside teaching.

Exile

When the National Socialists seized power in 1933, secular Jews like Anni Albers, or so-called 'half-Jews' like Hirschfeld-Mack, were confronted by a raft of restrictive anti-Semitic race laws. The Alberses were among the first wave of some 37 000 emigrants of Jewish origin who left Germany that year, after Josef was offered a teaching position at the progressive Black Mountain College in North Carolina. Hirschfeld-Mack's situation was more complex—his (non-Jewish) wife Elenor was disabled, and they had three young children. For several years he moved the family across Germany to teach in various progressive schools before the Nazis closed them down and excluded Jews from all cultural professions. Finally, he saw no option but to flee Germany for the United Kingdom in January 1936.

6 Jean Clay, 'Albers: three stages of a logic' (1968), reprinted in *Josef Albers: minimal means, maximum effect*, Fundación Juan March, Madrid, 2014, pp 337–38.

7 Forgács, p 93.

8 Mazdaznan was a neo-Zoroastrian cult that took off in America in the late nineteenth century and spread to Germany and Switzerland in the early twentieth century. It preached earthly renewal through a regime of breathing exercises, colonic irrigation and vegetarianism. Itten and his followers insisted on shaven heads and crimson robes.

9 Schwarzbauer with Bell, pp 49–63.

10 Josef Albers, 'Historical or contemporary?', originally published in German as 'Historische oder Jetzig?', *Junge Menschen* (Hamburg), vol 5, no 8, November 1924. Translated by Russell Stockman and reprinted in *Josef Albers: minimal means, maximum effect*, p 208.

11 T'ai Smith, *Bauhaus weaving theory: from feminine craft to mode of design*, Minnesota Press, Minneapolis, 2014, p 47.

12 Hirschfeld-Mack, 1963, pp 4, 5.

13 Smith, p 43.

Top	Ludwig Hirschfeld-Mack, *Bauhaus Ausstellung Weimar* (*Bauhaus exhibition, Weimar*) 1923, lithograph, sheet 9 × 14 cm
Bottom	Ludwig Hirschfeld-Mack, *Colour chart, blue, yellow, red on black* 1922, collage, 29.5 × 45.3 cm

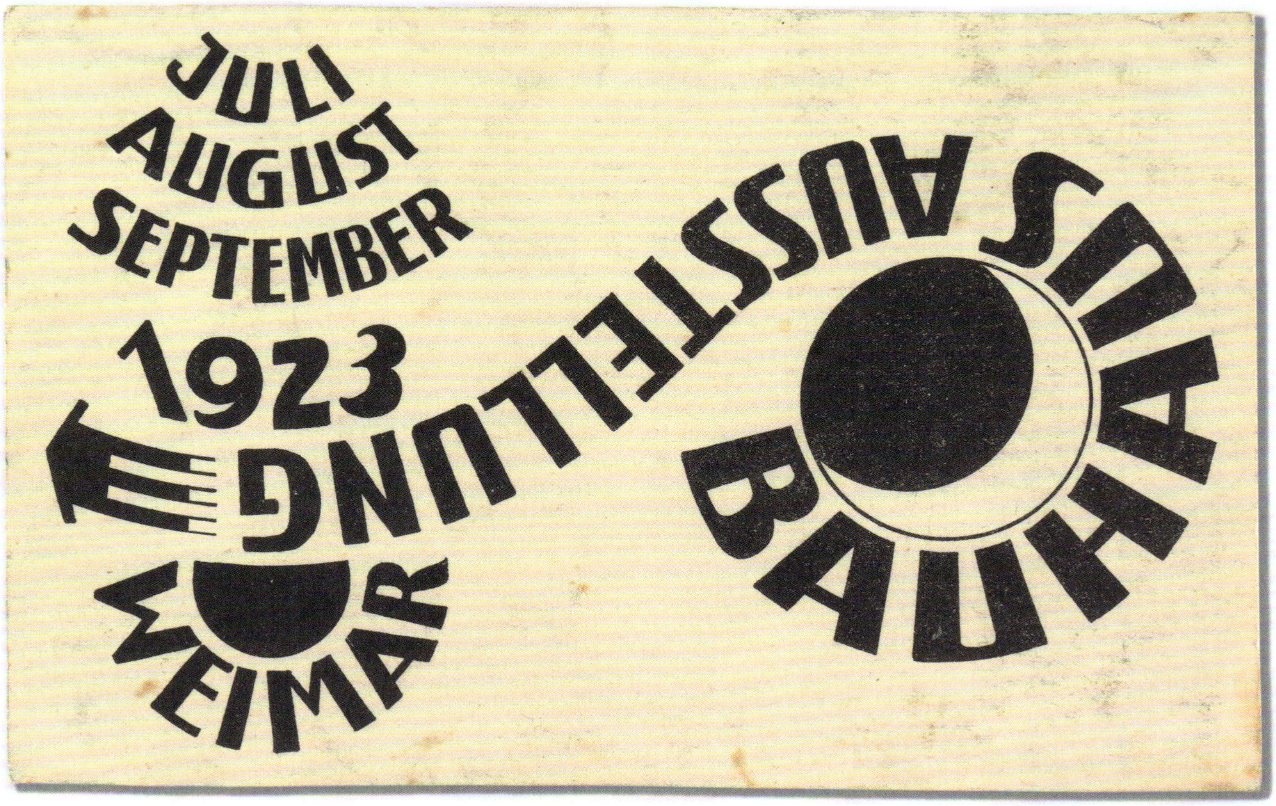

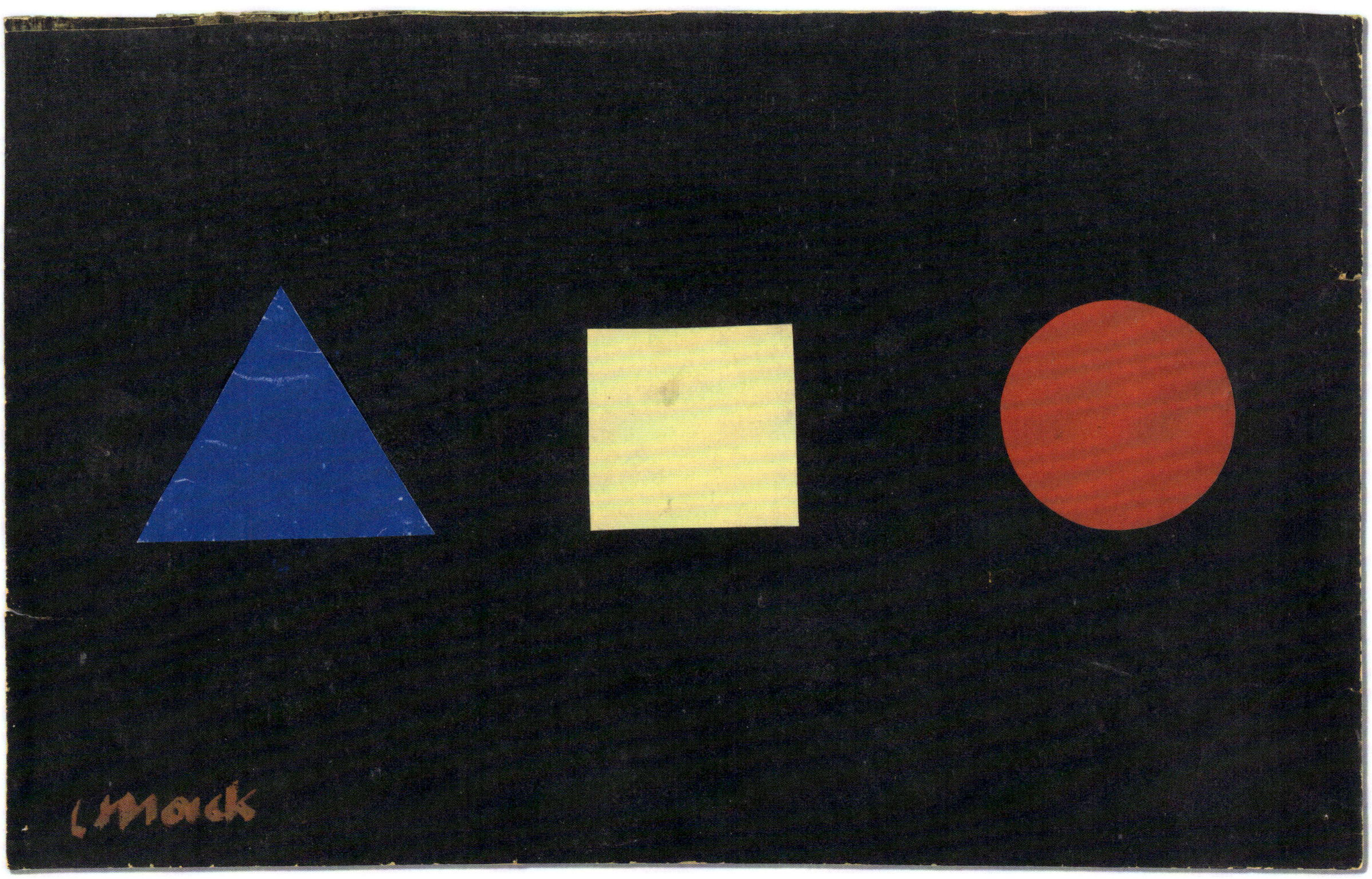

Below Ludwig Hirschfeld-Mack, *Postkarte zur Bauhaus-Ausstellung* (*Postcard for the Bauhaus-exhibition*) 1923, lithograph, sheet 10 × 15 cm

Next Ludwig Hirschfeld-Mack, *Ziehharmonika Spieler* (*Accordion player*) c 1922, watercolour and gouache on paper, 20.1 × 26 cm

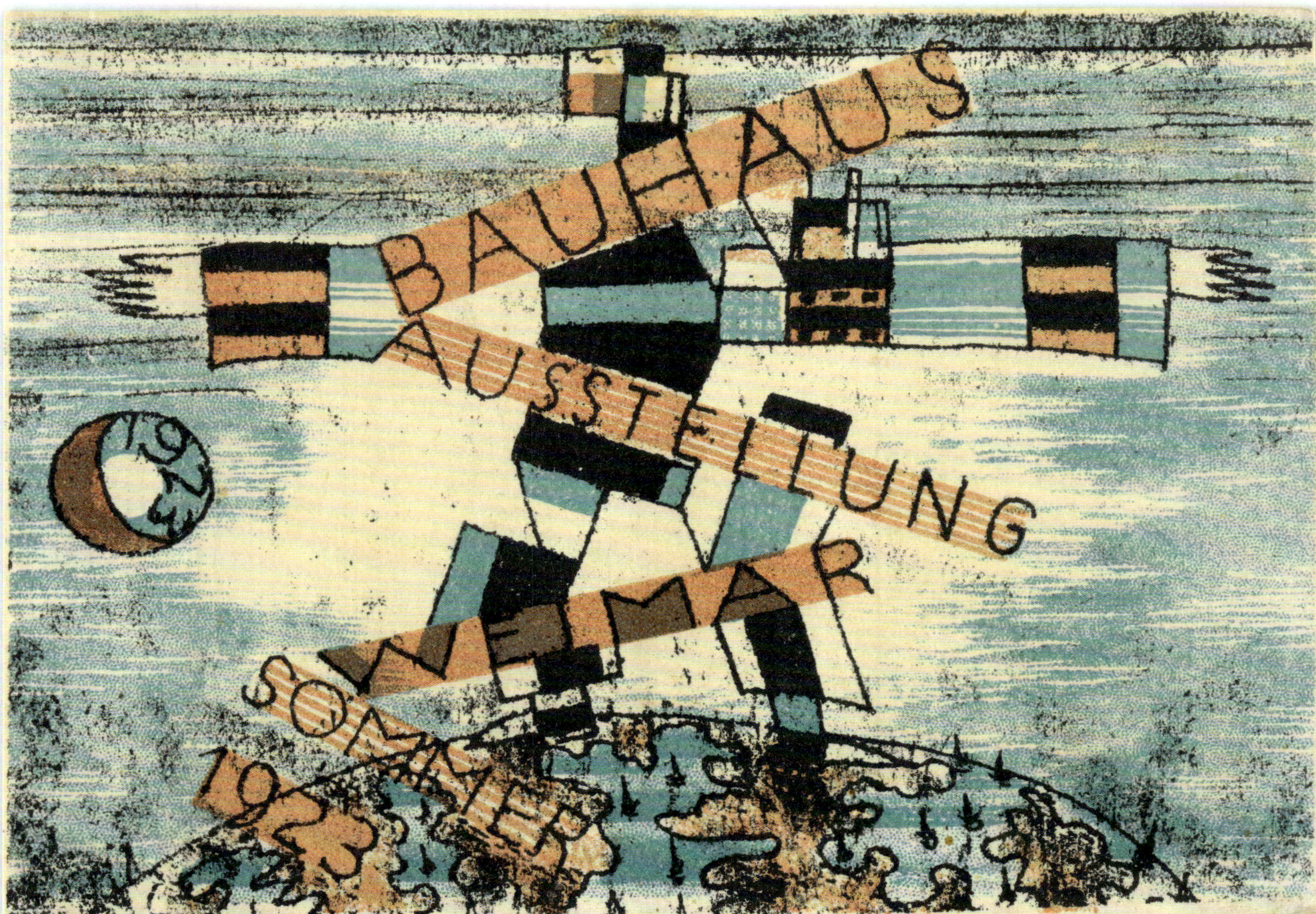

An intense correspondence began between the Alberses and Hirschfeld-Mack after he arrived in London. He saw it as a half-way stop en route to the United States. Like many other artists and intellectuals on the run from the Nazis, he held out hope for the possibility of finding work in the States. He appealed to '*Mein lieber Jupp*', as he called Josef Albers, who replied explaining the difficulties confronting immigrants, the attitude 'that foreigners are not wanted', and suggested contacting Sigmund Freud's son, the architect Ernst Freud, another refugee in the United Kingdom, who had three children at Dartington Hall, a progressive school in rural Devon partly inspired by the Bauhaus.[14] Nothing came of this suggestion. Over the following month, Albers became more positive, writing that 'people will be interested that Hirschfeld-Mack was at the Bauhaus', and urged him to send a curriculum vitae. He mentioned that 'before Christmas Gropius came from Harvard' and had told Anni there was a position for Hirschfeld-Mack. Albers went on to list their former colleagues who were now in the United States: 'Xanti [Alexander Schawinsky] at Black Mountain; Lajko [Marcel Breuer] at Harvard with Gropius; [László] Moholy-Nagy has opened the New Bauhaus in Chicago; Mies [Ludwig Mies van der Rohe] in NY.'[15] Albers continued to send a stream of potential contacts, from the Progressive Education Association in New York, Chicago and Indianapolis; the National Coordinating Committee for German Refugees; and the Institute for International Education, advising Hirschfeld-Mack to 'state the percentage of non-Aryan blood in his veins & the consequences for Hirschfeld-Mack and family in Germany'. He then included a personal reference, describing his friend as 'a person who is full of music and who has the native knack of instilling his own enthusiasm in children'.[16] Still nothing eventuated, so Hirschfeld-Mack took up an offer to coordinate a Quaker Subsistence Program for unemployed miners in Pontypool, South Wales.

Albers wrote in May and again in July, expressing relief that Hirschfeld-Mack had found work but asked whether he 'has given up his American plans or only postponed them?'[17] Albers appears to have continued to work behind the scenes, as Hirschfeld-Mack's eldest daughter Marga, who was with a Quaker refugee program in London, received a letter from Black Mountain College in mid 1940 informing her 'that everything is arranged for him and he is expected to start 9th September as students are expecting him'.[18] This missive came too late, for on 12 May 1940 Hirschfeld-Mack was rounded up and imprisoned as an 'enemy alien' along with over 70 000 Germans and Austrians, most of them Jewish, living in the United Kingdom. Two months later he was transported to Australia with over 2500 others on the infamous transport ship HMT *Dunera*. Throughout his internment, his letters to his daughters and family indicate that he still held out some hope of emigrating to the United States. In May 1941 a two-year contract arrived from Black Mountain College while he was still in detention in Australia; however by then, US immigration law had prohibited visas to 'any person who had blood relations in a German-controlled territory'.[19] In March 1942, following 22 months' incarceration, Hirschfeld-Mack was finally released, again at the intervention of Quaker connections, to teach art at Geelong Grammar School, a boys' boarding school with a progressive headmaster in the Victorian port city. He remained committed to teaching there for the next 15 years, despite an offer from the New Bauhaus in Chicago in 1947.

The Bauhaus reconstructed

The most sustained correspondence between them occurred after both Hirschfeld-Mack and Josef Albers retired in 1958. Josef spoke for them all when he wrote of finally wanting 'to have time for his own nonsense ... to paint and write very much more on art, education, aesthetics as ethics.'[20] Their renewed exchange was sparked off by

14 Josef and Anni Albers, letter to Hirschfeld-Mack, 1 February 1936, Unit 1: 1971.0009.0004, Hirschfeld-Mack Collection, UMA.

15 Josef Albers, letter to Hirschfeld-Mack, February 1936, Unit 1: 1971.0009.0005/4&5, Hirschfeld-Mack Collection, UMA.

16 Josef Albers, letter to Hirschfeld-Mack, 9 April 1936, Unit 1: 1971.0009.0005/1, Hirschfeld-Mack Collection, UMA.

17 Josef Albers, letter to Hirschfeld-Mack, 4 May 1936, Unit 1: 1971.0009.0005/3, Hirschfeld-Mack Collection, UMA.

18 Ludwig Hirschfeld-Mack, letter to daughter Marga Bell, 24 May 1941, quoted in Schwarzbauer with Bell, pp 168, 311.

19 Schwarzbauer with Bell, p 168.

20 Josef Albers, letter to Ludwig Hirschfeld-Mack, 7 June 1958, Unit 1: 1971.0009.0005/6, Hirschfeld-Mack Collection, UMA.

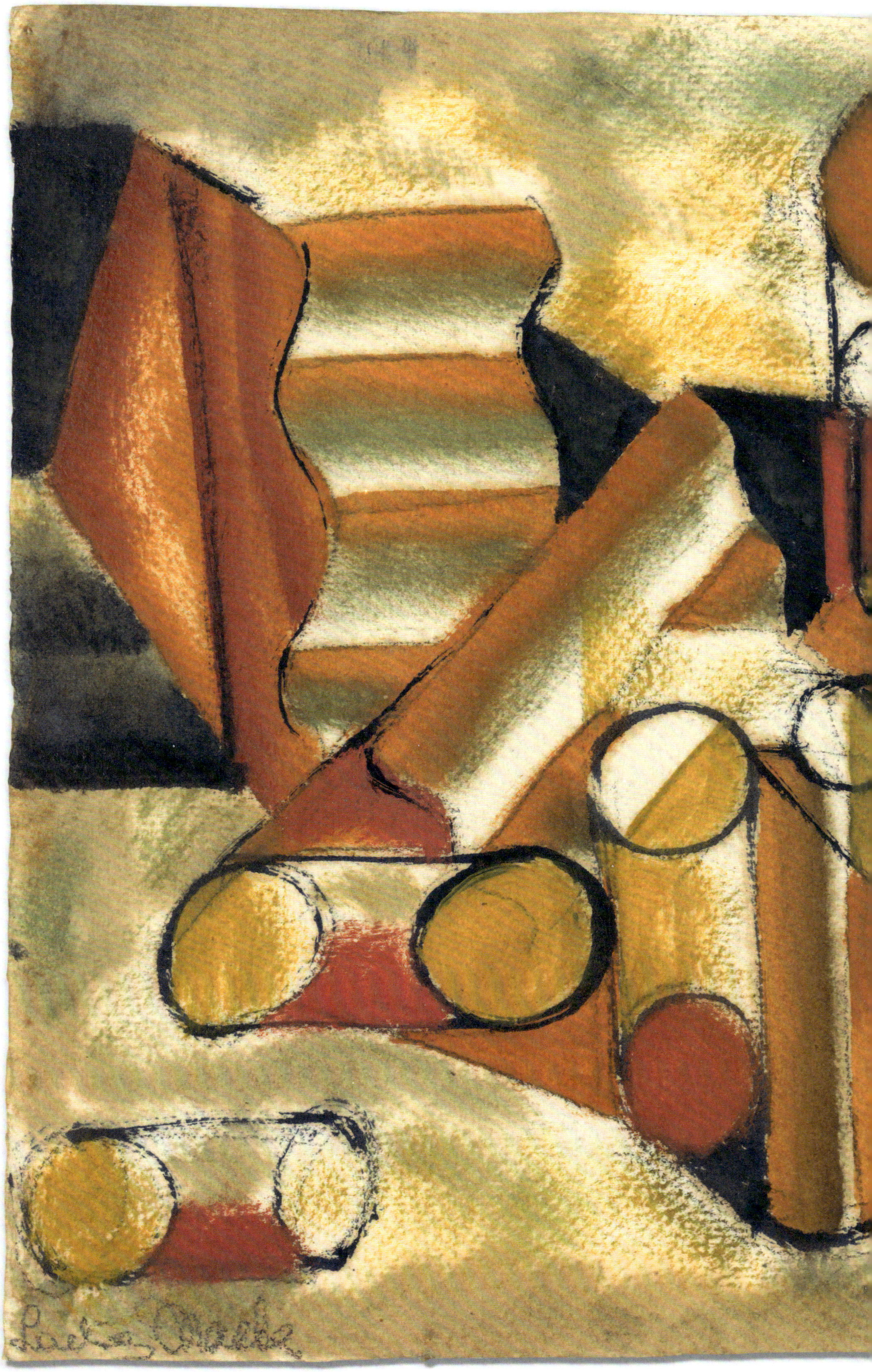

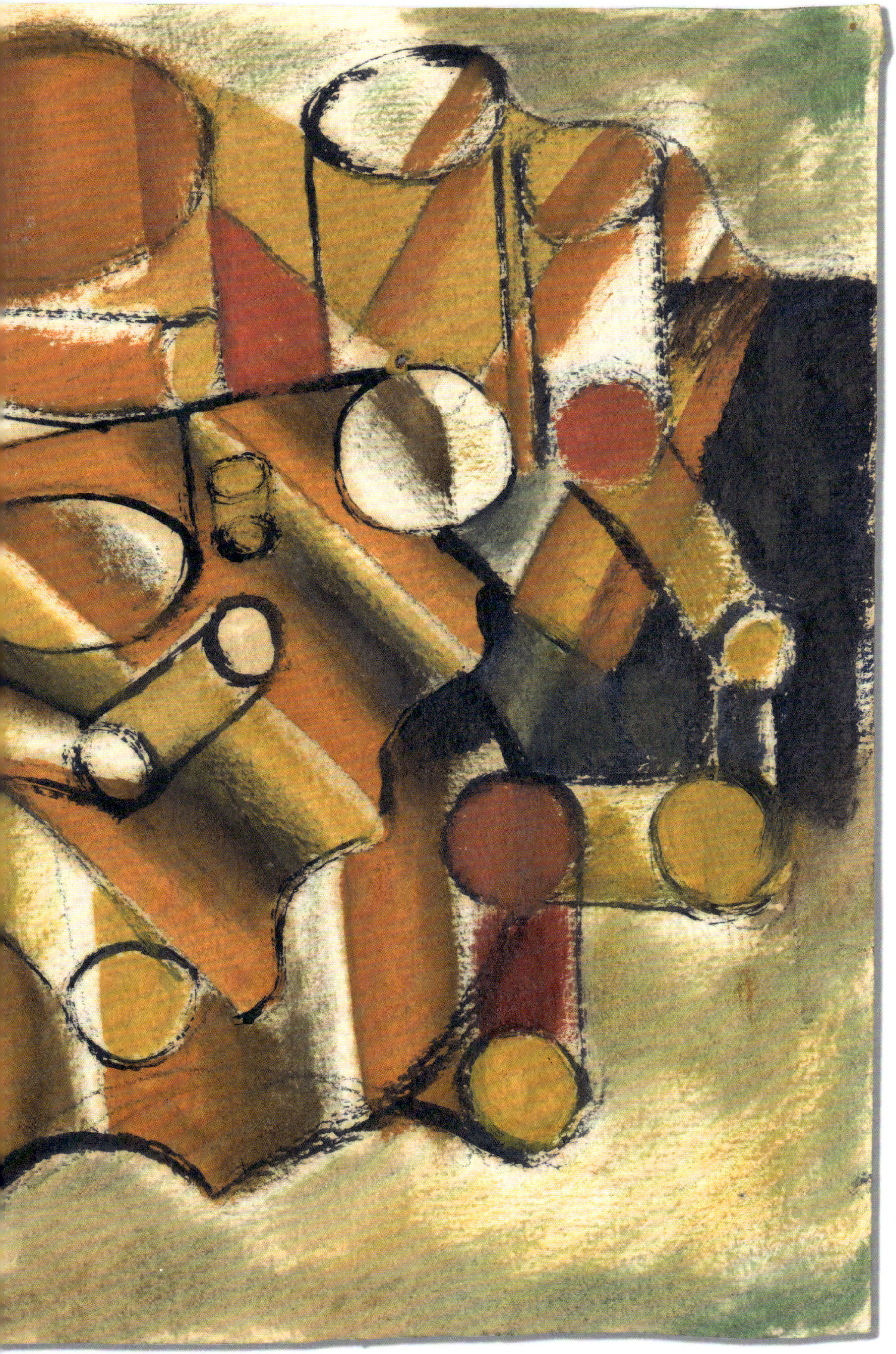

a new publication by Heinz Peters, titled *Die Bauhaus-Mappen: neue europäische Grafik, 1921–1923* (*Bauhaus portfolio: new European graphic art*) in 1957. Josef was outraged, largely on behalf of Hirschfeld-Mack, at this account of the Bauhaus print workshop: 'Let everyone see that the masters not only learnt from the journeymen but took over from them', he wrote, citing the covers that both had designed, which Peters had assumed to be solely the work of Paul Klee. He went further, expressing hope that Hirschfeld-Mack 'as the real producer of *Die Bauhaus-Mappen* will rectify this situation'.[21] Hirschfeld-Mack, who was travelling in Europe at the time, having been invited to remake his *Farbenlichtspiele* for the Bauhaus-Archiv, replied that as long as he could 'draw his lines, play his spinning tops and his music he does not ask for credit. Therefore Albers should not trouble himself.'[22]

A profound belief in an anti-individualistic creativity underpinned Hirschfeld-Mack's apparently self-deprecating response, as he later explained:

> At the Bauhaus—even in the beginnings at Weimar, I felt sometimes, too much effort was made by some people to propagate their own name and importance. When masters and apprentices were gathered for this now famous Weimar photo—I deliberately did not appear, because I felt then, there was too much emphasis on [the] individual for show. I remember I had several discussions about this problem in those days and I still maintain, that this special creative gift of the few, which lifts their work above average—belongs to humanity and is not for the benefit and fame for the individual—though I realize, we do not live in the Middle-ages, when artists worked for the 'praise of God' with complete disregard of their own posterity.[23]

The contact with his old Bauhaus friends appears to have spurred Hirschfeld-Mack to plan a Melbourne Bauhaus exhibition in 1961, coinciding with renewed interest both locally and internationally in his work. With the support of the young artist Clement Meadmore, Gallery A in Melbourne hosted an exhibition and published a catalogue that included Albers's print *Seclusion* 1942. Hirschfeld-Mack sent the Alberses his commentary from the catalogue and promised to 'write you soon at greater length and tell you more about this exhibition which will be an educational one with physiological experiments and not a sale exhibition'.[24] The day after the opening, Hirschfeld-Mack reported that 'a few hundred people had attended *Bauhaus Aspects & Influence*', explaining that the exhibition was 'mainly an educational one for students and secondary school students and … a preparation for teachers for the new Art Syllabus, 1963, which includes the study of the Bauhaus its history and influence in connection with "good design".'[25] He also mentioned that he had needed 'to reproduce my colour experiments of 1921–23 as my originals are all at the Bauhaus Archiv'.[26]

At the end of 1961 a parcel arrived from his friends, to which he responded:

> … your beautiful catalog of your latest works [the 1961 *Josef Albers* exhibition at the Stedelijk Museum, Amsterdam] and the interesting questions and answers. I will show and translate them to my pupils. The managing director of Gallery A was most impressed by your catalog. I like your concentration on one square in its composition and I can imagine meditation and concentration as they convey the greatest possible unity and simplicity. I am not so sure about the compositions with two units in one picture, the eye is not rested in one and is seeking for a third place to be satisfied—which is somehow invisible, setting the person looking at it in a state of restlessness. You probably intended to do this?[27]

21 Josef Albers, letter to Hirschfeld-Mack, 7 June 1958.

22 Ludwig Hirschfeld-Mack, letter to Josef Albers, July 1958, JA 4-50_1958-1965_Lud, JAAF.

23 Ludwig Hirschfeld-Mack, letter to Josef and Anni Albers, 21 July 1961, JA 4–50_1958–1965_Lud, JAAF.

24 Ludwig Hirschfeld-Mack, letter to Josef Albers, 24 June 1961, JA 4–50_1958–1965_Lud, JAAF; for an account of the exhibition see Ann Stephen, 'The Bauhaus: aspects and influence', in Philip Goad, Ann Stephen, Andrew McNamara et al (eds), *Bauhaus diaspora and beyond: transforming education through art, design and architecture*, Miegunyah Press, MUP, Carlton, 2019, ch 10.

25 Hirschfeld-Mack, letter to Josef and Anni Albers, 21 July 1961.

26 Ludwig Hirschfeld-Mack, letter to Josef Albers, 27 June 1961, JA 4–50_1958–1965_Lud, JAAF. Hirschfeld-Mack, with support from Sydney-based artist and teacher Lyndon Dadswell and Professor Joseph Burke in Melbourne, sought to bring Josef Albers to Australia for an exhibition and lecture tour, though this did not eventuate. Hirschfeld-Mack lists 26 colour charts that he sent to the Bauhaus Archiv.

27 Ludwig Hirschfeld-Mack to Josef and Anni Albers, 18 December 1961, JA 4–50_1958–1965_Lud, JAAF; listed among Hirschfeld-Mack's holdings are four Josef Albers catalogues, including the 1961 Stedelijk catalogue, 1971.0009.0048/2, Hirschfeld-Mack Collection, UMA.

His thoughtful response was entirely based on several black-and-white reproductions of the first of Albers's *Homage to the Square* series.

The Albers catalogue was a modest volume, as was Hirschfeld-Mack's small book *The Bauhaus: an introductory survey*, published two years later in 1963. The black-and-white illustrations succinctly surveyed the school's Weimar years: picturing Material Studies exercises from classes by Itten, Josef Albers and Moholy-Nagy; followed by his own Colour Experiments charts and Reflected Light Compositions; as well as products from all the workshops, including Josef's 1924 teacup from the metal workshop and Anni's 1925 knotted rug from the weaving workshop. Hirschfeld-Mack singled out Anni's book *On designing*, which advocated a collaborative ethic: 'if we, as designers, cooperate with the material, treat it democratically ... we will reach a less subjective solution'.[28] When the Alberses received copies of the book, it was Anni who responded warmly, though she was critical of its introduction by Gropius, accusing him of idealism which, she wrote, 'sounds like a late dream of his and hardly related to anything we knew at the time'.[29]

That year also saw the launch of *Interaction of colour*. Though initially a limited-edition unbound portfolio with some 150 prints by Albers and his students, it would become a widely published classic, making this aspect of Bauhaus material studies accessible to a mass audience. Hirschfeld-Mack responded with a long letter. As a former student of Hölzel himself, he recognised Albers's debt to his Stuttgart professor and his teachings on colour, listing them as: 'Contrast of colours in and for themselves, Light-dark contrast, Cold-warm contrast, Complementary/simultaneous contrasts, Quantity contrasts, Colour to non-colour contrasts.'[30] Albers's success was based on summarising earlier colour theories, such as Hölzel's, though stripped of symbolic or religious connotations in favour of a rational, scientific order.

Josef's book led Hirschfeld-Mack to reflect on his own lack of recognition, with some regret but without rancour. He wrote to his old friends about organising the first Bauhaus colour seminar:

> Unfortunately, the colour seminar at the Weimar Bauhaus in about 1922/23, which Klee and Kandinsky attended fairly regularly, is not mentioned in the new Bauhaus book [Hans M Wingler, *Bauhaus 1919–1933: Weimar Dessau Berlin*, 1962]. I very much regret that this was the only collective attempt to achieve objective results; I supplied the charts and colour tables, some of which are preserved in the Darmstadt archive. This seminar was not officially mentioned anywhere, nor could it be found in the syllabus, and probably Wingler concealed it, since, with the exception of my charts, he could not find any documents or evidence for the existence of this course. You are probably the only one who can remember. I remember that you couldn't come because of your glass workshop hours. Of course I still remember very well having produced a series of paste prints for Bauhaus folders—thanks to your help in design and cutting a plate. These are illustrated with some lithos by me and others in the new Bauhaus book (without naming names.)
>
> But I don't care about that! and everything that has to do with my name—mainly in connection with my work in the Bauhaus print shop—I should have done better at that time—a compromise—to maintain Elenor and the children with my work and at the same time to develop light shows etc—a divided life.
>
> I have always felt a shyness about publicity. I believe it is my destiny, within my limits, to give and to take nothing in return, so that today I am all about impact—without expecting a response. So there are probably several thousand paintings and monoprints in my studio and I have neither the time nor the urge to exhibit them.[31]

Hirschfeld-Mack then ends by mentioning his frustrations at his repeated attempts to have the Alberses visit:

> We had 'an Australian UNESCO Seminar on Art Education' at the Australian National University in Canberra in May 1963—with Herbert Read ... I tried in vain to get you both an invitation. I had to give a demonstration lesson and

28 Anni Albers, *On designing*, The Pellango Press, New Haven, 1959, quoted in Hirschfeld-Mack, 1963, p 10.

29 Anni Albers, letter to Ludwig Hirschfeld-Mack, 24 May 1964, Unit 1, 1971.0009.0005, Hirschfeld-Mack Collection, UMA.

30 Ludwig Hirschfeld-Mack, letter to Josef and Anni Albers, 2 June 1963, JA 4–50_1958–1965_Lud, JAAF. Translation by Andrew McNamara.

31 Hirschfeld-Mack, letter to Josef and Anni Albers, 2 June 1963.

> 2 lectures, mentioning Jupp's name several times as the originator of the material design.
>
> Although I will be 70 this year, I still ski, climb roofs and trees—and teach at a Kindergarten Training College in Melbourne 2 days a week—unfortunately Olive's health is not so good.[32]

A poignant letter followed 18 months later, from Hirschfeld-Mack's second wife Olive after his sudden death in January 1965, which ends the correspondence. She confesses that 'Although we have not met I feel I know you both for Ludwig so often spoke of you and Ermano and Ello Delugan [Hirschfeld-Mack's son-in-law and daughter] talked with us so enthusiastically in 1958 about [Josef's] time in Ulm.'[33]

Despite their very different trajectories and fortunes, these three Bauhäuslers maintained a strong sense of connection about art and teaching as a result of their formative years in Weimar. Their intimate correspondence about the school's history not only throws light on how a diaspora network was sustained but also on how they were each deeply invested in its contemporary legacy.

Dr Ann Stephen FAHA
Senior Curator Art
The University of Sydney
Chau Chak Wing Museum

32 Hirschfeld-Mack, letter to Josef and Anni Albers, 2 June 1963.

33 Olive Hirschfeld-Mack, letter to Josef and Anni Albers, 4 July 1965, JAAF. The Ulm school of design explicitly espoused a Bauhaus philosophy and in 1954 had invited Albers, among other Bauhäuslers, to teach.

Below Ludwig Hirschfeld-Mack giving a demonstration lesson to the Working Party of the Australian National Advisory Committee for UNESCO, Canberra, May 1963, photographer unknown, gelatin silver photograph, 50.7 × 20.4 cm

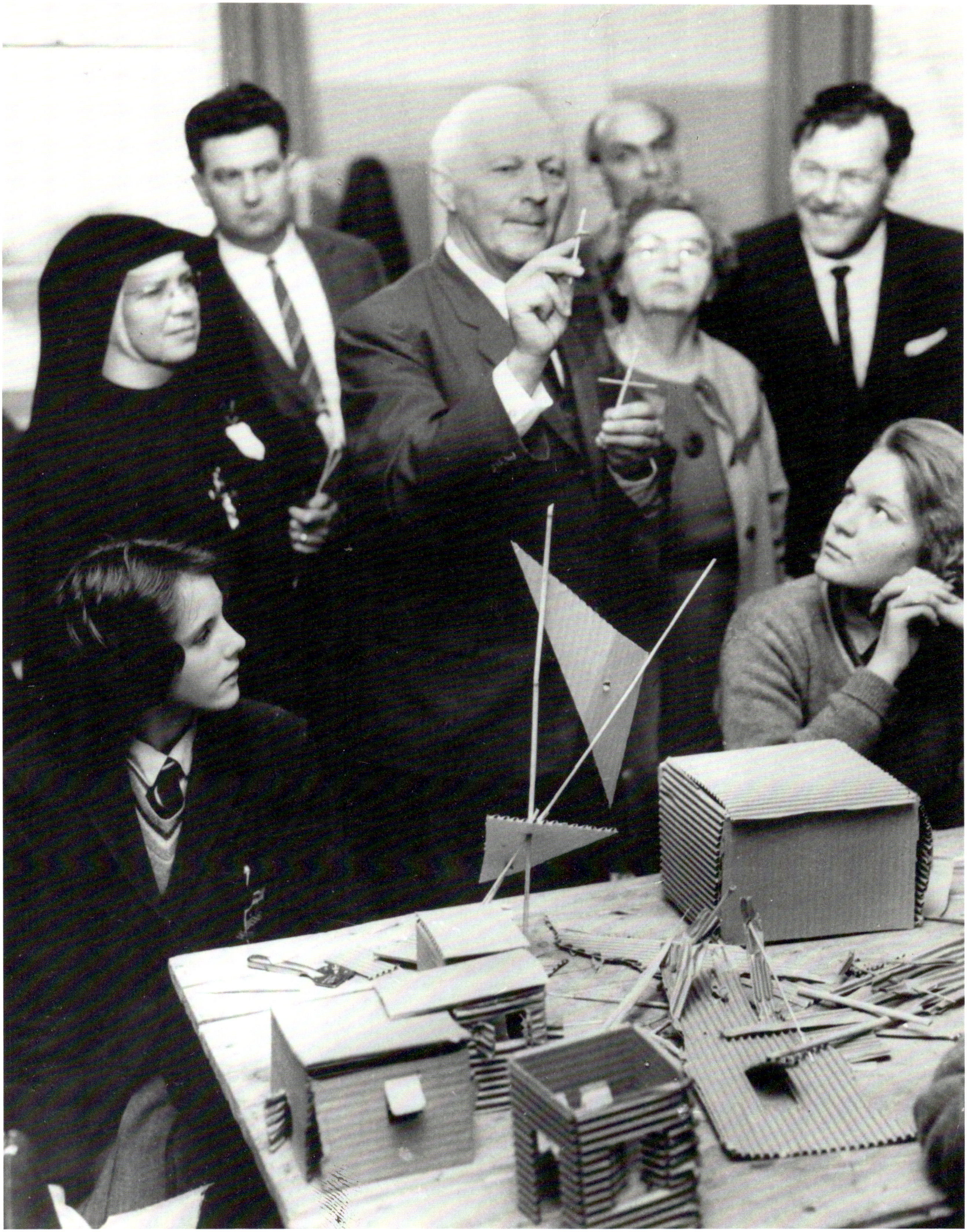

Below Ludwig Hirschfeld-Mack, *Aquarell III* 1919, watercolour over pencil with additions in varnish on paper, image 18.5 × 13.1 cm, sheet 24.6 × 16.3 cm

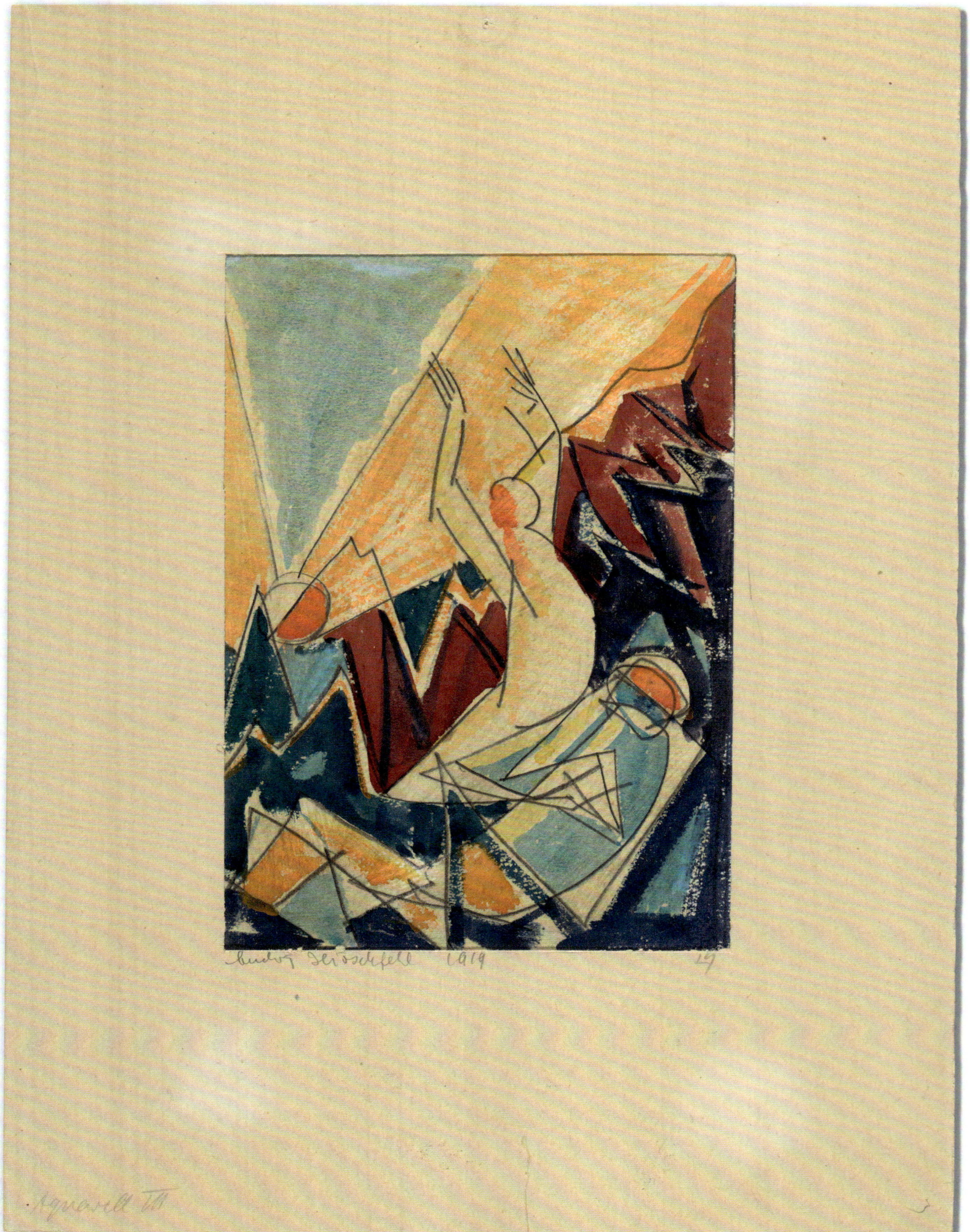

Below Ludwig Hirschfeld-Mack, Study for costume design 1920, watercolour over pencil on paper, 25.1 × 19.3 cm

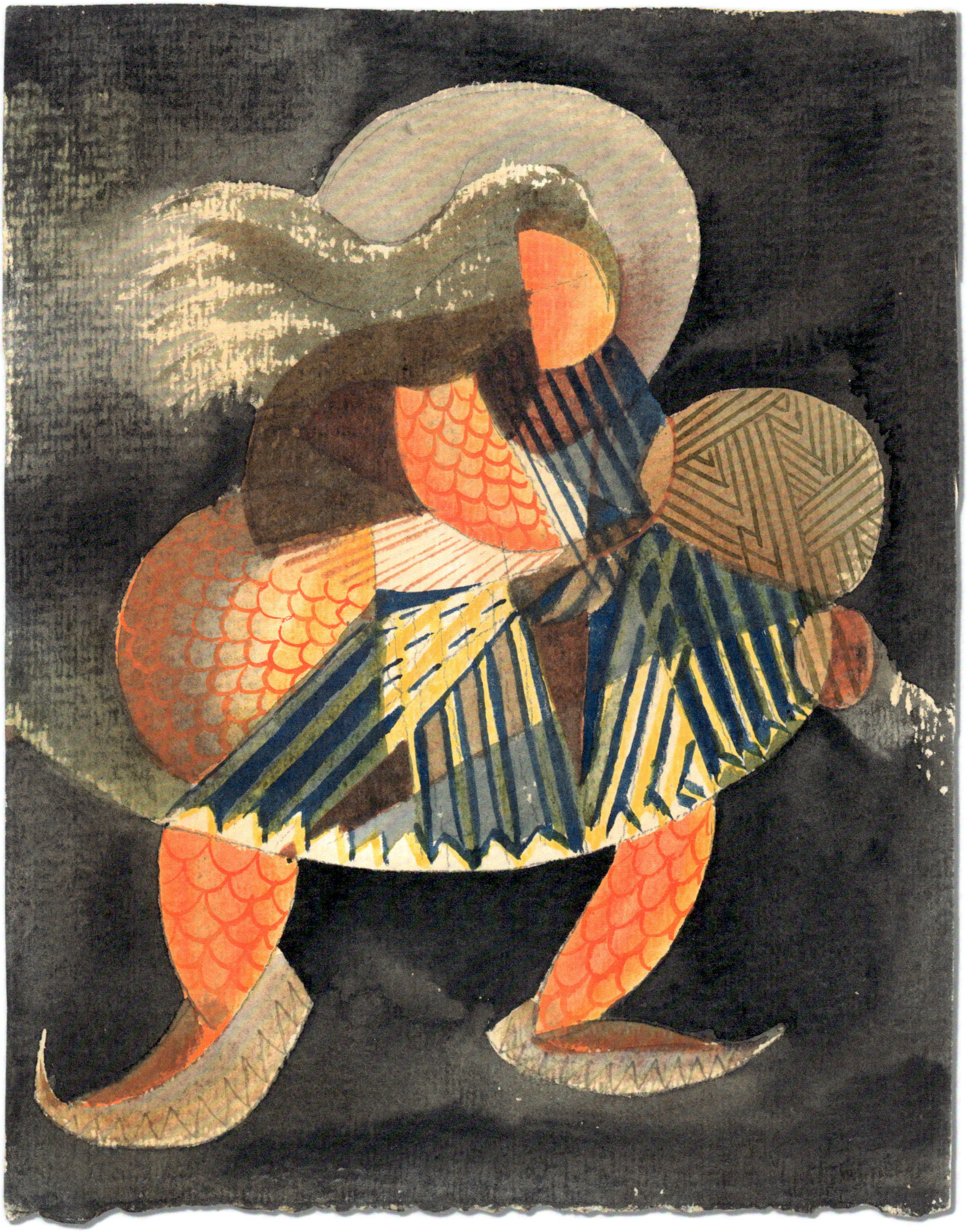

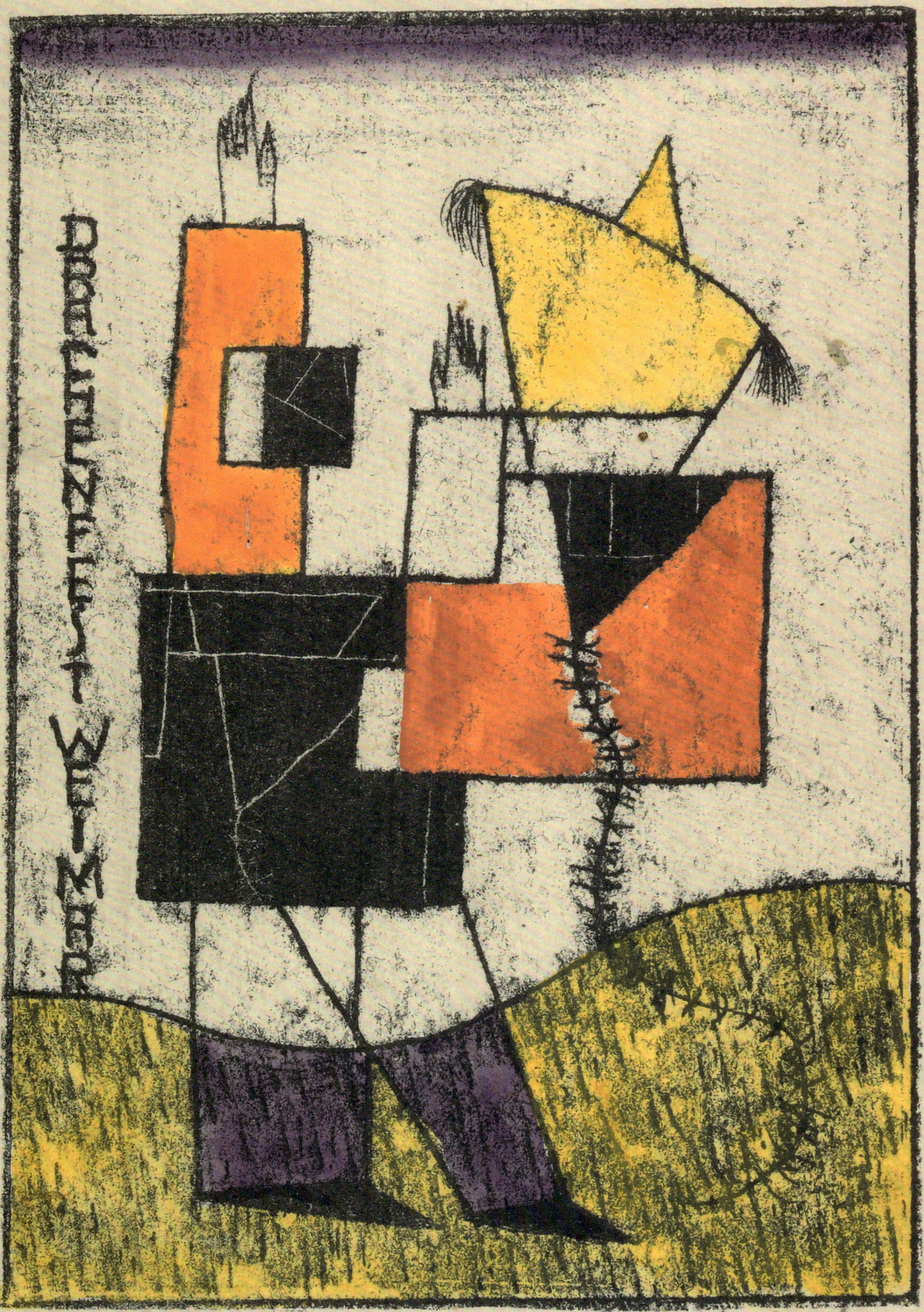

1922 L. Mack

Left Ludwig Hirschfeld-Mack, *Drachenfest Weimar* (*Kite festival, Weimar*) 1922, lithograph, hand-coloured in watercolour on card, image 12.6 × 8.6 cm, sheet 15.6 × 10.7 cm

Below Ludwig Hirschfeld-Mack, *Drachenfest Weimar* (*Kite festival, Weimar*) 1922, lithograph, hand-coloured in watercolour on card, image 9 × 12.5 cm, sheet 10.5 × 15.5 cm

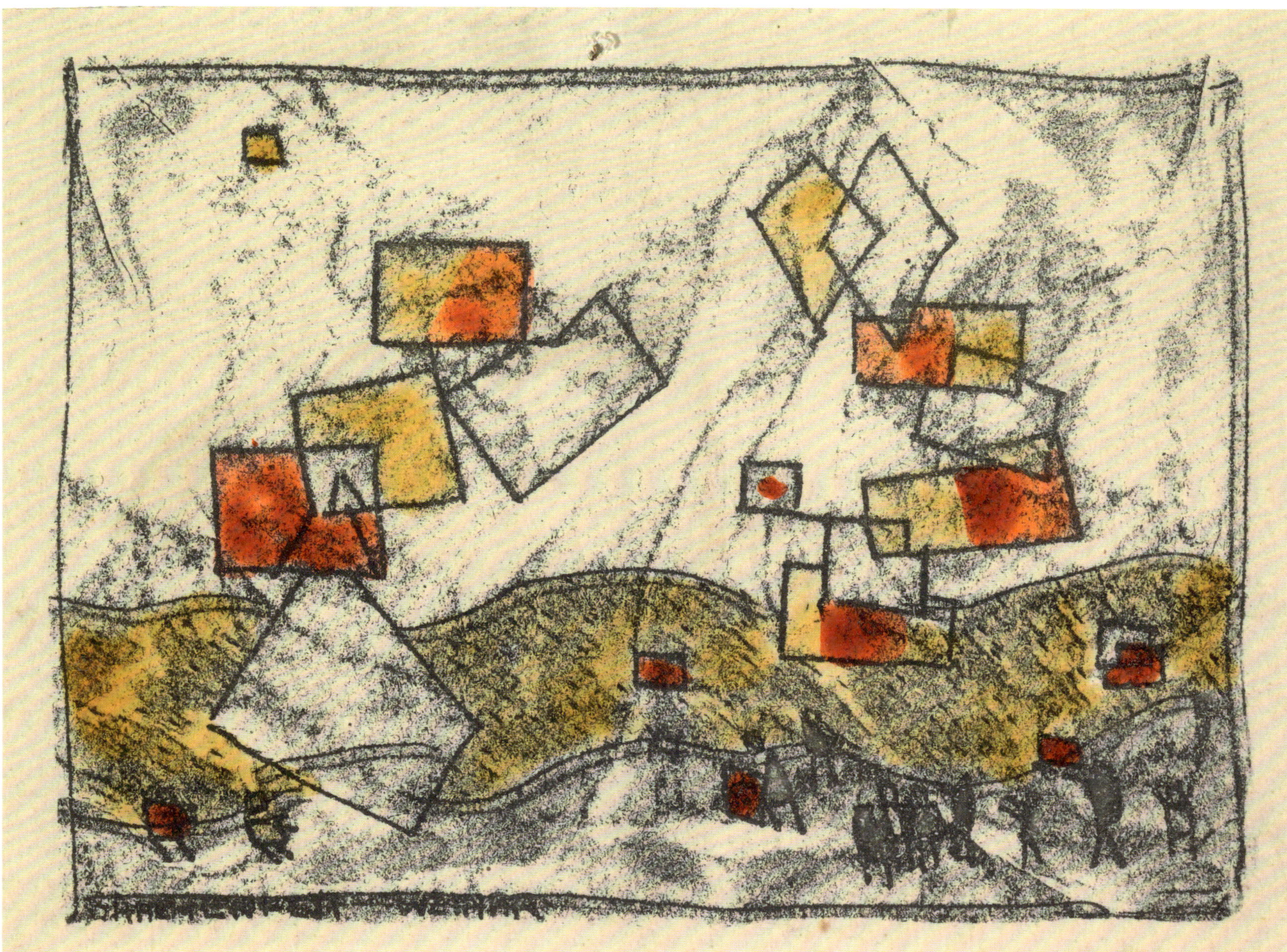

Below Paul Klee, *Laternenfest Bauhaus* (*Bauhaus Lantern Festival*) 1922, lithograph, sheet 9 × 13.5 cm

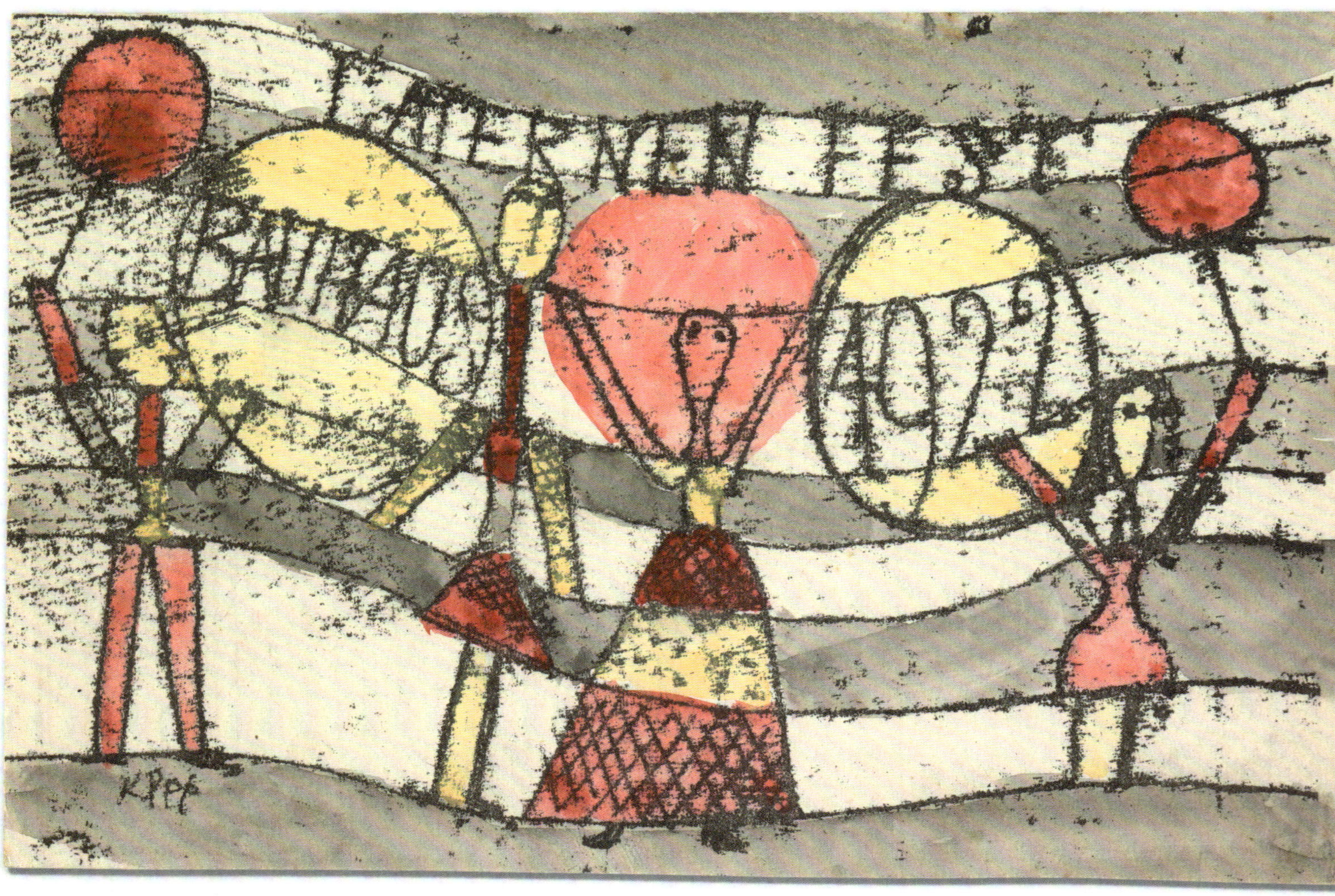

List of works

All works are from the collection of the National Gallery of Australia, unless otherwise stated.

Works are listed under artist surname, then chronologically, then alphabetically by title.

Collaborative works are listed under the first artist's surname.

Asterisks indicate works made at the Bauhaus.

Pre-Columbian textiles are listed separately at the end in alphabetical order of cultural group.

Measurements are height × width × depth.

The capitalisation and punctuation of titles of works of art by Anni Albers and Josef Albers are sourced from the following catalogues raisonnés published by the Josef and Anni Albers Foundation:

The prints of Anni Albers: a catalogue raisonné, 1963–1984 (2009)
The prints of Josef Albers: a catalogue raisonné, 1915–1976 (rev ed, 2010)

Anni Albers
Germany 1899 – United States 1994

Red Meander I 1969–70
screenprint, printed in colour inks, from two screens on Mohawk Superfine Bristol paper
image 50.7 × 41.7 cm
sheet 71.2 × 62.2 cm
26/50
edition of 50, plus 1 *hors commerce* print
printed by Sirocco Screenprints, North Haven, Connecticut
Purchased 1978
78.1365
p 129

Blue Meander 1970
screenprint, printed in colour inks, from two screens on Mohawk Superfine Bristol paper
image 49.3 × 40.6 cm
sheet 70.7 × 60.7 cm
40/75
edition of 75, plus 12 artist's proofs, 4 *hors commerce* prints
printed by Sirocco Screenprints, North Haven, Connecticut
Purchased 1978
78.1364
p 128

TR III 1970
embossing, from one zinc plate; silkscreen, printed in gold ink, from one screen on handmade Waterleaf paper
sheet 41.8 × 47 cm
right to print
edition of 60, plus 6 artist's proofs, right to print, printer's proof II, 3 Gemini impressions, cancellation proof
published by Gemini GEL, Los Angeles
Purchased 1973
73.846.3
p 61

Red Meander II 1970–71
screenprint, printed in colour inks, from two screens on Mohawk Superfine Bristol paper
image 50.7 × 40.7 cm
sheet 71.2 × 61.1 cm
artist's proof 6/10
edition of 75, plus 10 artist's proofs, 10 *hors commerce* prints
printed by Sirocco Screenprints, North Haven, Connecticut
Purchased 1978
78.1366
p 124

Mountainous III 1978
Mountainous IV 1978
Mountainous VI 1978
embossing, each printed from one magnesium plate on handmade TGL paper
image 47.2 × 43.7 cm (each)
sheet 56.6 × 52.7 cm (each)
right to print
edition of 20, plus 10 artist's proofs, right to print, printer's proof I, archive copy, cancellation proof
printed and published by Tyler Graphics Ltd, Bedford Village, New York
Purchased 1979
79.2923, 79.2924, 79.2926
p 130, p 125, p 131

Josef Albers
Germany 1888 – United States 1976

Zelte/Tents 1933
woodcut on lithographic paper
image 23.2 × 25.5 cm
sheet 29.2 × 31.9 cm
undesignated impression
edition unnumbered, probably of 20
printed by Ullstein Press, Berlin
Private collection, Gadigal Nura/Sydney
p 54

i 1934
linocut, printed in black ink, from one block on handmade paper
image 20.6 × 28.8 cm
sheet 32.3 × 40.1 cm
9/20
edition of 20
Purchased 1979
79.2271
p 155

Wings 1934
woodcut on Strathmore Highway paper
image 18.7 × 31.5 cm
sheet 20.6 × 33.6 cm
11/25
edition of 25; 4 proofs
Private collection, Gadigal Nura/Sydney
p 155

Study for *Biconjugate* c 1943
oil on paper
image and sheet 25.4 × 42 cm
Private collection, Gadigal Nura/Sydney
p 151

Study for *Vice Versa* c 1943
oil on paper
image and sheet 22.5 × 44.6 cm
Private collection, Gadigal Nura/Sydney
p 150

Study for *Oscillating* c 1945
oil on paper
image 30.5 × 22 cm
sheet 36.1 × 27.3 cm
Private collection, Gadigal Nura/Sydney
p 134

Study for *Variant/Adobe* c 1947
oil on paper
image and sheet 20.1 × 26.8 cm
Private collection, Gadigal Nura/Sydney
pp 56–57

Drawing for positioning of squares in printing of *White Line Squares* series c 1963
graphite pencil, coloured pencil on graph paper
47.7 × 52.6 cm
Purchased 1973
73.852
p 89

Homage to the Square: On an Early Sky 1964
oil on composition board
122.2 × 122.2 cm
Purchased 1981
81.3043
p 85

Collaged studies for *White Line Square II, V, VIII, IX, XIV* c 1966
collage of coloured paper on board
sheet 48.4 × 52.6 cm
Purchased 1973
73.853.A-E
p 8

Gouache studies for *White Line Square III* and *White Line Square IV* c 1966
gouache on paper
image (a) 30.2 × 15.2 cm
image (b) 30.5 × 15.2 cm (irreg)
Purchased 1973
73.854.A-B
p 78

Homage to the Square: Impartial 1966
oil on board
121.9 × 121.9 cm
Private collection, Gadigal Nura/Sydney
p 58

Oil studies for *White Line Square XIII* and *White Line Square XV* 1966
oil on paper
image (a) 33 × 18.8 cm
image (b) 33.6 × 18.6 cm (irreg)
Purchased with the assistance of the Orde Poynton Fund 2002
2002.1.1321
p 80

Oil studies for *White Line Square XIV* and *White Line Square X* 1966
oil on paper
image (a) 33 × 18.2 cm
image (b) 30.4 × 17.8 cm (irreg)
Purchased with the assistance of the Orde Poynton Fund 2002
2002.1.1320
p 81

Oil studies for *White Line Square XVI* and *White Line Square XII* 1966
oil on paper
image (a) 33.4 × 18.8 cm
image (b) 33.4 × 18.6 cm
Purchased with the assistance of the Orde Poynton Fund 2002
2002.1.1322
p 79

Preliminary drawing for *White Line Square I* 1966
fibre-tipped pen, coloured pencil and ballpoint pen on graph paper
35.6 × 43.2 cm
Purchased 1973
73.856
p 77

Printing order showing format for prints inclusive of *White Line Square I* to *White Line Square XVI* 1966
fibre-tipped pen, coloured pencil and ballpoint pen on wove paper
48.4 × 52.6 cm
Purchased 1973
73.855
p 88

White Line Square I 1966
White Line Square III 1966
White Line Square VI 1966
from the *White Line Squares (Series I)* 1966
lithographs, printed in colour inks, from three aluminium plates on Arches Cover paper
image 40 × 40 cm (each)
sheet 52.7 × 52.7 cm (each)
right to print
edition of 125, plus 15 artist's proofs
I: 10 trial proofs, right to print, printer's proof II, 2 Gemini impressions, cancellation proof
III: right to print, printer's proof II, 2 Gemini impressions, 10 progressive proofs, cancellation proof
VI: 5 trial proofs, right to print, printer's proof II, 2 Gemini impressions, cancellation proof
printed and published by Gemini GEL, Los Angeles
Purchased 1973
73.857.1, 73.857.3, 73.857.6
p 90, p 91, p 97

White Line Square XI 1966
White Line Square XIII 1966
White Line Square XV 1966
from the *White Line Squares (Series II)* 1966
lithographs, printed in colour inks, from three aluminium plates on Arches Cover paper
image 40 × 40 cm (each)
sheet 52.7 × 52.7 cm (each)
right to print
edition of 125, plus 10 artist's proofs
XI: 5 trial proofs, right to print, printer's proof II, 2 Gemini impressions, 8 progressive proofs, 3 colour trial proofs, cancellation proof
XIII: 5 trial proofs, right to print, printer's proof II, 2 Gemini impressions, cancellation proof
XV: 10 trial proofs, right to print, printer's proof II, 2 Gemini impressions, cancellation proof
printed and published by Gemini GEL, Los Angeles
Purchased 1973
73.857.11, 73.857.13, 73.857.15
p 98, p 99, p 100

Folio I, folder 8
from *Formulation : Articulation* 1972
screenprint, printed in colour inks, from multiple stencils on Mohawk Superfine Bristol paper
image 15.8 × 44 cm
sheet 38.2 × 50.7 cm
undesignated impression
edition of 1000
printed by Sirocco Screenprints, North Haven, Connecticut
published by Ives-Sillman, Inc, New Haven, Connecticut
Purchased 1973
73.482.8
pp 158–59

Folio I, folder 22
from *Formulation : Articulation* 1972
screenprint, printed in colour inks, from multiple stencils on Mohawk Superfine Bristol paper
image 33.3 × 34.6 cm
sheet 38.2 × 50.7 cm
undesignated impression
edition of 1000
printed by Sirocco Screenprints, North Haven, Connecticut
published by Ives-Sillman, Inc, New Haven, Connecticut
Purchased 1973
73.482.22
p 50

Folio I, folder 24
from *Formulation : Articulation* 1972
screenprint, printed in colour inks, from multiple stencils on Mohawk Superfine Bristol paper
image (a) 28.7 × 29.6 cm
image (b) 28.7 × 36.5 cm
sheet 38.2 × 50.8 cm (folded)
undesignated impression
edition of 1000
printed by Sirocco Screenprints, North Haven, Connecticut
published by Ives-Sillman, Inc, New Haven, Connecticut
Purchased 1973
73.482.24.1–73.482.24.2
p 136, p 149

Folio II, folder 12
from *Formulation : Articulation* 1972
screenprint, printed in colour inks, from multiple stencils on Mohawk Superfine Bristol paper
image 25.5 × 32.9 cm
sheet 38.2 × 50.8 cm
undesignated impression
edition of 1000
printed by Sirocco Screenprints, North Haven, Connecticut
published by Ives-Sillman, Inc, New Haven, Connecticut
Purchased 1973
73.482.45
p 135

Gray Instrumentation Ia 1974
Gray Instrumentation Ib 1974
Gray Instrumentation Ic 1974
Gray Instrumentation Id 1974
Gray Instrumentation Ie 1974
Gray Instrumentation If 1974
Gray Instrumentation Ig 1974
Gray Instrumentation Ih 1974
Gray Instrumentation Ii 1974
Gray Instrumentation Ij 1974
Gray Instrumentation Ik 1974
Gray Instrumentation Il 1974 (not exhibited)
from the *Gray Instrumentation I* series 1974
screenprints, printed from four screens in light blue-grey, blue-grey, medium violet-grey and dark violet-grey on Arches 88 paper
image 28 × 28 cm (each)
sheet 48.2 × 48.2 cm (each)
right to print
edition of 36, plus 10 artist's proofs
Ia, *Ic*, *Ig*, *Ih*, *Ij* & *Il*: colour trial proof, right to print, printer's proof I, archive copy
Ib: colour trial proof, special (presentation) proof, right to print, printer's proof I, archive copy
Id: 4 trial proofs, right to print, printer's proof I, archive copy
Ie, *Ik*: 2 trial proofs, right to print, printer's proof I, archive copy
If: trial proof, right to print, printer's proof I, archive copy
Ii: 2 colour trial proofs, right to print, printer's proof I, archive copy
printed and published by Tyler Graphics Ltd, Bedford Village, New York
Purchased 1975
75.553.9–75.553.20
pp 20–31

Studies for Ken [*Gray Instrumentation II* series] 1974
8 collages of thin, cream hand-cut tissue paper adhered to thick buff cardboard
image 12.8 × 12.6 cm (each)
sheet 25 × 20.3 cm (each)
Gift of Kenneth Tyler 2002
2002.1.2002–2002.1.2009
pp 12–19

Gray Instrumentation IIa 1975
Gray Instrumentation IIb 1975
Gray Instrumentation IIc 1975
Gray Instrumentation IId 1975
Gray Instrumentation IIe 1975
Gray Instrumentation IIf 1975
Gray Instrumentation IIg 1975
Gray Instrumentation IIh 1975
Gray Instrumentation IIi 1975 (not exhibited)
Gray Instrumentation IIj 1975
Gray Instrumentation IIk 1975
Gray Instrumentation IIl 1975
from the *Gray Instrumentation II* series 1975
screenprints, printed from four screens in turquoise blue-grey, medium blue-grey, light green-grey and pale green-grey on Arches 88 paper
image 27.8 × 27.8 cm (each)
sheet 48.2 × 48.2 cm (each)
right to print
edition of 36, plus 10 artist's proofs
IIa, *IIb*, *IIe*, *IIh*, *IIi*, *IIj* & *IIl*: 2 trial proofs, right to print, printer's proof I, archive copy
IIc, *IIf*: 2 colour trial proofs, right to print, printer's proof I, archive copy
IId: 3 trial proofs, right to print, printer's proof I, archive copy
IIg: 4 trial proofs, right to print, printer's proof I, archive copy
IIk: colour trial proof, right to print, printer's proof I, archive copy
printed and published by Tyler Graphics Ltd, Bedford Village, New York
Purchased 1975
75.554.9–75.554.20
p 36

Bauhaus Dessau weaving workshop

Weaving study, furnishing fabric swatch c 1926 *
wool, cotton and rayon
11.8 × 20.2 cm
Purchased with the assistance of Dame Elisabeth Murdoch 1988
88.1680
p 66

Herbert Bayer designer
Austria 1900 – United States 1985
Walter Gropius designer
Germany 1883 – United States 1969
László Moholy-Nagy editor
Hungary 1895 – United States 1946

Staatliches Bauhaus in Weimar 1919–1923 1923 *
letterpress and lithograph
25.1 × 25.5 cm
edition of 2600: 2000 in German, 300 in English, 300 in Russian
published by Bauhaus Verlag, Weimar
National Gallery of Australia Research Library Rare Book collection
p 43

Lena Bergner
Germany 1906–1981

Textile design for throw rug 1928 *
watercolour on paper
30.1 × 20.2 cm
Purchased by the Arthur Boyd Drawing Fund 1988
88.1669
p 65

Textile design with yarn sample 1928 *
watercolour and pencil on paper with wool sample
16.5 × 13 cm
Purchased with the assistance of Dame Elisabeth Murdoch 1988
88.1674
p 64

Weaving sample, swatch for clothing fabric 1930 *
handwoven cotton and rayon
11.4 × 10.4 cm
Purchased with the assistance of Dame Elisabeth Murdoch 1988
88.1683
p 52

Weaving study, fabric swatch for divan cover 1930 *
handwoven wool, cotton and rayon
14.6 × 8.6 cm
Purchased with the assistance of Dame Elisabeth Murdoch 1988
88.1684
p 67

Max Dupain photographer
Australia 1911–1992
Harry Seidler architect
Austria 1923 – Australia 2006

Harry Seidler's Thurlow House, Blakehurst, NSW June 1954
gelatin silver photograph, cardboard
58.1 × 47.5 cm
Gift of Harry Seidler 2001
2001.223
p 172

Harry Seidler architecture, Horwitz House, Sussex Street, Haymarket, Sydney, exterior November 1955
gelatin silver photograph, cardboard
59.1 × 47.8 cm
Gift of Harry Seidler 2001
2001.228
p 171

Harry Seidler architecture, Printers Union, Sydney, exterior (since demolished) January 1959
gelatin silver photograph, cardboard
47.5 × 59.7 cm
Gift of Harry Seidler 2001
2001.232
p 170

Harry Seidler architecture, Blues Point Tower apartments, McMahons Point, Sydney 1962
gelatin silver photograph, cardboard
58.2 × 48.6 cm
Gift of Harry Seidler 2001
2001.237
p 169

Ludwig Hirschfeld-Mack
Germany 1893 – Australia 1965

Aquarell III 1919 *
watercolour over pencil with additions in varnish on paper
image 18.5 × 13.1 cm
sheet 24.6 × 16.3 cm
Gift of Olive Hirschfeld 1979
79.852
p 204

Study for costume design 1920 *
watercolour over pencil on paper
25.1 × 19.3 cm
Gift of Olive Hirschfeld 1979
79.856
p 205

Not titled 1921–22 *
oil on canvas
77 × 53.5 cm
Purchased 2023
2023.69
p 192

Colour chart, blue, yellow, red on black 1922 *
collage of hand-cut paper painted in gouache on painted textured wallpaper
29.5 × 45.3 cm
Gift of Chris Bell 2015
2015.989
p 195

Drachenfest Weimar (*Kite festival, Weimar*) 1922 *
lithograph, printed in black ink, from one stone; hand-coloured in watercolour on card
image 12.6 × 8.6 cm
sheet 15.6 × 10.7 cm
Poynton Bequest 2023
2023.85
p 206

Drachenfest Weimar (*Kite festival, Weimar*) 1922 *
lithograph, printed in black ink from one stone; hand-coloured in watercolour on card
image 9 × 12.5 cm
sheet 10.5 × 15.5 cm
Poynton Bequest 2023
2023.86
p 207

Ziehharmonika Spieler (*Accordion player*) c 1922 *
watercolour and gouache on paper
20.1 × 26 cm
Gift of Olive Hirschfeld 1979
79.865AB
pp 198–99

Bauhaus Ausstellung Weimar (*Bauhaus exhibition, Weimar*) 1923 *
lithograph, printed in black ink, from one stone on card
sheet 9 × 14 cm
Poynton Bequest 2023
2023.84
p 195

Postkarte zur Bauhaus-Ausstellung (*Postcard for the Bauhaus-exhibition*) 1923 *
lithograph, printed in colour inks, from multiple stones on card
sheet 10 × 15 cm
Donated through the Australian Government's Cultural Gifts Program by Penelope Seidler AM in memory of Harry Seidler AC 2010
2010.13
p 196

Piano accordion c 1933–36
wood, vinyl, pearl shell, leather, metal, paper, paint
16.9 × 30 × 35.7 cm
Gift of Chris Bell 2015
2015.1002
p 190

Colour chord (Queen Mary) c 1936–39
wood, wire
11.7 × 97.5 × 12.1 cm
Gift of Chris Bell 2015
2015.997
p 191

Optischer Farbmischer (*Optical colour mixer*) 1950s
wood; drawing in fibre-tipped colour pen on paper
10 × 6.8 (diam) cm (each)
Gift of Chris Bell 2015
2015.1000.1–-2015.1000.5
p 189

Stringed instrument (12 strings) 1950s
wood, wire
8 × 25.5 × 37.5 cm
Gift of Chris Bell 2015
2015.996
p 190

Paul Klee
Switzerland 1879–1940

Laternenfest Bauhaus (*Bauhaus Lantern Festival*) 1922 *
lithograph, printed in black ink, from one stone; hand-coloured in watercolour on card
sheet 9 × 13.5 cm
Poynton Bequest 2023
2023.83
p 208

Die erhabene Seite. Postkarte zur Bauhaus-Ausstellung (*The sublime side. Postcard for the Bauhaus-exhibition*) 1923 *
lithograph, printed in colour inks from multiple stones on card
sheet 15 × 10 cm
Donated through the Australian Government's Cultural Gifts Program by Penelope Seidler AM in memory of Harry Seidler AC 2010
2010.11
p 40

László Moholy-Nagy
Hungary 1895 – United States 1946

Postkarte zur Bauhaus-Ausstellung (*Postcard for the Bauhaus-exhibition*) 1923 *
lithograph, printed in colour inks, from multiple stones on card
sheet 15 × 10 cm
Donated through the Australian Government's Cultural Gifts Program by Penelope Seidler AM in memory of Harry Seidler AC 2010
2010.12
p 41

Hilde Reindl
Germany 1909–1990

Textile design c 1928 *
watercolour and pencil on paper
image 10 × 10 cm
sheet 13.8 × 13.6 cm
Purchased 1988
88.1667
p 68

SI designer
after Josef Albers

Teacup and saucer 1926 *
electroplated metal, wood handle, glass liner
5.5 × 13.1 (diam) cm (each)
manufactured by Berliner Electro Plated Waren Fabrik, Berlin
Purchased 1984
84.245.A-C, 84.247.A-C
p 6

Lotte Stam-Beese
Germany 1903 – Netherlands 1988

Group-portrait, weaving workshop at the Bauhaus, Dessau 1928 *
gelatin silver photograph
image 8.4 (diam) cm
Purchased 1984
1984.2945
p 132

Gunta Stölzl
Germany 1897 – Switzerland 1983

Textile design c 1926 *
watercolour, gouache and pencil on paper
image 31 × 19 cm
sheet 35.8 × 25 cm
Purchased 1988
88.1678
p 53

Unidentified student, Bauhaus Dessau

Study executed in Paul Klee's course 1927 *
watercolour on paper
image 10.5 × 10.5 cm
Purchased by the Arthur Boyd Drawing Fund 1988
88.1668
p 44

Unknown photographer

Ludwig Hirschfeld-Mack giving a demonstration lesson to the Working Party of the Australian National Advisory Committee for UNESCO, Canberra, May 1963
gelatin silver photograph
50.7 × 20.4 cm
Gift of Chris Bell 2015, National Gallery of Australia Art Archive
p 203

Wilhelm Wagenfeld
Germany 1900–1990

Kubus-Geschirr (*Cube-tableware*) 1938 *
press-moulded glass
16.5 × 18 × 18 cm
Purchased from Gallery Restaurant Funds 1987
87.354.1-10.A-B
p 34

Pre-Columbian textiles

Ica-Chincha people
South coast, Peru 1100–1476 CE

Tabard c 1300 CE
feathers and cotton
142 × 80.2 cm
Purchased 1981
81.1924
p 113

Moche people
North coast, Peru 100–800 CE

Stirrup vessel with a geometric design c 600 CE
ceramic
24 × 14.5 (diam) cm
Purchased 1983
83.293
p 115

Paracas or Nazca people
South coast, Peru 800 BCE – 800 CE

Textile fragment (split-weave tapestry fragment of a border with step and spiral motifs) c 200 BCE – 200 CE
wool and cotton
16 × 42.8 cm
Purchased 1974
74.397.5
p 121

Sicán-Lambayeque people
North coast, Peru 750–1375 CE

Beaker 900–1100 CE
gold: hammered, embossed, annealing and repoussé
13.2 × 10 (diam) cm
Gift of American Friends of the National Gallery of Australia, Inc, New York, NY, USA, made possible with the generous support of Nora Wise in memory of her husband John Wise 1986
86.698
p 114

Wari (Huari) people
Central, south and north Peru 500–1000 CE

Tunic 500–800 CE
wool and cotton
185 × 106.8 cm
Purchased 1982
82.1370
p 46

Band 600–1000 CE
wool and cotton
81.8 × 6.6 cm
Purchased 1981
81.1622
p 133

Band 600–1000 CE
wool and cotton
49 × 7.6 cm
Purchased 1981
81.1623
p 47

Curator's acknowledgements
Imogen Dixon-Smith

I would like to start by thanking Nick Mitzevich, director of the National Gallery, for providing me with the opportunity and support to work on a dream project—to research and reflect on the unparalleled life and work of Anni and Josef Albers and delve into the manifold connections here in Australia to the couple and their time at the Bauhaus.

I am indebted to the artists themselves, Anni and Josef Albers, for a vast body of work, both artistic and educational, that has encouraged me to look at the world anew and, in the words of Anni, 'breathe with a different kind of happiness'. Their dedication to an unpretentious and affecting art is still as relevant today as it was when Josef's paint was still wet and Anni's weft traversed her loom. I am grateful to the Josef and Anni Albers Foundation for its support of the development of the exhibition and publication, and for the work director Nicholas Fox Weber and curator Brenda Danilowitz carry out to keep the artists' spirit alive. Special thanks to assistant curator and digital manager Amy Jean Porter, whose swift provision of materials from the archive meant that geography presented no barrier to my research.

I would like to acknowledge the unwavering generosity of Kenneth Tyler AO through the Tyler Charitable Foundation. His ongoing support for the development of National Gallery exhibitions and publications that make the art of America's foremost modernists accessible to Australian audiences is both admirable and invaluable. Encountering the can-do attitude of his workshops through the works and resources held in the Kenneth E Tyler Collection and archive has provided endless inspiration. Thanks is also extended to Sara Laser, assistant to Kenneth E Tyler, for her continued support to the International Prints and Drawings department.

I am grateful to Penelope Seidler AM for her generous contribution to this project. Hearing her fond and insightful recollections of the relationship between the Alberses and architect Harry Seidler was one of the most enjoyable parts of realising this project. The research support provided by her family was also of great assistance. A special mention also to Professor Philip Goad for bringing his architectural expertise to this discussion.

Thank you also to the other contributors to this publication, Nicholas Fox Weber, Ann Stephen and Jordan Troeller, who have shared their immense knowledge of the Alberses and the Bauhaus with passion and flair. Reading through the texts brought me great joy as the threads of the exhibition started to be woven together.

For their work on this publication, special thanks to the National Gallery's Penny Sanderson, publishing manager, and Meagan Down, publishing assistant manager, who seamlessly marry proficiency in their field with warmth and humour. They are ably assisted by our contractors: thank you to Linda Michael for her thoughtful editing, to Clare WIlliamson for her meticulous proofreading, and to Stuart Geddes and Žiga Testen for the exquisitely considered design of the publication.

Thank you to Adam Lindsay, deputy director, for his support of the exhibition and stewardship of the National Gallery's dynamic exhibition program. I extend acknowledgements to other current and former colleagues at the Gallery, without whose support and hard work this project would have remained merely a good idea. I am grateful to Ellie Misios, Monica Tran and Eliza Williams for their work across copyright and permissions. Thanks also to Maryanne Voyazis in Foundation, Sophie Hunter in Executive and Samantha Pollock in Registration for liaising with the exhibition's lenders and supporters. For the enormous amount of work that goes on behind the scenes in preparing works for exhibition, I would like to thank Andrea Wise, James Ward, Fiona Kemp, Micheline Ford, Sarah McHugh, Courtney Crane, Kim Goldsmith and Jocelyn Evans in Conservation and Masahiro Asaka in Mountcutting. Thanks also to Eleni Kypridis and Brooke Shannon for imaging the works so they can sing on these pages. For her sensitive yet punchy exhibition design, thank you to Aislinn King. I am grateful also for the support of the exhibition coordinators Rowena Paget and Aaron Walker.
To my curatorial colleagues, whose advice is always both sound and inspiring, thank you, particularly to Carol Cains, Russell Storer, Dr Deborah Hart, Dr Sarina Noordhuis-Fairfax, Sally Foster, Elspeth Pitt, Dr Shaune Lakin, Lucina Ward, Dr Rebecca Edwards, Annie O'Hehir, Beatrice Thompson, Kira Godoroja-Prieckaerts, Deirdre Cannon and Vy Tsan. Lastly, special thanks to David Greenhalgh, whose knowledge of the Kenneth E Tyler Collection and archive is unparalleled and whose tireless dedication to its care and promotion is admirable. His willingness to track down a footnote at the final hour should also be acknowledged.

National Gallery acknowledgements

The Hon Anthony Albanese MP, Prime Minister of Australia

Governing Ministers

The Hon Tony Burke MP, Minister for the Arts
Susan Templeman MP, Special Envoy for the Arts

National Gallery Council

Ryan Stokes AO, Chair
Abdul-Rahman Abdullah
The Hon Richard Alston AO
Esther Anatolitis
Ilana Atlas AO
Stephen Brady AO CVO
Helen Cook
Alison Kubler
Dr Nick Mitzevich, Director
Sally Scales
Prof Sally Smart

National Gallery Foundation

His Excellency General the Hon David Hurley AC, DSC (Retd), Patron of the National Gallery Foundation
Stephen Brady AO CVO, Chair
Philip Bacon AO, Deputy Chair
Julian Beaumont OAM
Anthony Berg AM
Robyn Burke
Julian Burt
Terrence Campbell AO
Sue Cato AM
The Hon Ashley Dawson-Damer AM
James Erskine
Tim Fairfax AC
Andrew Gwinnett
Hiroko Gwinnett
John Hindmarsh AM
Wayne Kratzmann AM
The Hon Dr Andrew Lu AM
Dr Peter Lundy RFD, Secretary
Michael Maher
Dr Michael Martin
Dr Nick Mitzevich, Director
Roslyn Packer AC
Penelope Seidler AM
Ezekiel Solomon AM
Kerry Stokes AC
Ryan Stokes AO
Ray Wilson OAM

National Gallery Executive

Dr Nick Mitzevich, Director
Adam Lindsay, Deputy Director
Susie Barr, Assistant Director, Marketing, Communications and Visitor Experience
Sophie Gray, Project Director, Capital Works Taskforce
Alison Halpin, Chief Operating Officer
Bruce Johnson McLean, Wierdi/Birri-Gubba peoples, Assistant Director, First Nations Engagement, Head Curator, First Nations Art
Felicity McGinnes, Chief Finance Officer
Helen Gee, Sophie Hunter, Jennifer Barrett and Elizabeth Smith, Directorate

Curator

Imogen Dixon-Smith, Kenneth E Tyler Curator, International Prints and Drawings

First Nations Engagement Team

Bruce Johnson McLean, Wierdi/Birri-Gubba peoples, Assistant Director, First Nations Engagement, Head Curator, First Nations Art
Cara Kirkwood, Mandandanji/Mithaka peoples, Head of First Nations Engagement and Strategy

National Gallery Project Team

Natalie Beattie, Head of Registration, and staff
Samantha Braniff, Head of Partnerships, and staff
Jade Carson, Chief Information Officer, and staff
Carol Cains, A/Head Curator, International Art, and staff
Georgia Close, Head of National Learning, and staff
Tracy Cooper-Lavery, Head of Art Across Australia, and staff
Terri Dwyer, Head of Human Resources, and staff
Mary Fisher, Head of Financial Accounting, and staff
Stefan Giammarco, Head of Visitor Experience, and staff
Deborah Hart, Head Curator, Australian Art, and staff
Greg Ible, Head of Estate Management, and staff
Cara Kirkwood, Mandandanji/Mithaka peoples, Head of First Nations Engagement and Strategy, and staff
Elizabeth Little, Manager Research Library and Archives, and staff
Marika Lucas-Edwards, Principal Content Strategist and Digital Strategist, and staff
Elizabeth Malone, Head of Commercial Operations, and staff
Laura McElhinney, Head of Financial Planning and Analysis, and staff
Fiona McQueenie, Head of Communications, and staff
Dominique Nagy, Head of Exhibitions, and staff
Kanesan Nathan, Head of Marketing, and staff
Kirsti Partridge, A/Head of Governance and Strategic Planning, and staff
Maryanne Voyazis, Head of Development and Executive Director, National Gallery Foundation, and staff
Debbie Ward, Head of Conservation, and staff
Daryl West-Moore, Head of Creative Studio, and staff
Kerry White, A/Head of Capital Works Taskforce, and staff
Jan Wojna, Head of Project Management Office, and staff

Photograph credits

All reproductions of works of art from the collection of the National Gallery of Australia are courtesy of the Gallery's Digital team, unless otherwise stated in captions accompanying reproductions.

Transcript credits

All transcripts of telephone conversations are held in the Kenneth E Tyler Collection archive, box 3, folder 5, National Gallery of Australia.

Anni Albers, phone conversation with Kenneth Tyler, 3 September 1968: pp 69–76.

Josef Albers, phone conversation with Kenneth Tyler, 3 September 1968: pp 101–12.

Josef Albers, phone conversation with Kenneth Tyler, c1966: pp 137–48.

Josef Albers, phone conversation with Kenneth Tyler, c1966: front and back cover (excerpts), pp 173–88.

Published on the occasion of the exhibition *Anni and Josef Albers*
8 June – 22 September 2024
National Gallery of Australia
Ngunnawal Country
Parkes Place East, Parkes
ACT 2600

The National Gallery of Australia is an Australian Government Agency.

A catalogue record for this work is available from the National Library of Australia.

Title: Anni and Josef Albers
Editor: Imogen Dixon-Smith*
ISBN: 9780642335043
First published: June 2024

Managing Editor: Meagan Down*
Design: Stuart Geddes and Žiga Testen
Text editor: Linda Michael
Proofreader: Clare Williamson
Imaging: Sam Cooper, Eleni Kypridis, Brooke Shannon and David McClenaghan* (unless otherwise noted)
Rights and permissions: Ellie Misios and Monica Tran*
Publishing Manager: Penny Sanderson*
Pre-press: Splitting Image
Printed by: die Keure, Bruges
Cover photos: Kenneth Tyler and Anni Albers review proofs for *TR I*, photo by Malcolm Lubliner: front cover top; Josef Albers and Kenneth Tyler, photo by William Crutchfield: front cover bottom; Portrait of Josef Albers, photo by Malcolm Lubliner: back cover top; Kenneth Tyler and Anni Albers, photo by Malcolm Lubliner: back cover bottom. All photos taken in 1969 at Anni and Josef Albers's home and studio in New Haven, Connecticut, and held in the Kenneth E Tyler Collection archive, National Gallery of Australia.

* National Gallery of Australia